RAILWAY APTITUDE TEST

A COMPREHENSIVE BOOK ON RAILWAY APTITUDE & PSYCHOLOGICAL TESTS

For the Centralised Recruitment of

Assistant Station Master, Traffic Assistant, Assistant Loco-Pilot, Diesel/Electrical Assistant-Pilot, Motorman, Station Controller, Train Operator, Rail Conductor etc.

by
RPH Editorial Board

Ramesh Publishing House, New Delhi

Published by
O.P. Gupta *for* Ramesh Publishing House

Admin. Office
12-H, New Daryaganj Road, Opp. Officers' Mess,
New Delhi-110002 ✆ 23261567, 23275224, 23275124

E-mail: info@rameshpublishinghouse.com
Website: www.rameshpublishinghouse.com

Showroom
● Balaji Market, Nai Sarak, Delhi-6 ✆ 23253720, 23282525
● 4457, Nai Sarak, Delhi-6, ✆ 23918938

Book Code: R-1532

10th Edition : 1803

ISBN: 978-93-5012-305-8

CONTENTS

RAILWAY APTITUDE TEST

1. An Introduction 1

2. Intelligence Test 2

3. Similarity Test 20

4. Memory Test 59

5. Spatial Scanning Test 69

6. Brick Test 84

7. Yes or No Test 122

8. Digit Search Test 134

9. Selective Attention Test 138

10. Table Test or Column-Row Test 147

11. Shape, Size and Colour Test 154

12. Personality Test 175

13. Information Ordering Test 189

TEST PAPERS (SOLVED) 205-232

AN INTRODUCTION

After the Written Test, Railway Recruitment Board, conducts Aptitude Test for the post of Assistant Station Master, Traffic Assistant and Assistant Loco-Pilot or Diesel/Electrical Assistant-Pilot etc. Aptitude Test is conducted for those candidates who qualify the Written Test.

Aptitude Test is conducted to test the Mental Ability and Personality of the candidates. Aptitude Tests for different posts have abit different test factors.

The test factors of the Aptitude Test for the post of Assistant Station Master/Traffic Assistant/Assistant Loco-Pilot/Diesel/Electrical Assistant-Pilot etc. are explained in detail with examples so that the candidates may attempt maximum number of questions in minimum possible time.

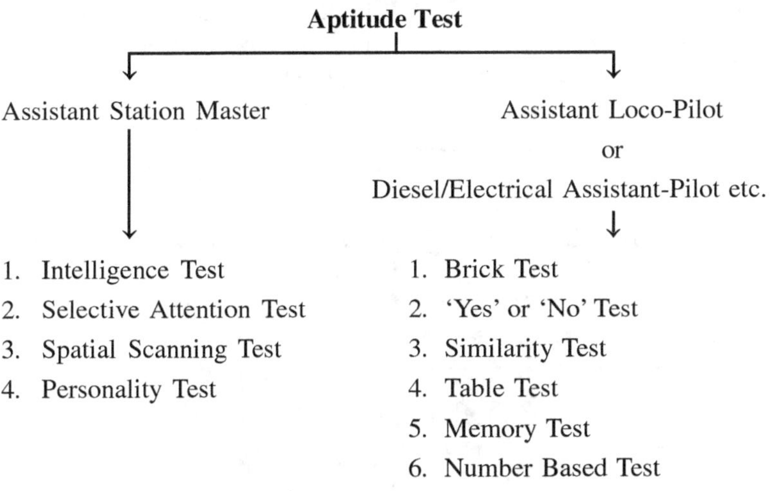

Note: Each test has a different time-limit which is informed to candidates during the test-session itself. The candidates have to solve different test-questions within the stipulated time.

Rly Apt (E)–1

INTELLIGENCE TEST
(Odd/Dissimilar Figure Test)

In this part of test, a set of figures are given, such that, except one all have similar features/characteristics. We are required to select the figure which differs from other figures in the given set. In this test, we study problems with five figures, out of which four are alike in same manner. We have to select the exclusively different figure in the given set.

Example:

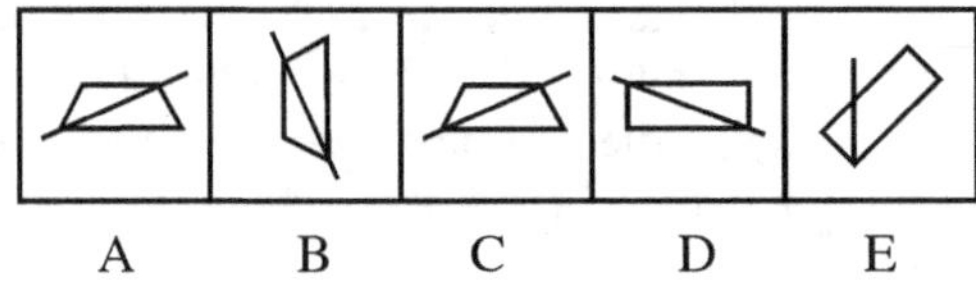

A   B   C   D   E

Explanation: Except in figure "E", in all other figures the median passes through the two corners of the given geometrical figure. In figure "E", the median passes through an angle and one side of the parallelogram.

EXERCISE-1

Directions (Qs. 1-25) : *Out of the given five figures, four are similar in a certain way. One figure is not like the other four. That means four figures form a group. The question is which one of the figures does not belong to this group.*

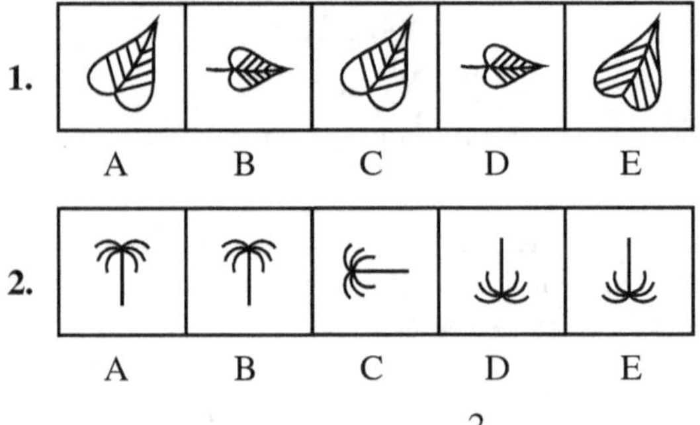

A   B   C   D   E

2

3.

4.

5.

6.

7.

8.

9.

10.

11.

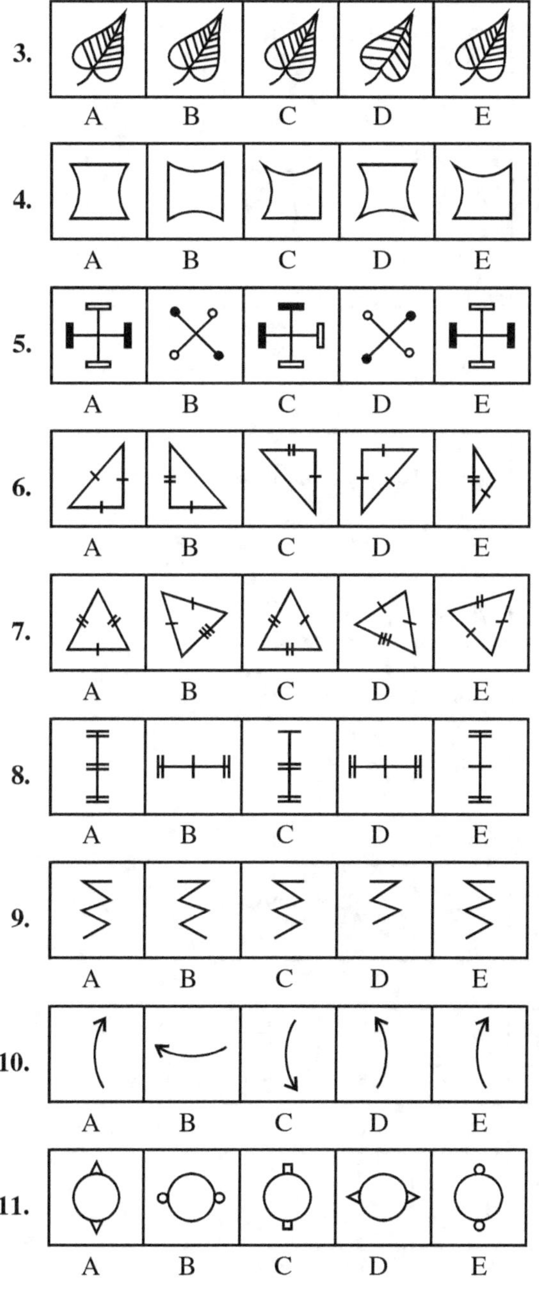

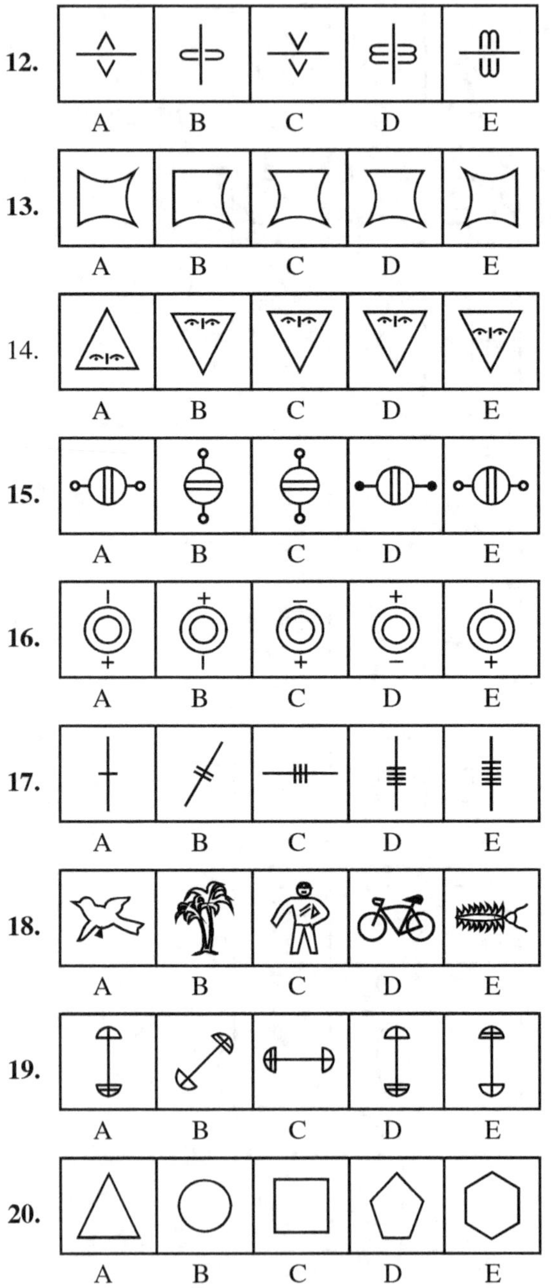

12. A B C D E
13. A B C D E
14. A B C D E
15. A B C D E
16. A B C D E
17. A B C D E
18. A B C D E
19. A B C D E
20. A B C D E

21. 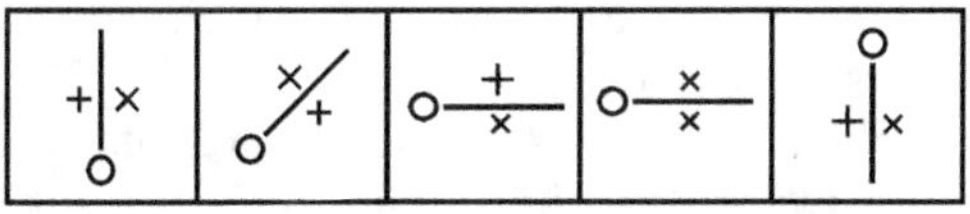

A B C D E

22. 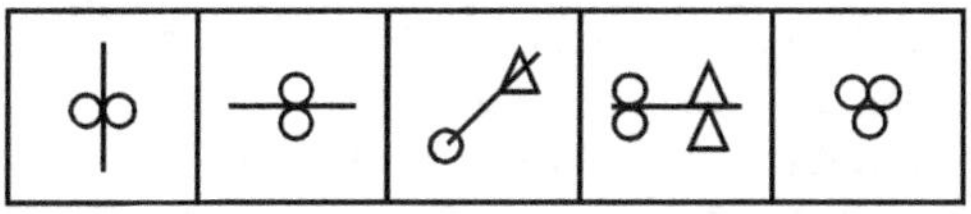

A B C D E

23. 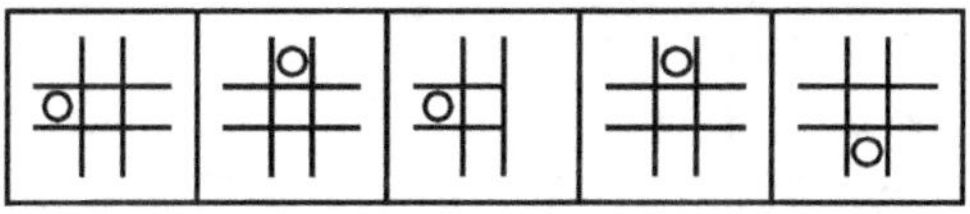

A B C D E

24. 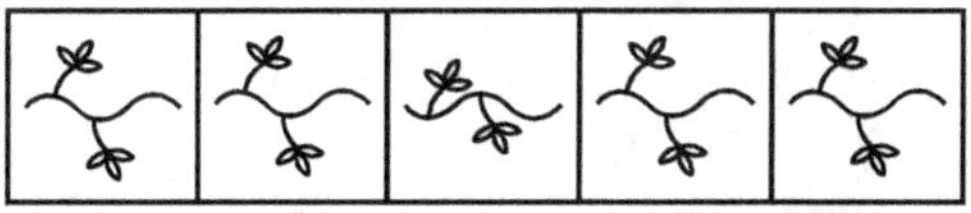

A B C D E

25. 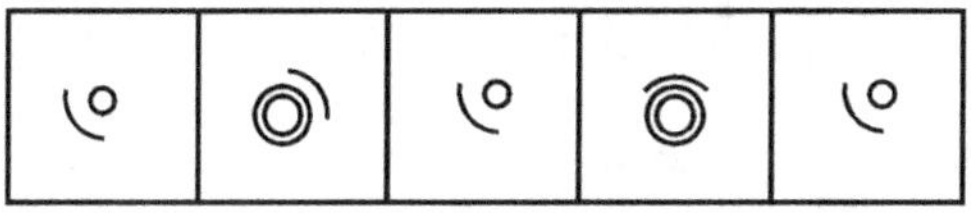

A B C D E

ANSWERS

1	**2**	**3**	**4**	**5**	**6**	**7**	**8**	**9**	**10**
E	C	D	D	C	E	E	A	D	B
11	**12**	**13**	**14**	**15**	**16**	**17**	**18**	**19**	**20**
C	C	B	A	D	C	D	D	D	B
21	**22**	**23**	**24**	**25**					
D	E	C	C	D					

EXPLANATIONS

1. Except "E" all the figures make acute angle in the inside of the leaf, whereas in the fifth figure the angle is obtuse.

2. Each figure indicates a tree which is vertical. In the figure "C" it is horizontal.

3. In all the figures veins form acute angle while in the figure "D" veins form obtuse angle.

4. Except "D" all the rectangles' have two sides curved whereas in figure "D" three sides are curved.

5. In each figure except "C" two lines cross perpendicularly with rectangles or circle at two ends white and at two ends black, but in figure "C" black and white rectangle is adjoining each other.

6. Except "E" all the triangles are right angle traingles.

7. Except "E" each triangle has five dashes.

8. Every figure has a straight line with five dashes whereas the first figure has straight lines with six dashes.

9. Each figure is a series of five lines but figure "D" is a series of four lines.

10. The arrow in all the figures have vertical direction, while in the figure "B" it is in horizontal direction.

11. While figure "A" rotates 90° to get figure "D" and the figure "B" rotates 90° to get figure "E" not the figure "C".

12. In all the figures, the design is in opposite direction while in the figure "C" it is in same direction.

13. Answer figure have three curves and one straight line while the figure "B" has two straight lines.

14. Except "A" all the base line of the triangle are in the upper position.

15. The small circles on each side are white in all figures but these are black in figure "D".

16. Except "C" each figure has a sign of addition (+) and a vertical sign while the figure "C" has one (+) and one horizontal sign.

17. Except "D" each figure turns 45° while the figure "D" turn 90° from the figure "C".

18. Except "D" all are living things.

19. Except "D" all figures rotates 135° in anticlockwise direction but "D" does not hold this rule.

20. Each figure is enclosed by straight lines while the "B" is enclosed by circle.

21. A straight line and sign of addition (+) rotate in clockwise direction except "D".

22. There is one straight line in every figures but "E" has no any straight line.

23. Except "C" all figures have two pairs of parallel lines with one circle cross each other.

24. The leaves are added only on emerged portion of curved line. But option C does follow the rule.

25. The curve makes some angle with the base whereas in figure "D" it is parallel to the base.

EXERCISE-2

Directions (Qs. 1-25) : *Out of given five figures four are similar in a certain way while one figure is different from the other four figures. In other words, four figures out of five figures form a group. Find the odd figure in each question.*

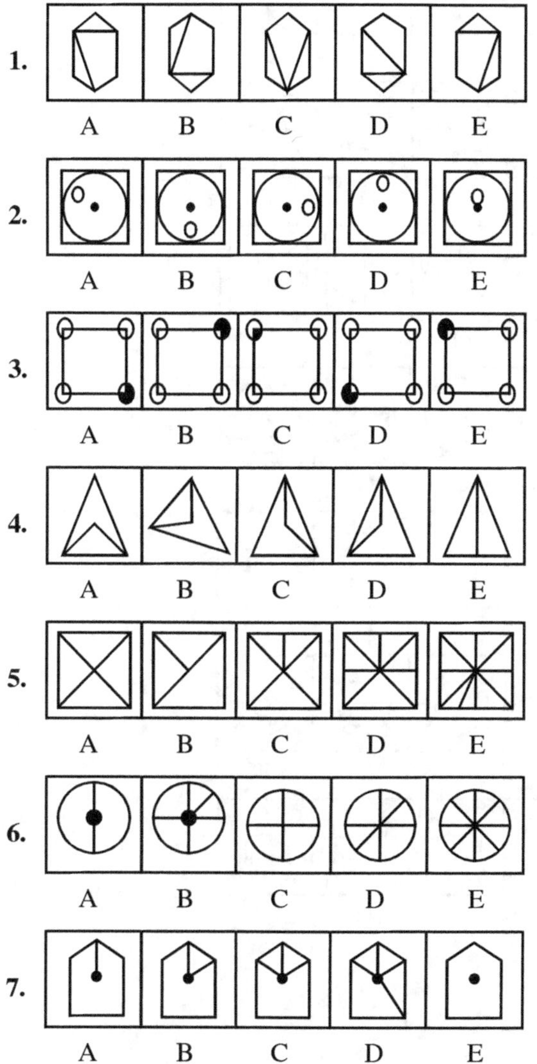

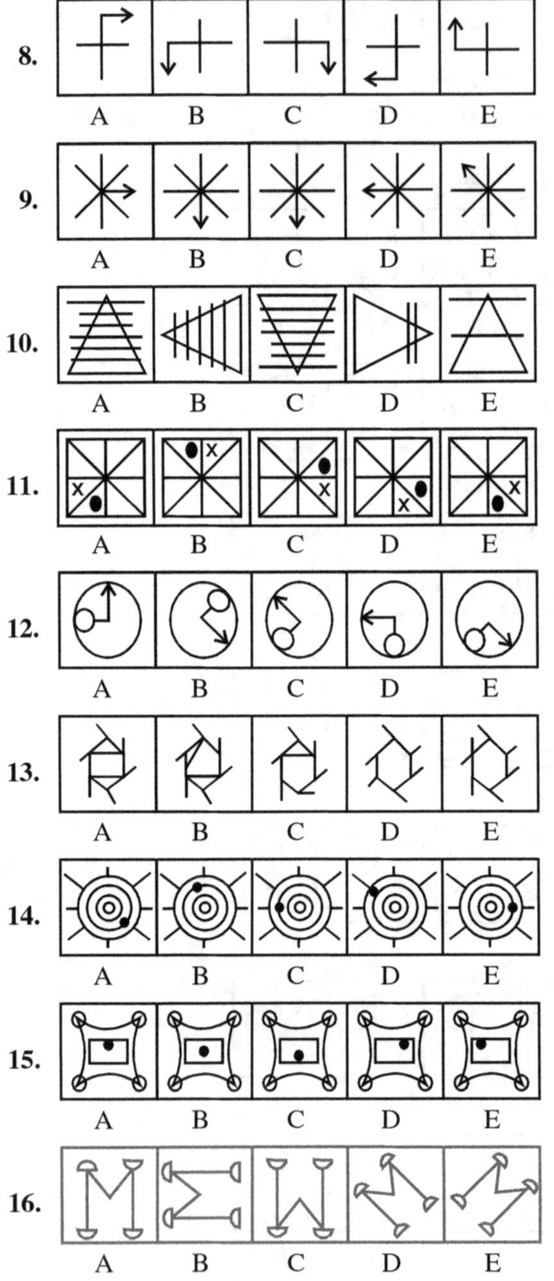
8.
A   B   C   D   E
9.
A   B   C   D   E
10.
A   B   C   D   E
11.
A   B   C   D   E
12.
A   B   C   D   E
13.
A   B   C   D   E
14.
A   B   C   D   E
15.
A   B   C   D   E
16.
A   B   C   D   E

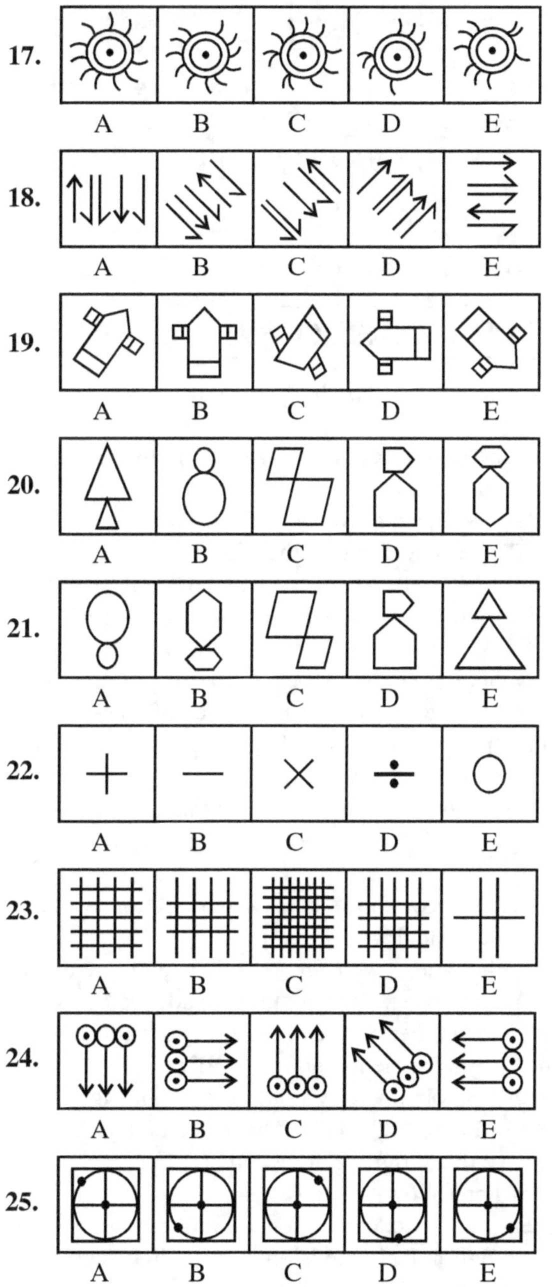

17.
A   B   C   D   E

18.
A   B   C   D   E

19.
A   B   C   D   E

20.
A   B   C   D   E

21.
A   B   C   D   E

22.
A   B   C   D   E

23.
A   B   C   D   E

24.
A   B   C   D   E

25.
A   B   C   D   E

ANSWERS

1	2	3	4	5	6	7	8	9	10
D	E	C	E	A	B	E	B	A	B

11	12	13	14	15	16	17	18	19	20
E	E	E	D	B	A	D	D	C	A

21	22	23	24	25
D	E	C	A	D

EXPLANATIONS

1. Except option D the diagonals of hexagon touch the alternate vertex.
2. In all other figures the smaller circle is away from the centre but in figure "E" it touches the centre.
3. In all other figures the outer part of one of the circles is shaded while in figure "C" the inner part of the circle is shaded.
4. In all other figures there are two line segments inside the triangle but in figure "E" there is only one line segment inside the triangle.
5. In all other figures there are odd number of lines inside the main design but in figure "A" there are even number of lines.
6. In all other figures there are even number of radii but in figure "B" there are odd number of radii.
7. In all other figures there are some line segments inside the pentagon but in figure "E" there is no line segments inside the pentagon.
8. In all other figures the arrow shows clockwise direction while in figure "B" it shows anticlockwise direction.
9. In all other figures there are seven line segments and one arrow but in figure "A" there are six line segments and one arrow.
10. In all other figures the number of line segments is even. But there are 5 (odd number) line segments in figure "B".
11. All other figures can be obtained by rotating any one figure but in figure "E" the position of "O" and "X" have been interchanged.
12. If we move clockwise in the figure, circle comes before the arrow. But option E does not follow the rule.
13. Eight line segments are needed to construct the four figures except the figure in option E. It needs only seven line segments.

14. In all other figures the black dot is located on the second circle from the outside but in figure "D" it is located between the first and the second circles.

15. In all other figures the black dot is located on the periphery of the rectangle but in figure "B" it is on the centre of the rectangle.

16. In all other figures the four semi-circles point towards the same direction but in figure "A" the upper left semi-circle is opposite to the other three semi-circles.

17. Except in figure "D" in all other figures the number of curved lines is odd.

18. Except in figure "D" in all other figures one arrow faces opposite diretion.

19. Except in figure "D" in all other figures the larger figure is pentagon.

20. In all other figures the smaller design is superimposed on the larger design but in figure "A" the larger design is superimposed on the smaller design.

21. In all other figures the larger design is superimposed on the smaller design while in "D" the smaller design is superimposed on the larger design.

22. In all other figures mathematical sign is given but in figure "E" a geometric figure (circle) is given.

23. In all other figures there is difference of one between the vertical and horizontal lines but in figure "C" there are equal number of vertical and horizontal lines.

24. In all other figures then is a dot in the centre of the each circle attached to the arrow but it is not so in figure "A".

25. In all other figures the black dot touches only circle but in figure "D" it touches both the circle and the square.

EXERCISE-3

Directions (Qs. 1-25) : *Four of the following five figures in each question given below are similar in a certain way and hence form a group. One figure is not like the other four. The question is, which one of the five figures does not belong to that group?*

1. 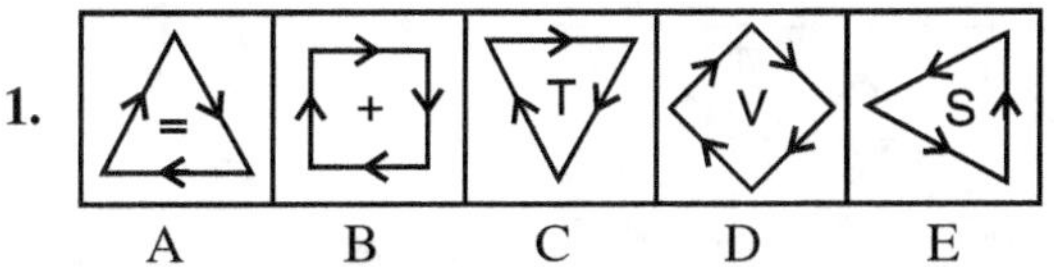
A   B   C   D   E

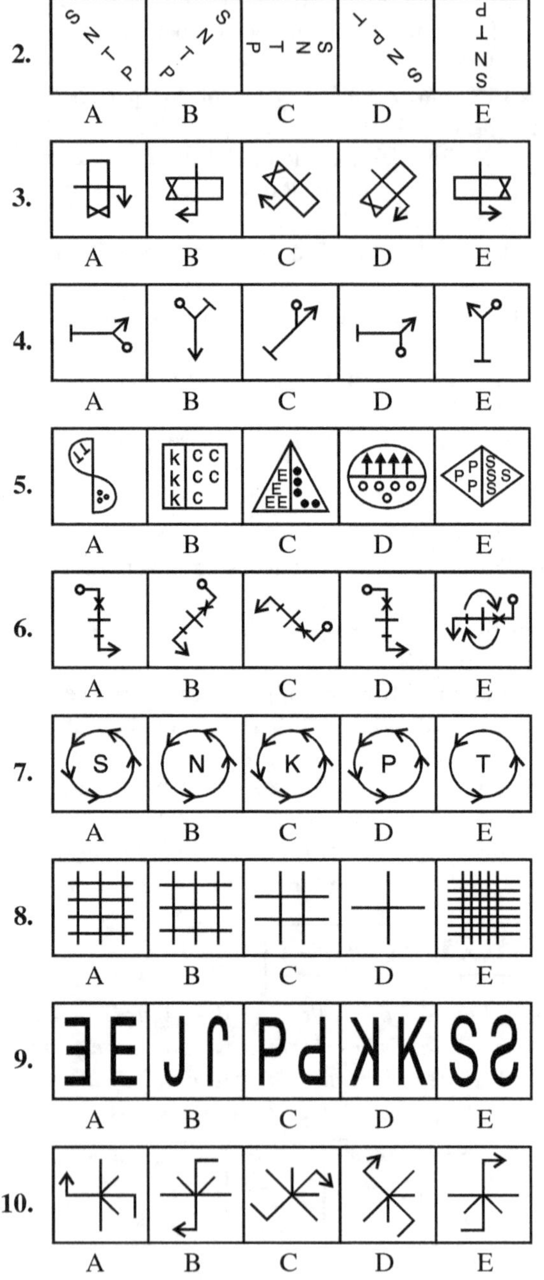

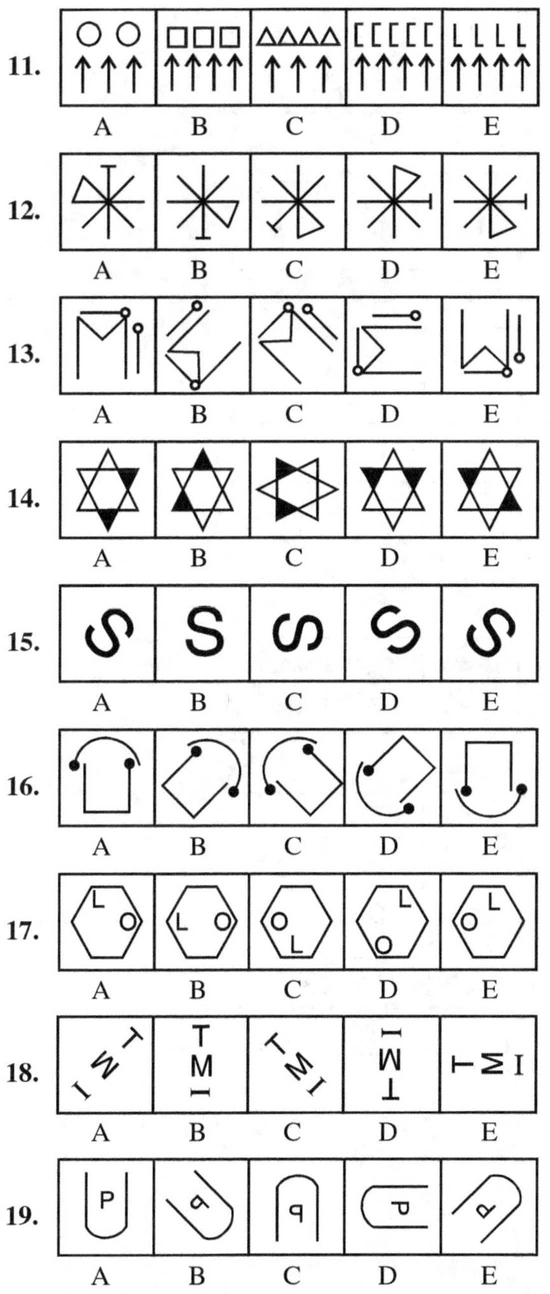

11.   A   B   C   D   E

12.   A   B   C   D   E

13.   A   B   C   D   E

14.   A   B   C   D   E

15.   A   B   C   D   E

16.   A   B   C   D   E

17.   A   B   C   D   E

18.   A   B   C   D   E

19.   A   B   C   D   E

20.

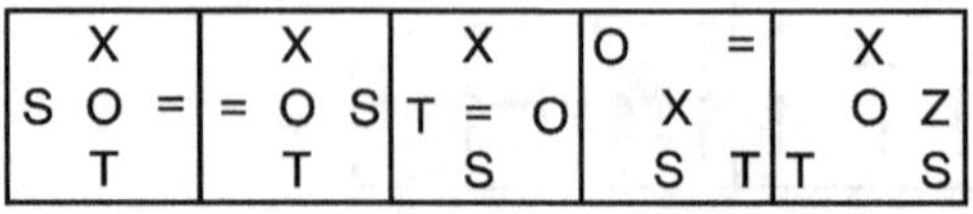

A	B	C	D	E
X S O = T	X = O S T	X T = O S	O = X S T	X O Z T S

21.

A	B	C	D	E
A	O	P	E	I

22.

A	B	C	D	E
E	J	O	T	E

23.

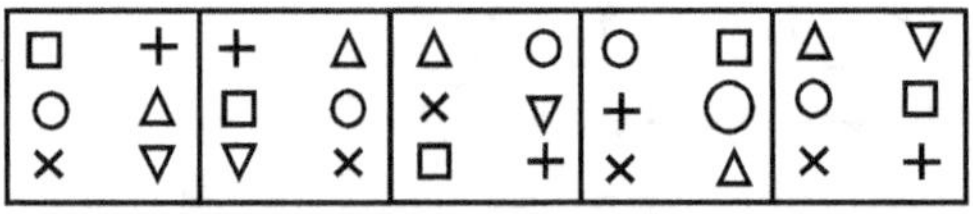

A	B	C	D	E
□ + ○ △ × ▽	+ △ □ ○ ▽ ×	△ ○ × ▽ □ +	○ □ + ○ × △	△ ▽ ○ □ × +

24.

A	B	C	D	E

25.

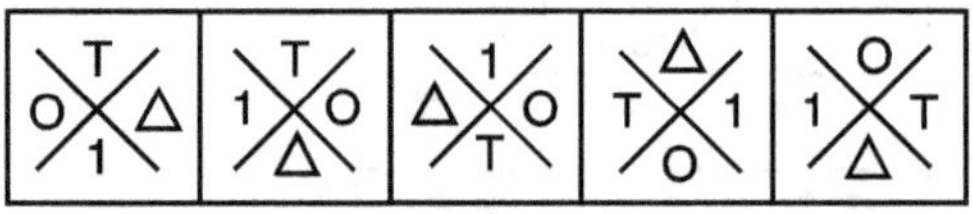

A	B	C	D	E

ANSWERS

1	2	3	4	5	6	7	8	9	10
E	D	E	C	B	E	B	D	C	C

11	12	13	14	15	16	17	18	19	20
E	E	E	E	D	B	D	A	C	E

21	22	23	24	25
C	E	D	D	B

EXERCISE-4

Directions (Qs. 1-25): *Out of the given five figures, four are similar in a certain way. One figure is not like the other four. That means four figures form a group. The question is : which one of the figures does not belong to this group?*

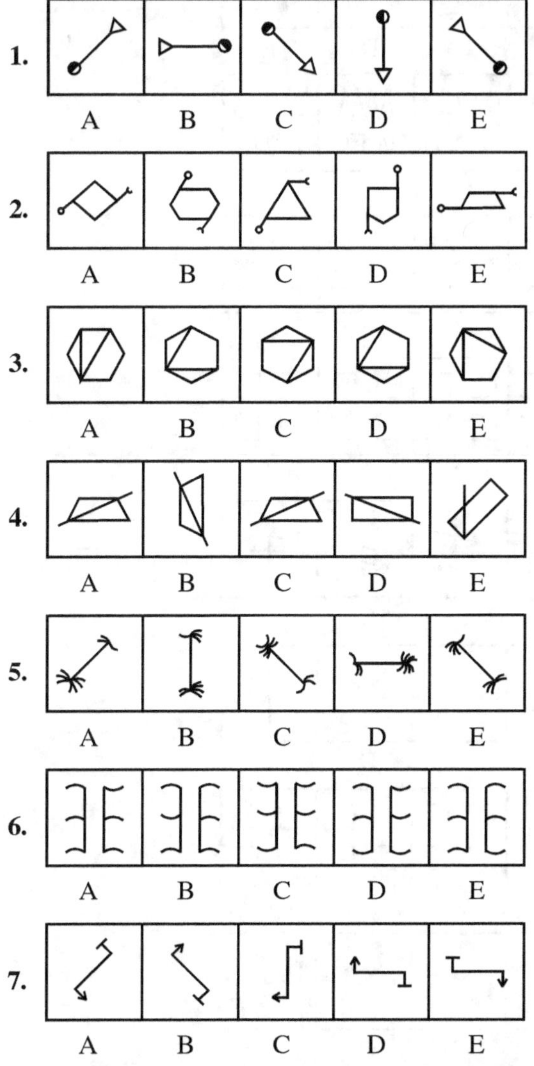

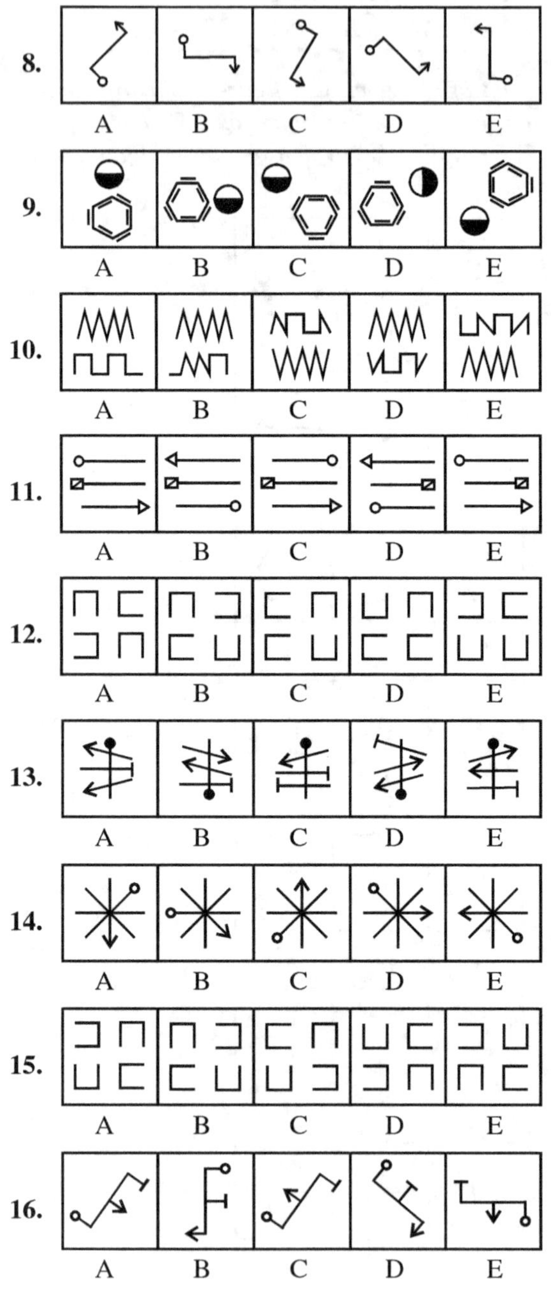

8.   A   B   C   D   E

9.   A   B   C   D   E

10.   A   B   C   D   E

11.   A   B   C   D   E

12.   A   B   C   D   E

13.   A   B   C   D   E

14.   A   B   C   D   E

15.   A   B   C   D   E

16.   A   B   C   D   E

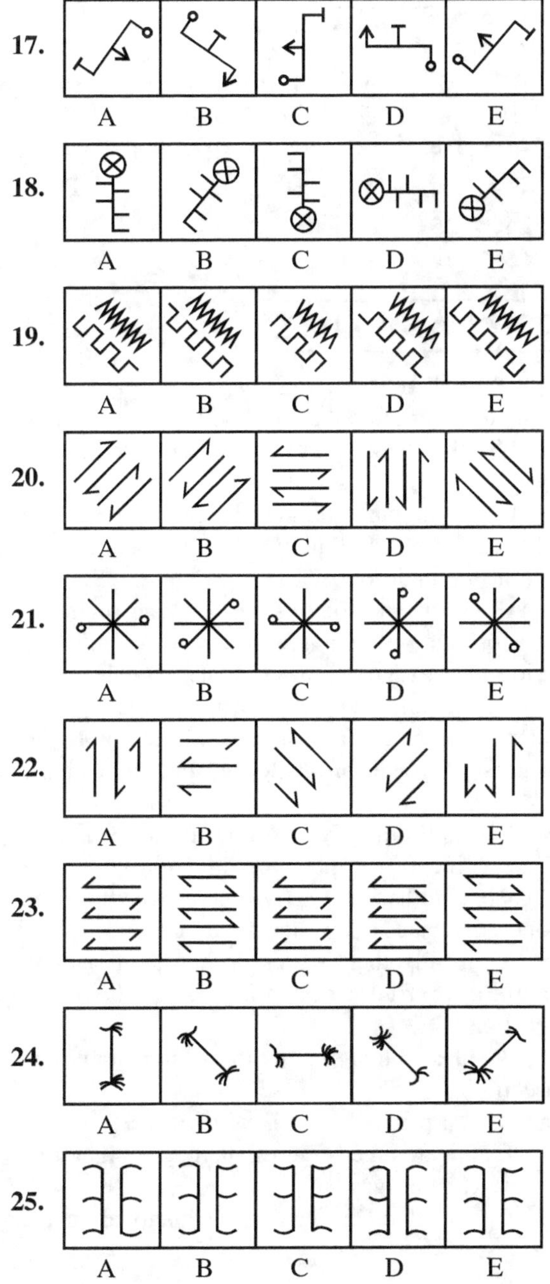

17. A B C D E

18. A B C D E

19. A B C D E

20. A B C D E

21. A B C D E

22. A B C D E

23. A B C D E

24. A B C D E

25. A B C D E

Rly Apt (E)–2

ANSWERS

1	2	3	4	5	6	7	8	9	10
B	C	A	E	D	D	A	B	D	E

11	12	13	14	15	16	17	18	19	20
C	B	C	B	A	A	D	B	A	B

21	22	23	24	25
A	A	D	C	B

EXPLANATIONS

1. Except in figure "B" in all other figures the shaded part of the circle is at right angle or in a straight line with respect to line segment. In figure "B" the shaded part of the circle is obliquely placed with respect to the line segment.

2. Except in figure "C" in all other figures the pinhead and the arrow are parallel to each other. In figure "C" the two designs are placed at an angle at an angle of 135°.

3. Except in figure "A" in all other figures the two line segments inside the hexagon form an obtuse angle. In figure "A" the two line segments inside the hexagon form an actue angle.

4. Except in figure "E", in all other figures the median passes through the two corners of the given geometrical figure. In figure "E", the median passes through an angle and one side of the parallelogram.

5. Except in figure "D", in all other figures, four and three curves attached to the line segment face the same direction.

6. Except in figure "D" in all other figures five curves face the same direction while one curve faces opposite directions.

7. Except in figure "A" in all other figures the design moves in clock wise direction. In figure "A" the design moves in anticlockwise direction.

8. Except in figure "B" in all other figures the design rotates in anticlockwise direction.

9. In figure "D", the shaded part of circle is vertical.

10. Except in figure "E" in all other figures there are eight line segments each in the two designs.

11. Except in figure "C" in all other figures the diagonal in the square is similar.

12. Except in figure "B" in all other figures two designs out of four designs face the same directions.

13. Except in figure "C" in all other figures there are two arrows ($\rightarrow$) and one (T). In figure ''C'' there are two (T) and one arrow ($\rightarrow$).

14. Except in figure "B" in all other figures the arrow is two steps ahead in closkwise direction of the circle.

15. Except in figure "A" in all other figures the design rotates in clockwise diretion. In figure "A" the design rotates in anticlockwise direction.

16. In figure "A" the designs "T" and "$\rightarrow$" face same direction while in other figures they face different directions.

17. Except in figure "D" in all other figures the designs "T" and "$\rightarrow$" face different directions.

18. In figure "B" there is a continuous stright line.

19. Except in figure "A" in all other figures the number of line segments of both the designs is the same.

20. In figure "B" the attached line segments of the two middle lines should be opposite to one another to maintain the alternating series.

21. Except figure "A" all other figures show movement in clockwise direction. The design of figure "A" shows movement in anticlockwise direction.

22. Except in figure "A" in all other figures two adjacent line segment have arrow heads facing the same direction.

23. Except in figure "D" in all other figures bent line segments are placed at the upper and lower sides. alternatively.

24. Except in figure "C" in all other figures the three and four curves attached to the line segment face same direction.

25. Except in figure "B" in all other figures five curves face the same direction and only one curve faces opposite direction. In figure "B" four curves face the same direction and the other two curves face opposite direction.

SIMILARITY TEST

In this type of test, there are two sets of figures. One set is 'Problem Figure' while the other is 'Answer Figures'. The candidates are required to select one of the figures from the 'Answer Figures' which also exhibits the same characteristics.

Example:

Problem Figure   **Answer Figures**

Explanation: E (All the elements of the problem figure are present in the figure E).

EXERCISE-1

Directions (Qs. 1-20) : *In each of the following questions an unnumbered figure is followed by four numbered figures. The unnumbered figure resembles with one of the four numbered figures. The number of that figure is your answer.*

Problem Figure   **Answer Figures**

Problem Figure　　　　　**Answer Figures**

3.

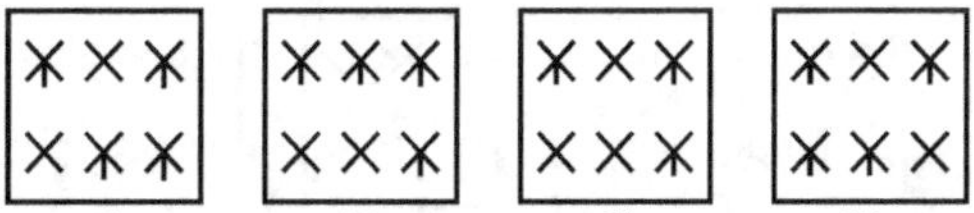

A　　　　B　　　　C　　　　D

4.

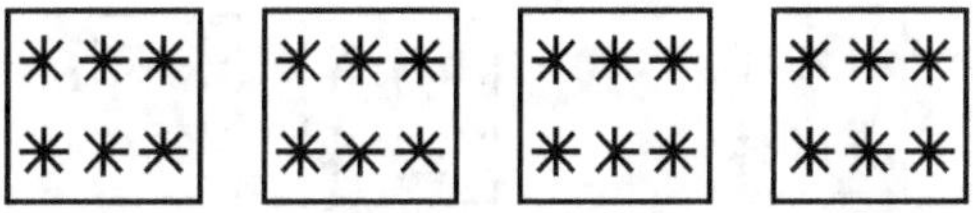

A　　　　B　　　　C　　　　D

5.

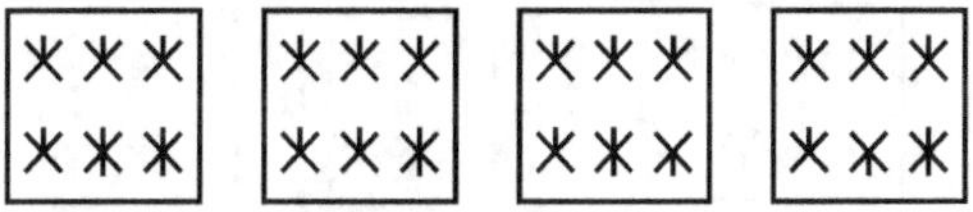

A　　　　B　　　　C　　　　D

6.

A　　　　B　　　　C　　　　D

7.

A　　　　B　　　　C　　　　D

8.

A　　　　B　　　　C　　　　D

9.

A　　　　B　　　　C　　　　D

10.

A　　　　B　　　　C　　　　D

11.

A　　　　B　　　　C　　　　D

Problem Figure   **Answer Figures**

12.

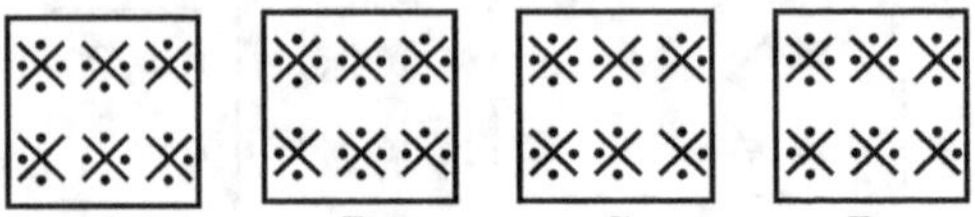

A   B   C   D

13.

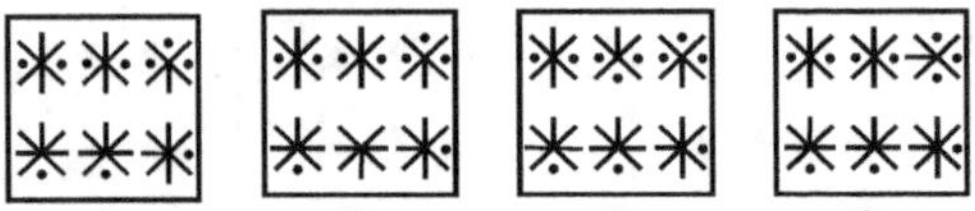

A   B   C   D

14.

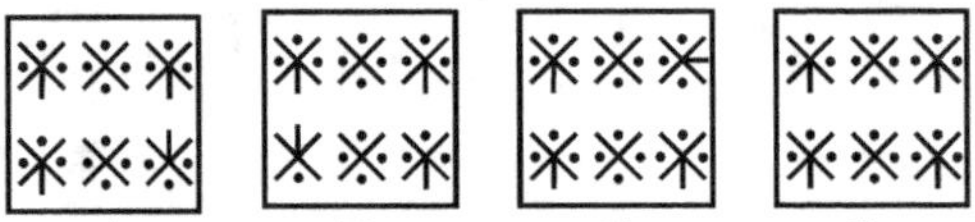

A   B   C   D

15.

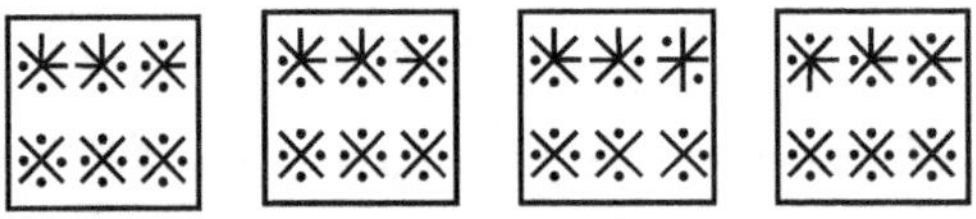

A   B   C   D

16.

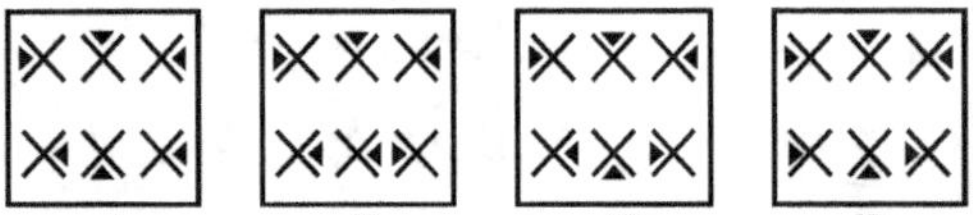

A   B   C   D

17.

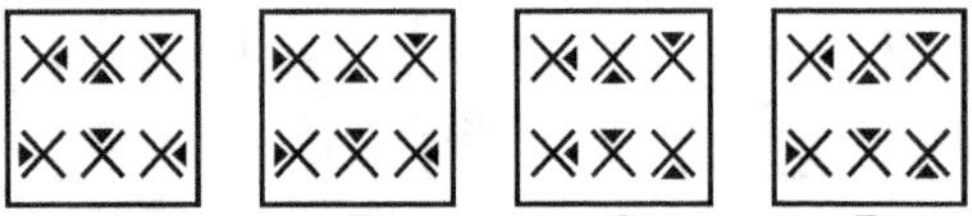

A   B   C   D

18.

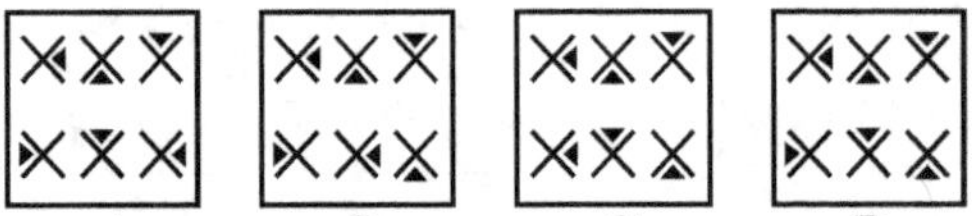

A   B   C   D

19.

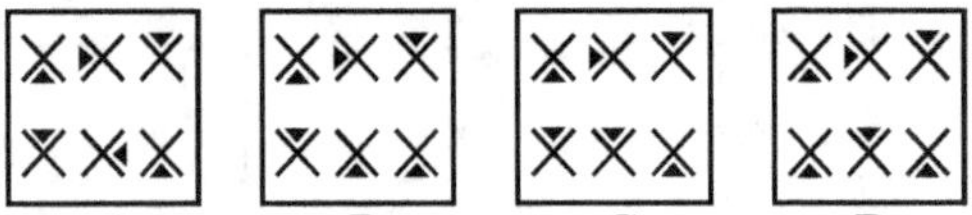

A   B   C   D

20.

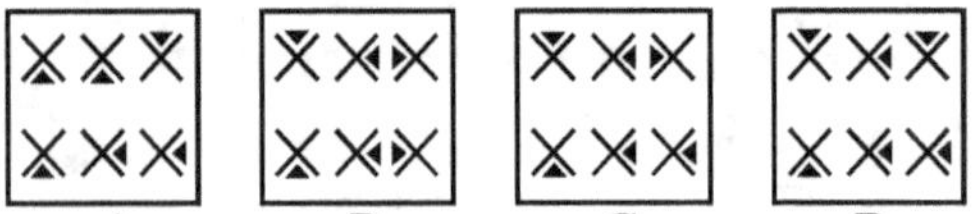

A   B   C   D

ANSWERS

1	2	3	4	5	6	7	8	9	10
D	B	C	A	C	C	B	D	A	C

11	12	13	14	15	16	17	18	19	20
B	A	A	D	A	C	B	D	A	C

EXERCISE-2

Directions (Qs. 1-40) : *In each of the following questions, there are two sets of figures. One set is 'Problem Figure' while the other is 'Answer Figures'. Find out which one of the answer figures should be same as problem figure.*

Problem Figure   **Answer Figures**

1.

2.

3.

4.

5.

6.

Problem Figure **Answer Figures**

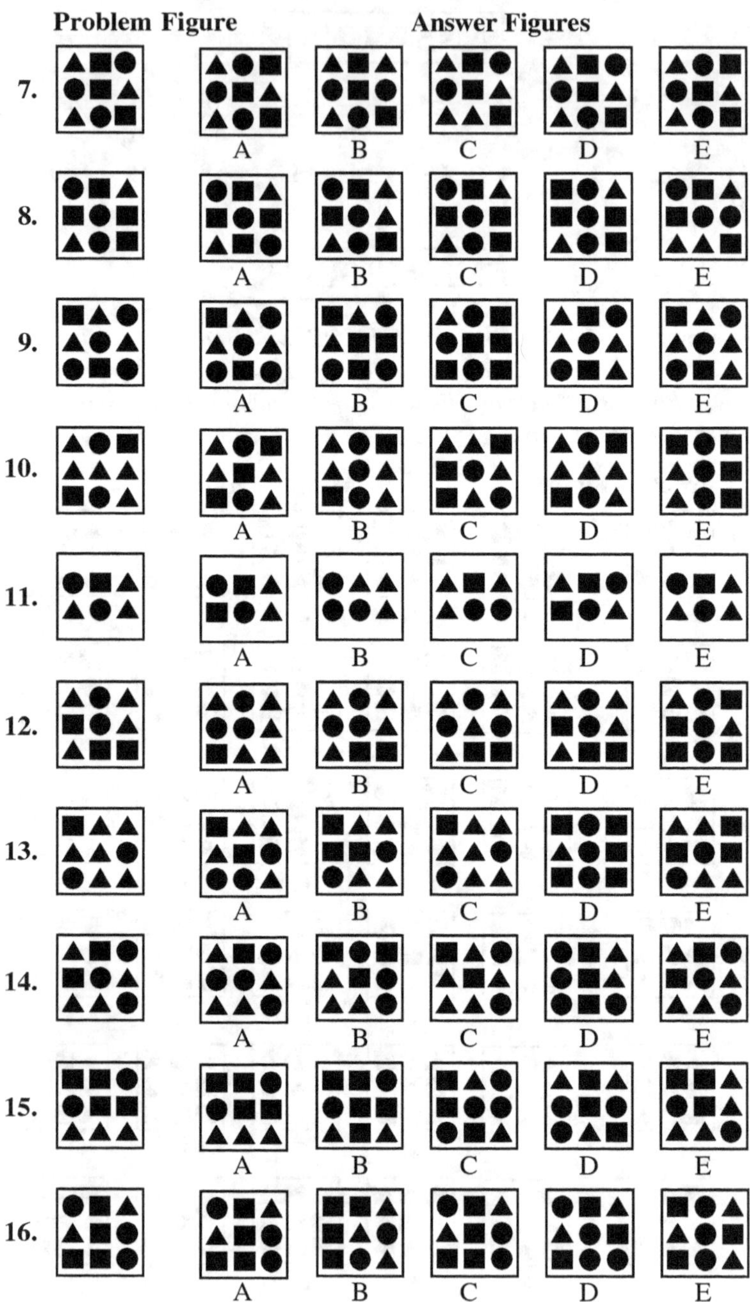

Problem Figure   **Answer Figures**

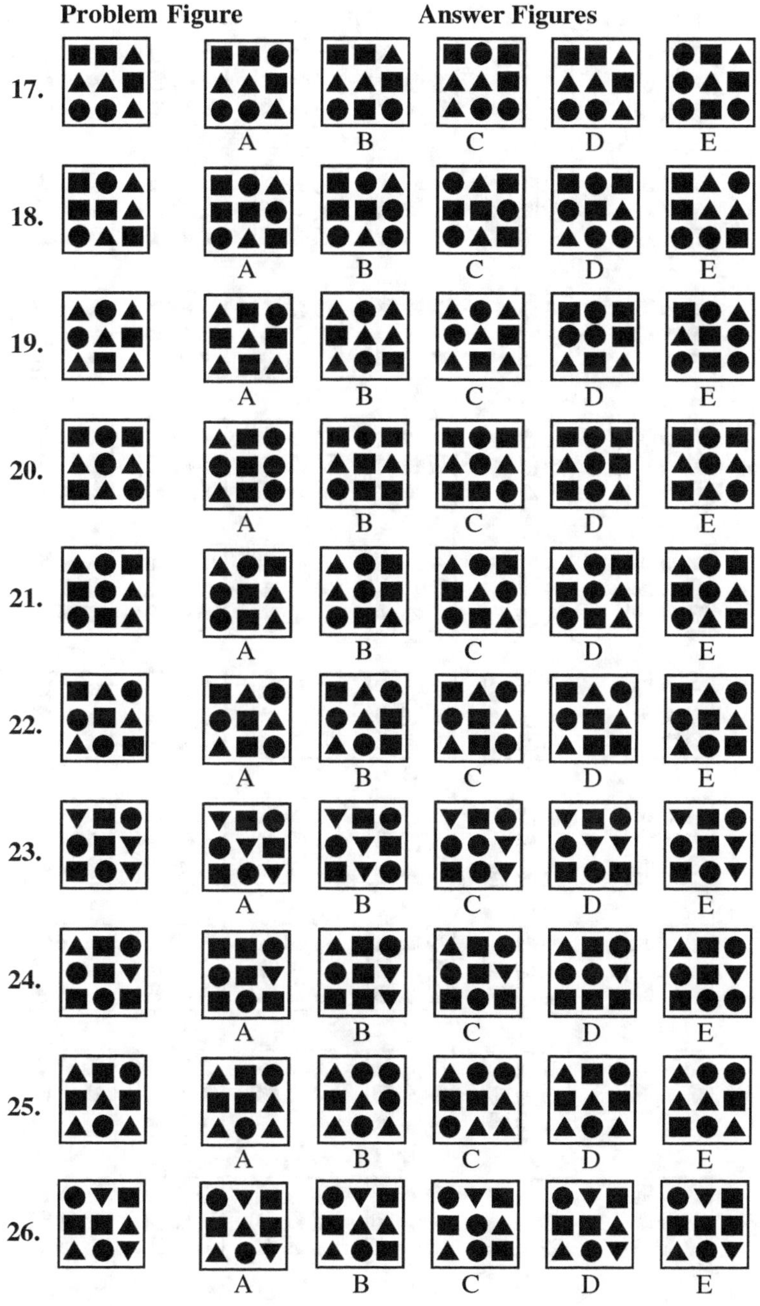

Problem Figure **Answer Figures**

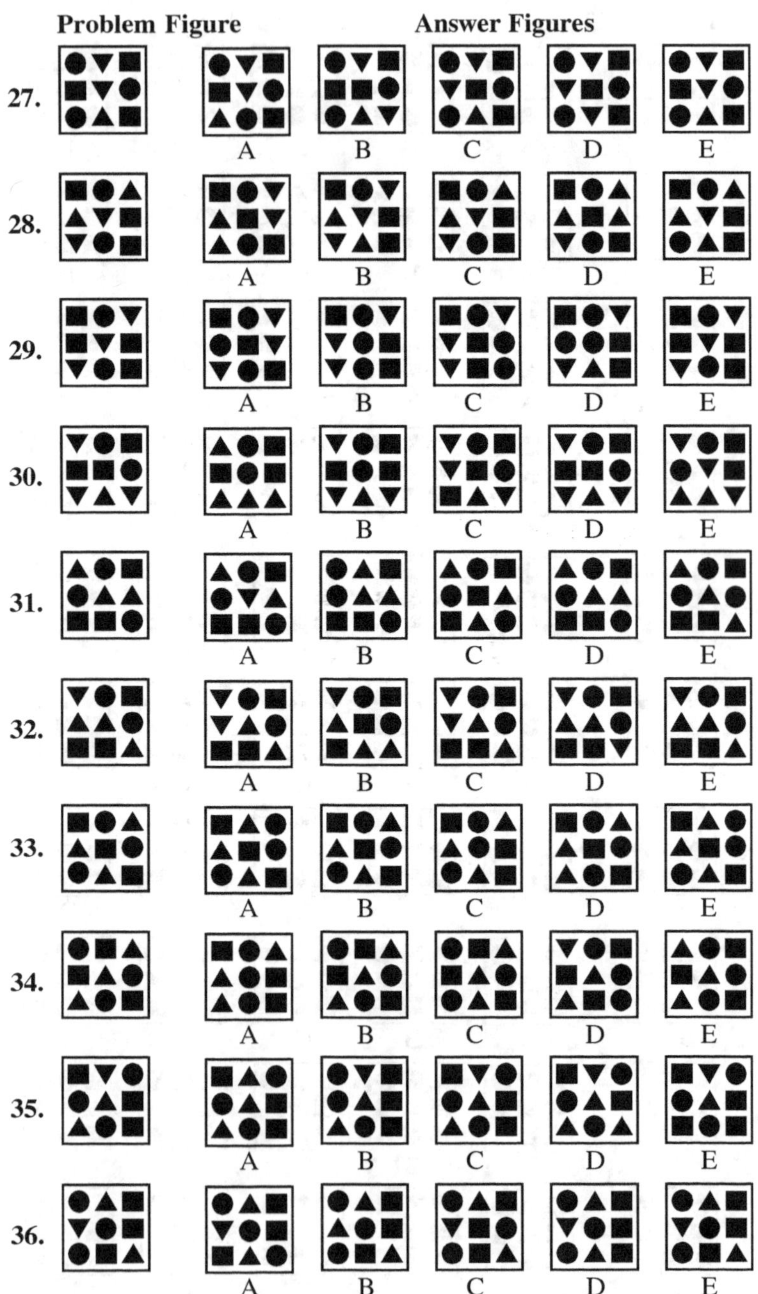

27.

28.

29.

30.

31.

32.

33.

34.

35.

36.

Problem Figure   **Answer Figures**

37.

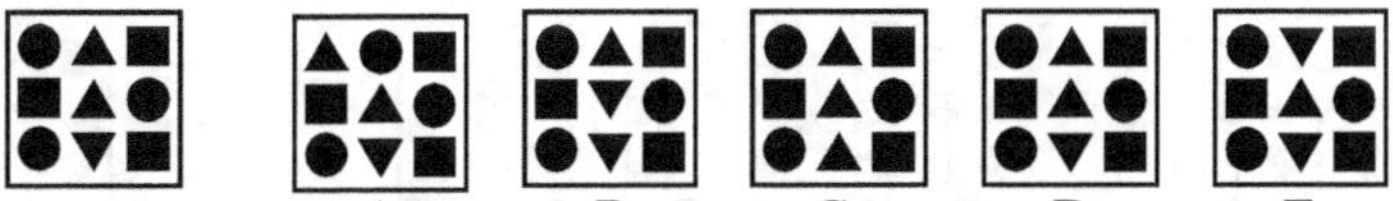

        A   B   C   D   E

38.

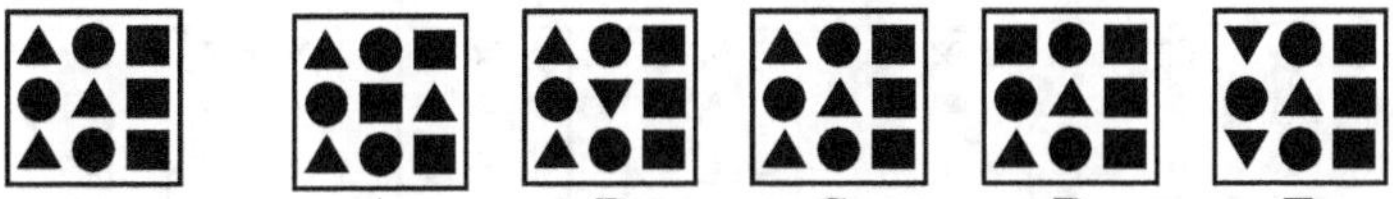

        A   B   C   D   E

39.

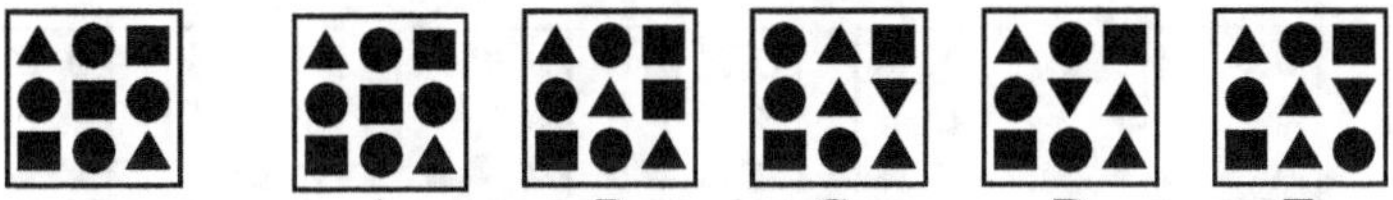

        A   B   C   D   E

40.

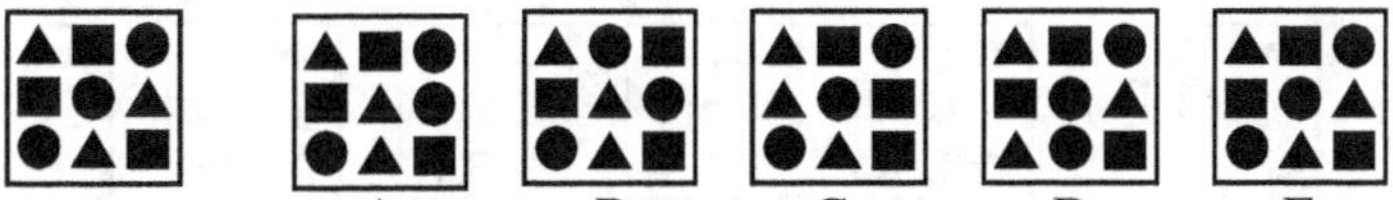

        A   B   C   D   E

ANSWERS

1	2	3	4	5	6	7	8	9	10
B	C	A	E	E	B	D	C	A	D

11	12	13	14	15	16	17	18	19	20
E	D	C	E	A	C	D	A	C	E

21	22	23	24	25	26	27	28	29	30
D	E	E	C	D	D	E	C	E	D

31	32	33	34	35	36	37	38	39	40
D	E	B	B	C	E	D	C	A	E

EXERCISE-3

Directions (Qs. 1-40) : *In each of the following questions, there are two sets of figures. One set is 'Problem Figure' while the other is 'Answer Figures'. Find out which one of the answer figures should be same as problem figure.*

Problem Figure   **Answer Figures**

1.

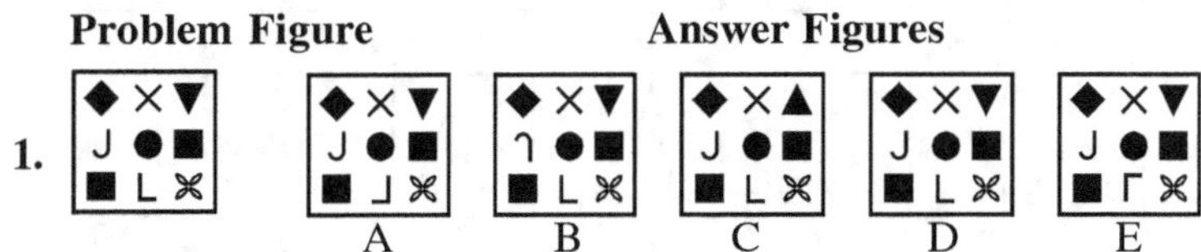

        A   B   C   D   E

Problem Figure   **Answer Figures**

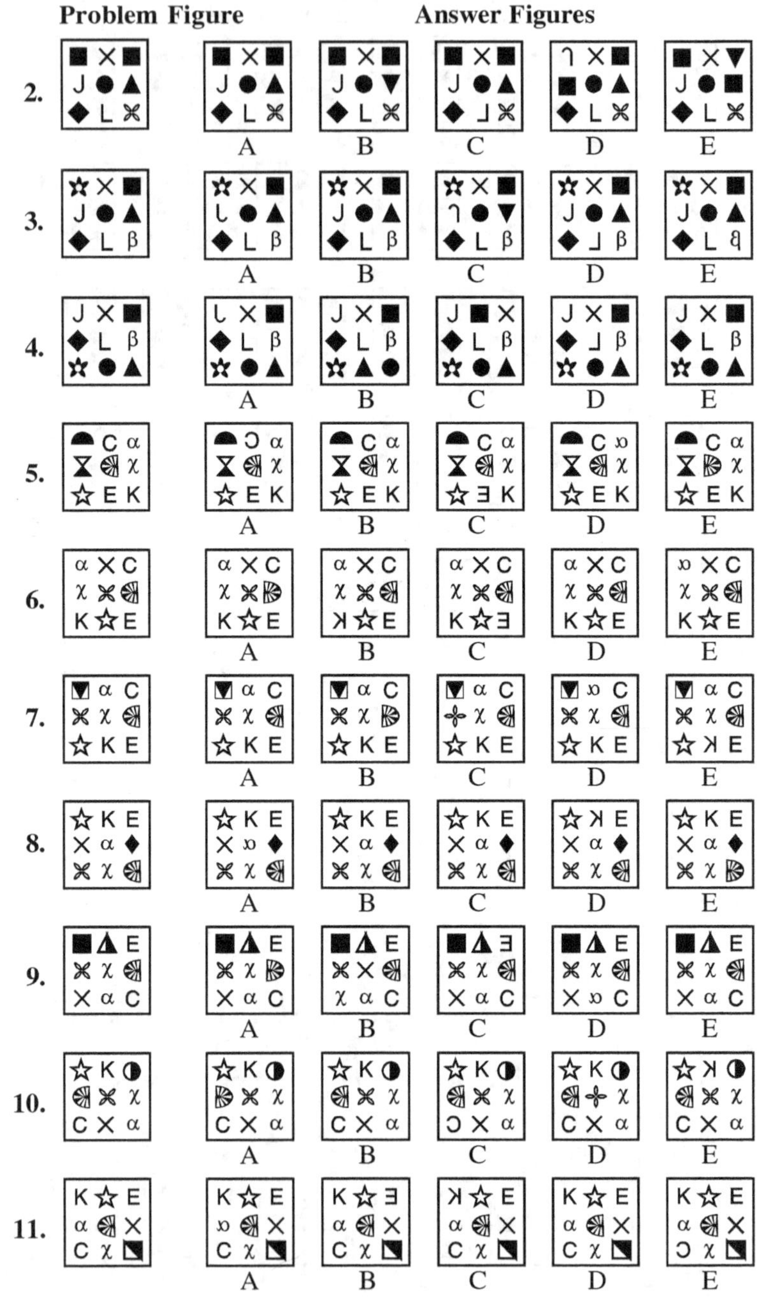

Problem Figure   **Answer Figures**

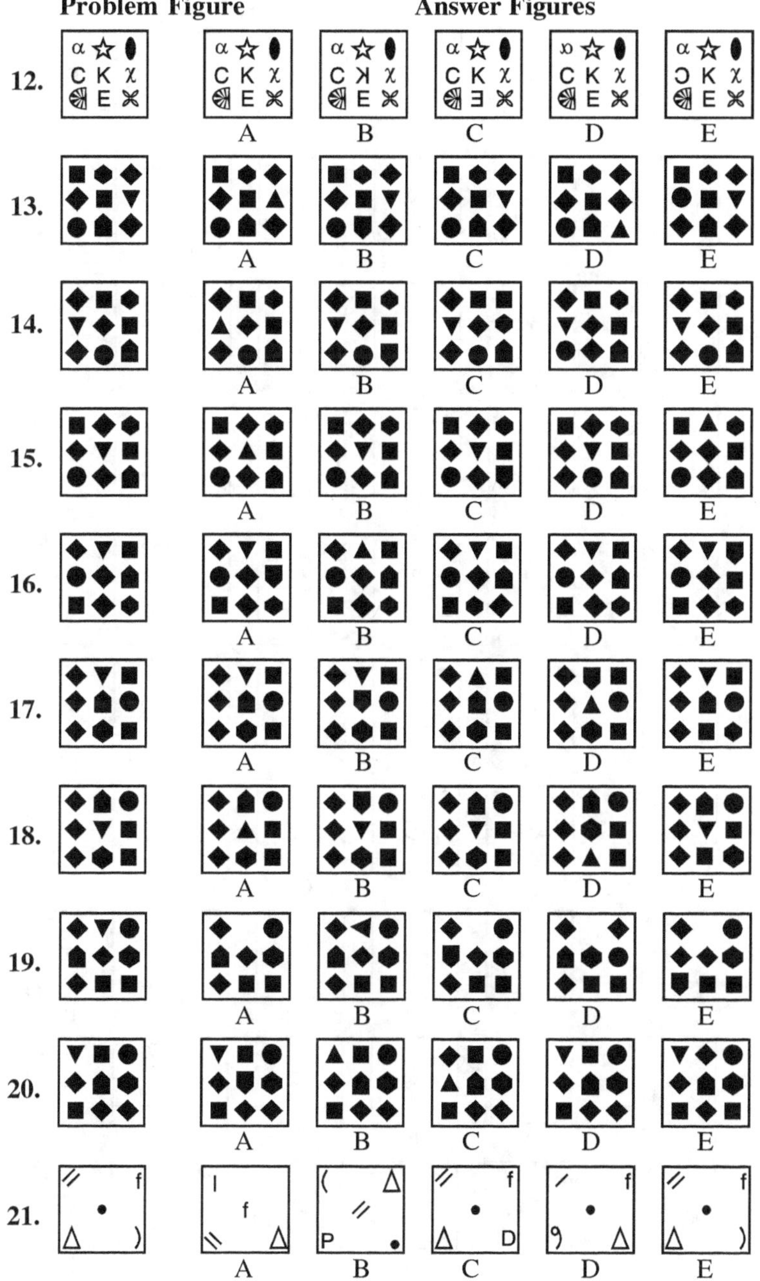

Problem Figure   Answer Figures

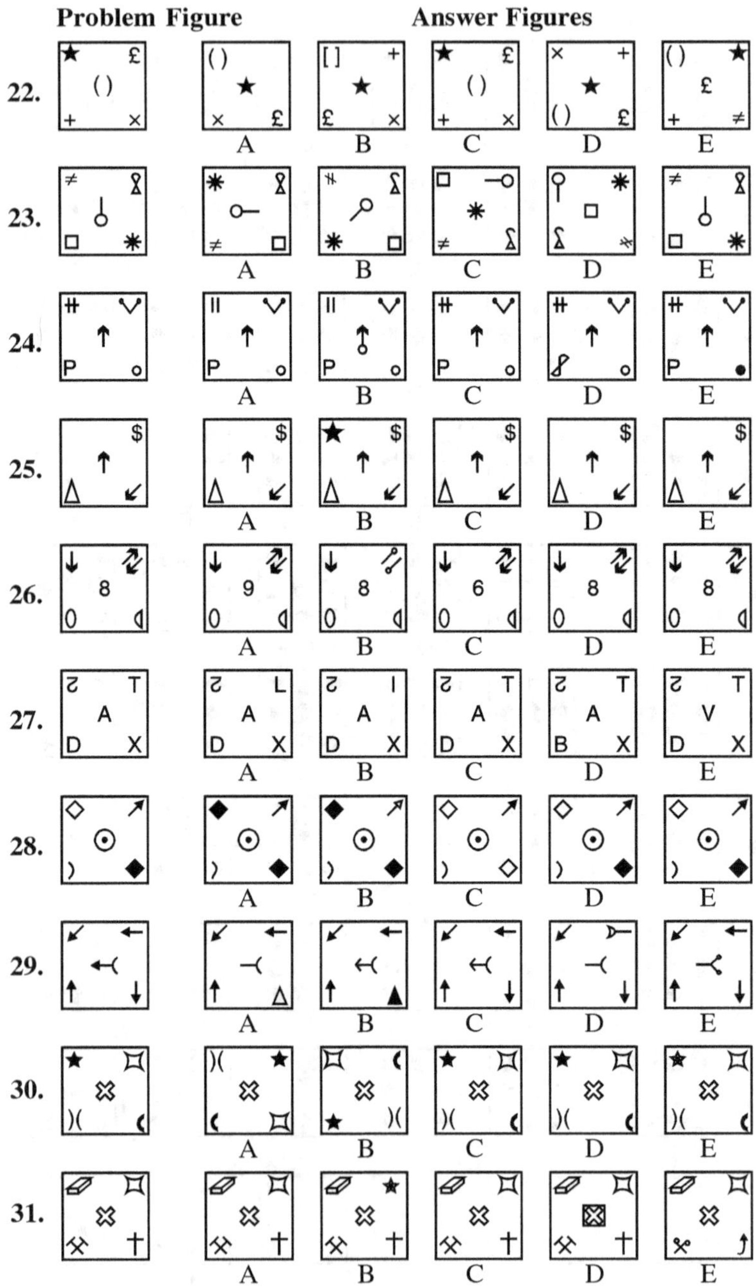

Problem Figure   **Answer Figures**

32.

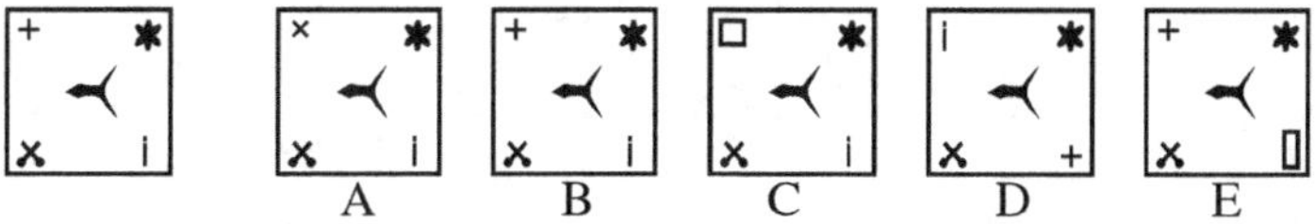

A   B   C   D   E

33.

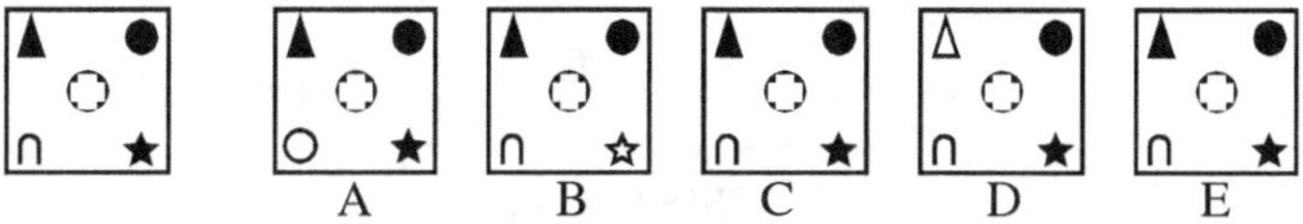

A   B   C   D   E

34.

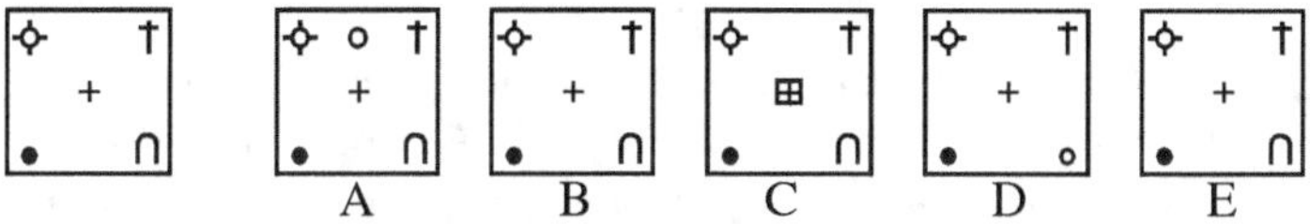

A   B   C   D   E

35.

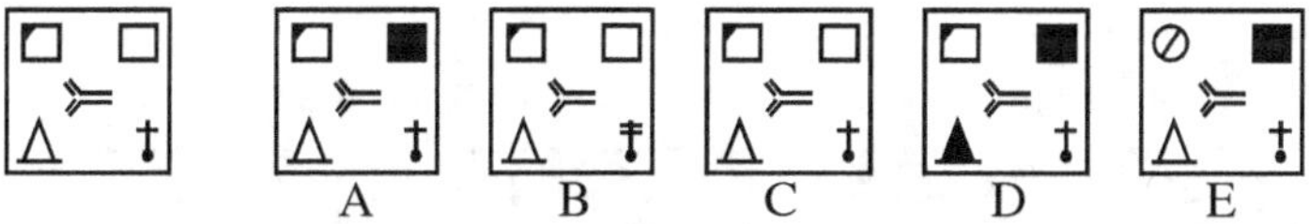

A   B   C   D   E

36.

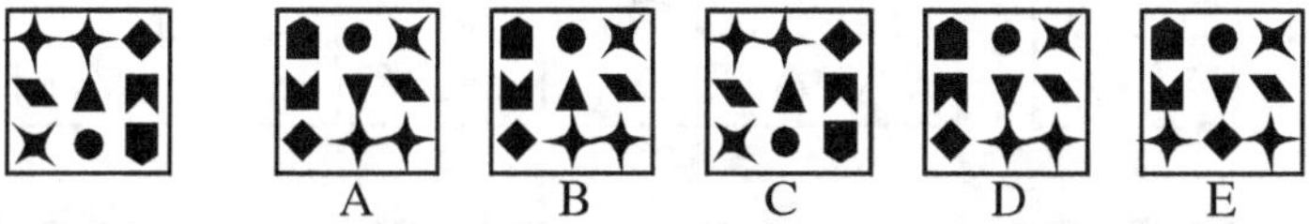

A   B   C   D   E

37.

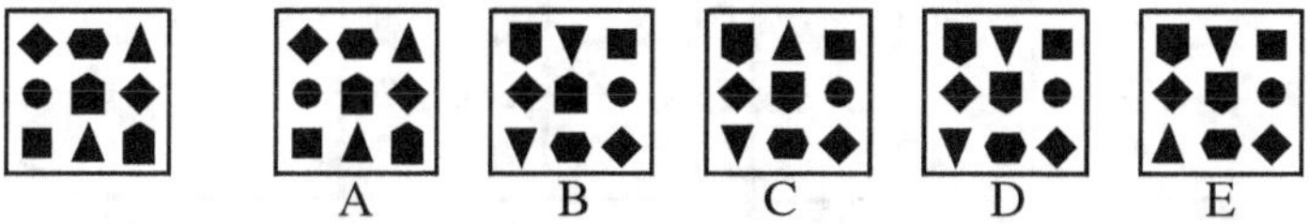

A   B   C   D   E

38.

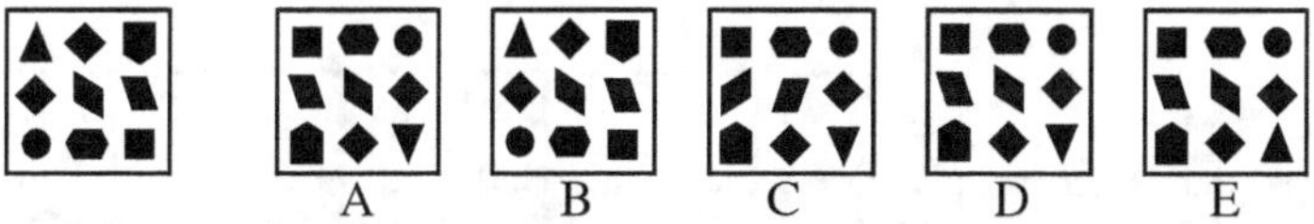

A   B   C   D   E

39.

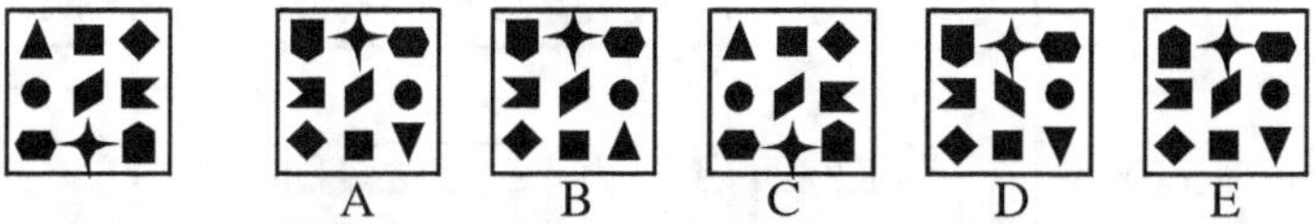

A   B   C   D   E

40.

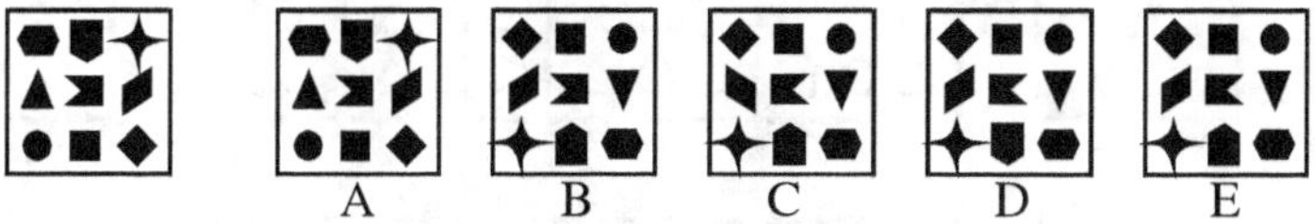

A   B   C   D   E

ANSWERS

1	2	3	4	5	6	7	8	9	10
D	A	B	E	B	D	A	C	E	B

11	12	13	14	15	16	17	18	19	20
D	A	C	E	B	D	A	C	B	D

21	22	23	24	25	26	27	28	29	30
E	C	E	C	D	E	C	D	C	D

31	32	33	34	35	36	37	38	39	40
A	B	E	E	C	C	A	B	C	A

EXERCISE-4

Directions (Qs. 1-40) : *In each of the following questions, there are two sets of figures. One set is 'Problem Figure' while the other is 'Answer Figures'. Find out which one of the answer figures should be same as problem figure.*

Problem Figure   **Answer Figures**

Problem Figure   **Answer Figures**

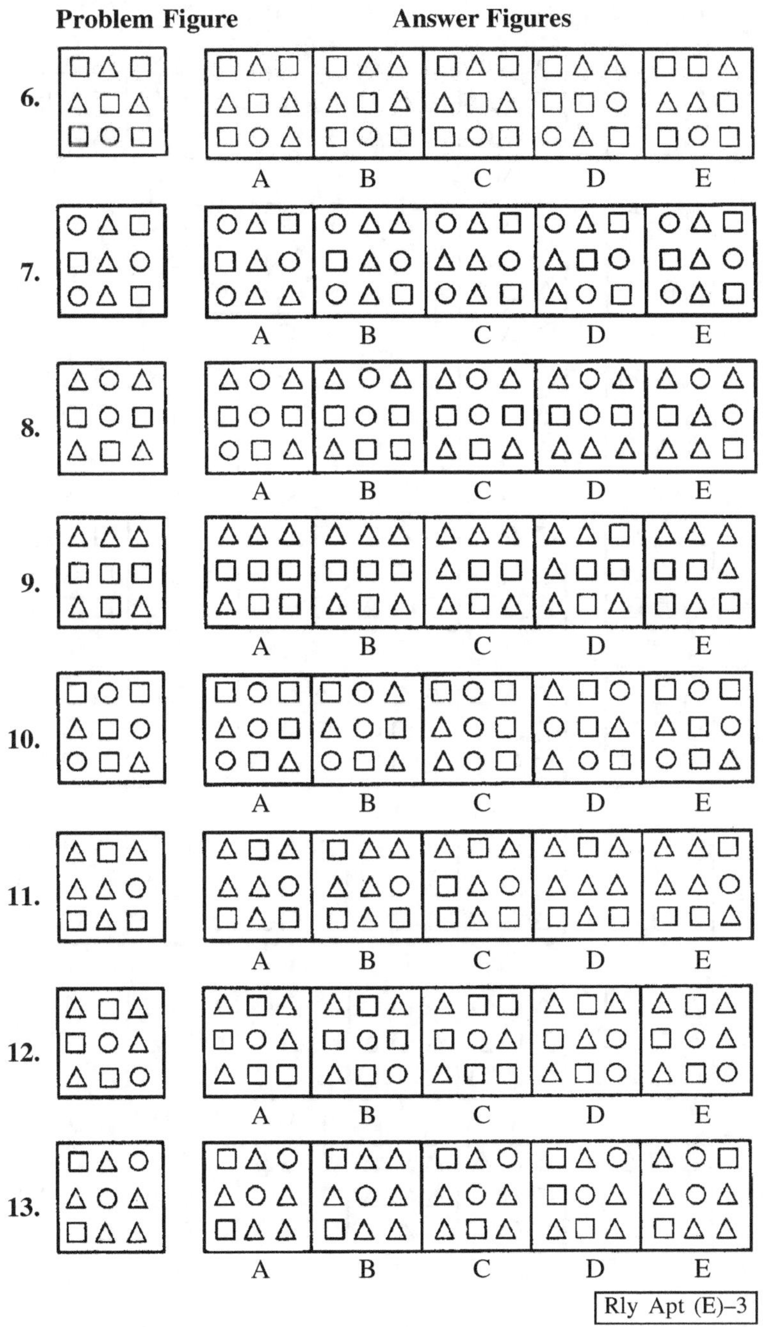

Problem Figure   **Answer Figures**

14.

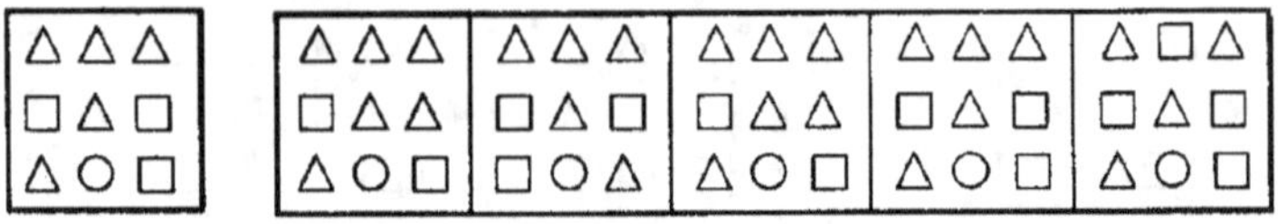

A   B   C   D   E

15.

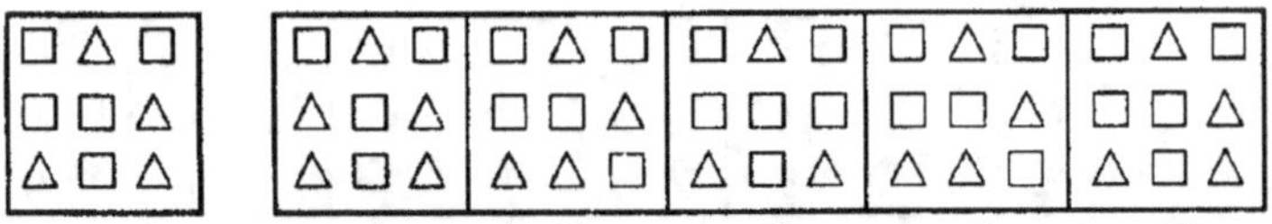

A   B   C   D   E

16.

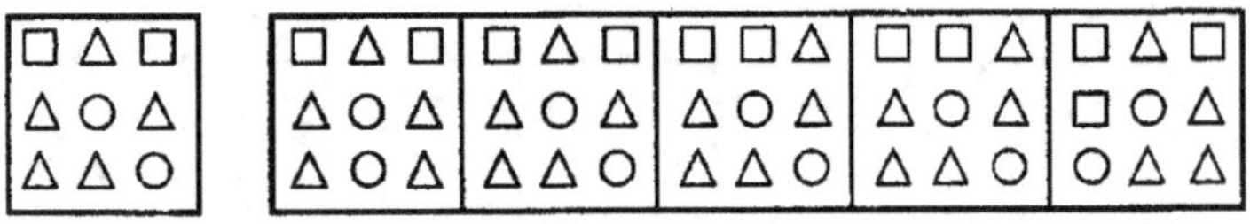

A   B   C   D   E

17.

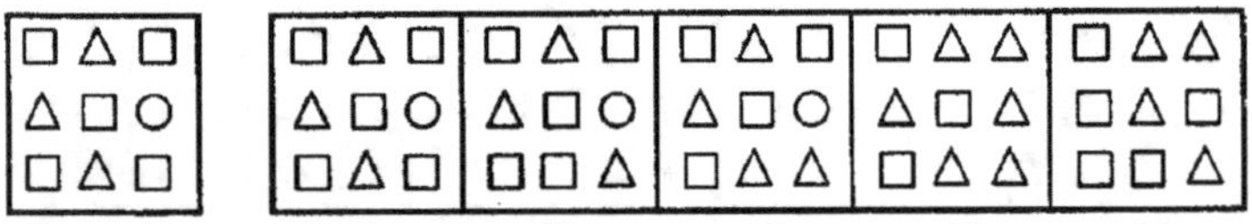

A   B   C   D   E

18.

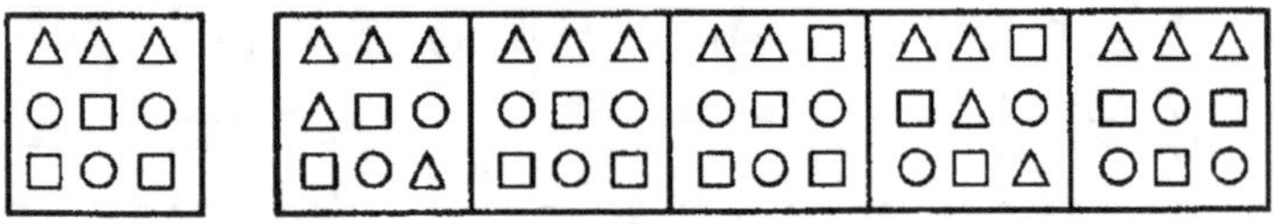

A   B   C   D   E

19.

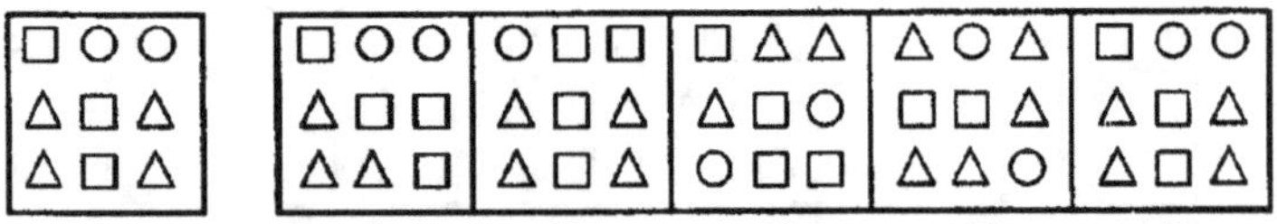

A   B   C   D   E

20.

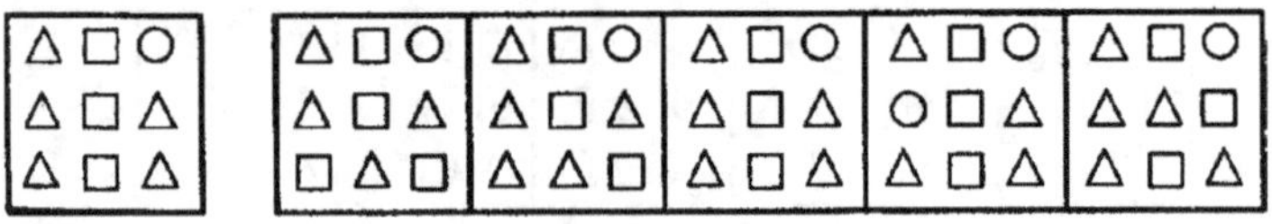

A   B   C   D   E

21.

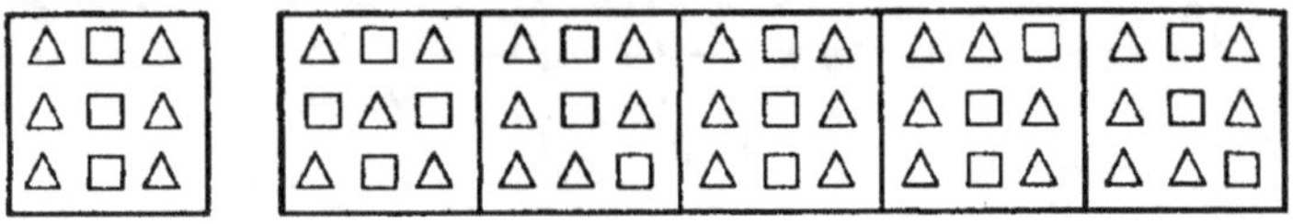

A   B   C   D   E

Problem Figure　　　　　　　**Answer Figures**

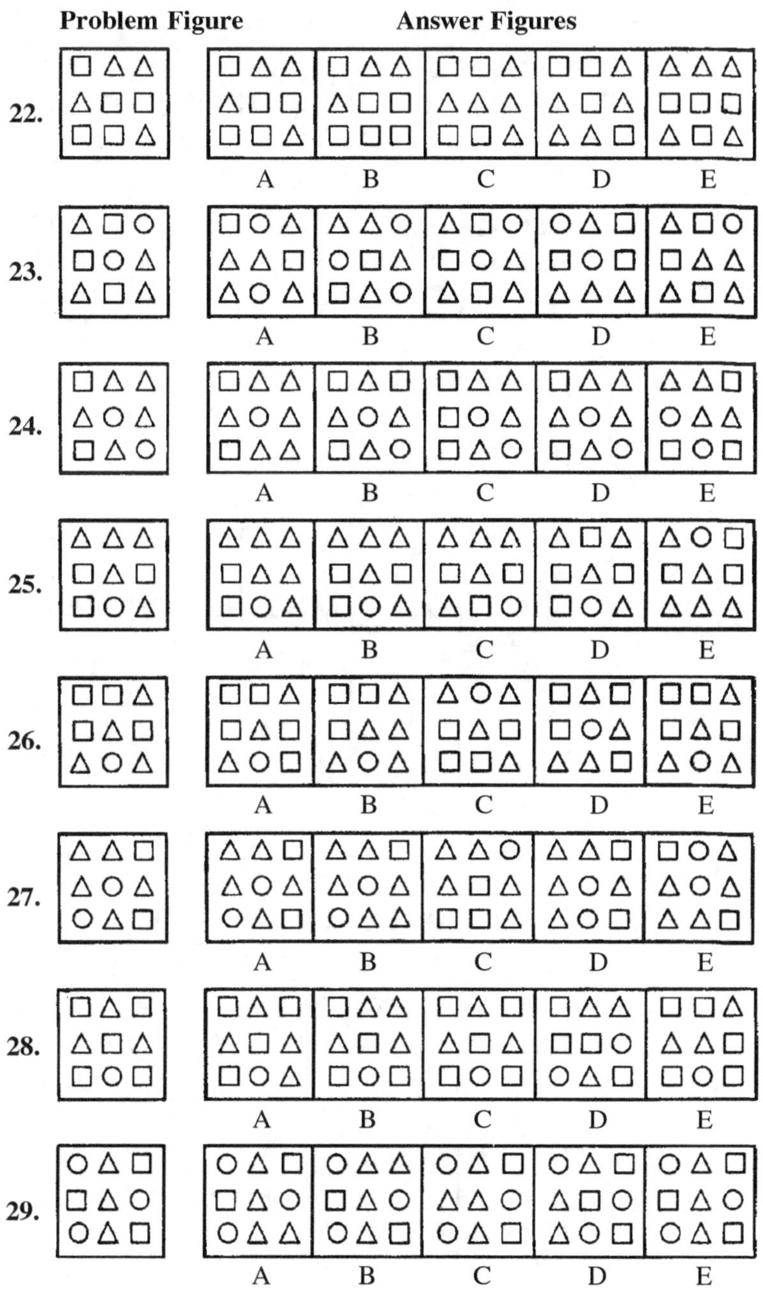

Problem Figure   **Answer Figures**

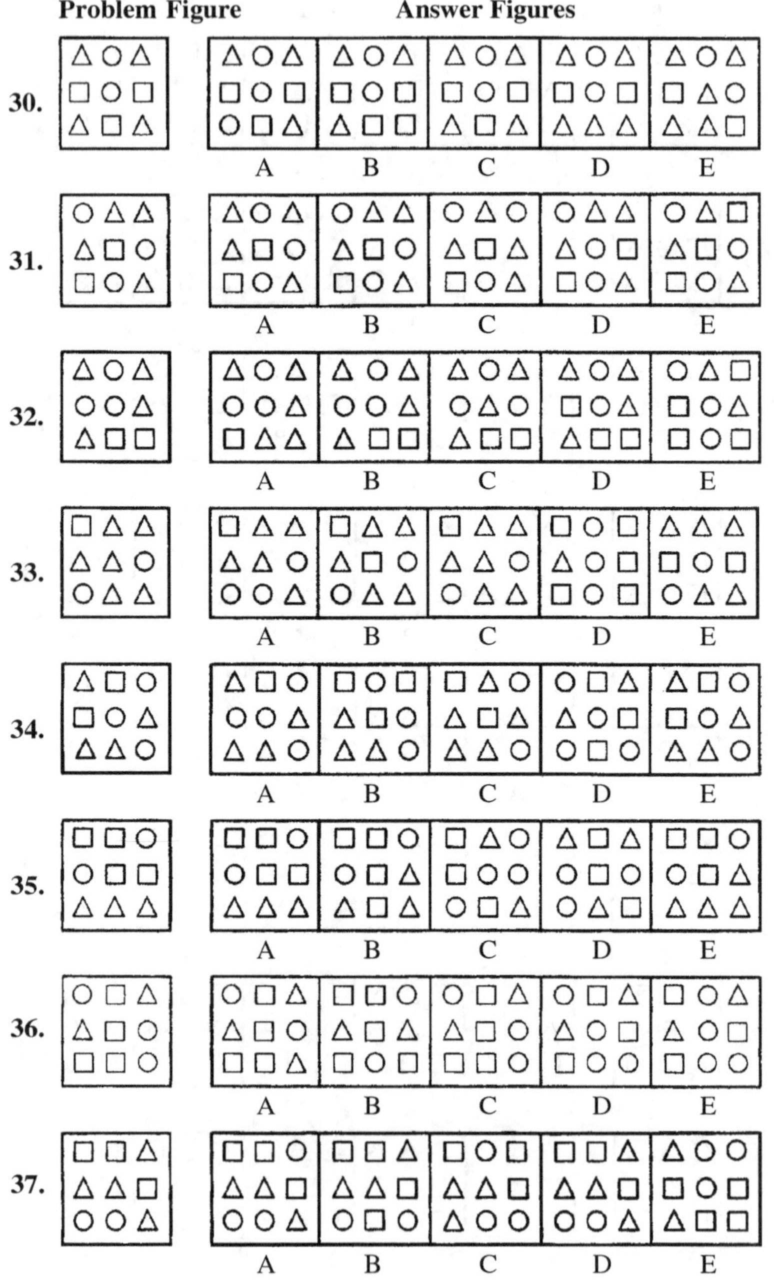

Problem Figure **Answer Figures**

38.

| □ ○ △ |
| □ □ ○ |
| ○ △ □ |

□ ○ △	□ ○ △	○ △ ○	□ ○ □	□ △ ○
□ □ ○	□ □ ○	□ □ ○	○ □ △	□ △ △
○ △ □	○ △ ○	○ △ □	△ ○ ○	△ ○ □
A	B	C	D	E

39.

| △ ○ △ |
| □ △ □ |
| △ □ △ |

△ □ ○	△ ○ △	△ ○ △	□ ○ □	□ ○ □
□ △ □	□ △ △	□ △ □	○ ○ □	△ □ ○
△ □ △	△ ○ □	△ □ △	△ □ △	○ □ △
A	B	C	D	E

40.

| □ ○ □ |
| △ ○ △ |
| □ △ ○ |

△ □ ○	□ ○ □	□ ○ □	□ △ □	□ ○ △
○ □ △	△ □ △	△ ○ △	△ ○ □	△ ○ △
△ □ ○	○ □ □	□ △ ○	□ ○ △	□ △ ○
A	B	C	D	E

ANSWERS

1	2	3	4	5	6	7	8	9	10
C	C	B	E	A	C	E	C	B	E

11	12	13	14	15	16	17	18	19	20
A	E	A	D	E	B	A	B	E	C

21	22	23	24	25	26	27	28	29	30
C	A	C	D	B	E	A	C	E	C

31	32	33	34	35	36	37	38	39	40
B	B	C	E	A	C	D	A	C	C

EXERCISE-5

Directions (Qs. 1-72): *In the following questions similar type of figures are given on the top and these figures have been reproduced below in five boxes which are marked as A, B, C, D and E. You have to select the one figure from the five figures given below which is exact reproduction of the question figure given on the top. Indicate your answer by blackening the appropriate circle on the Answer Sheet.*

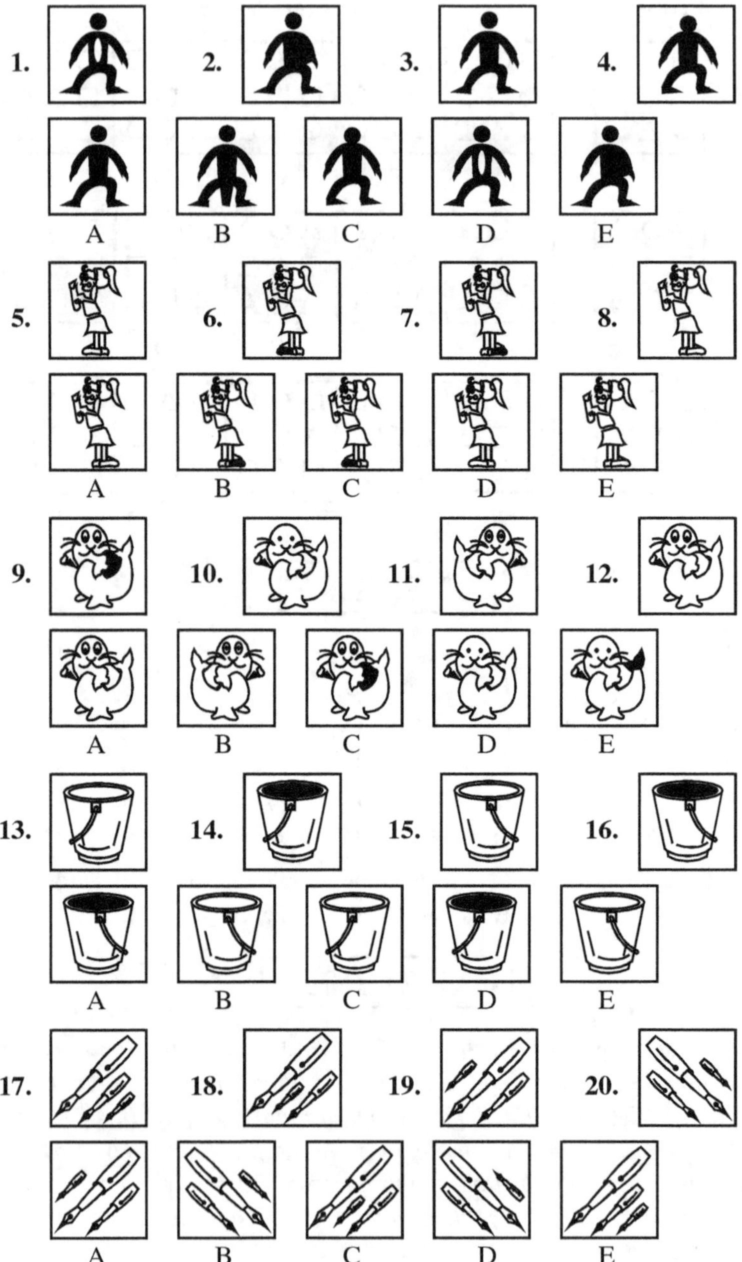

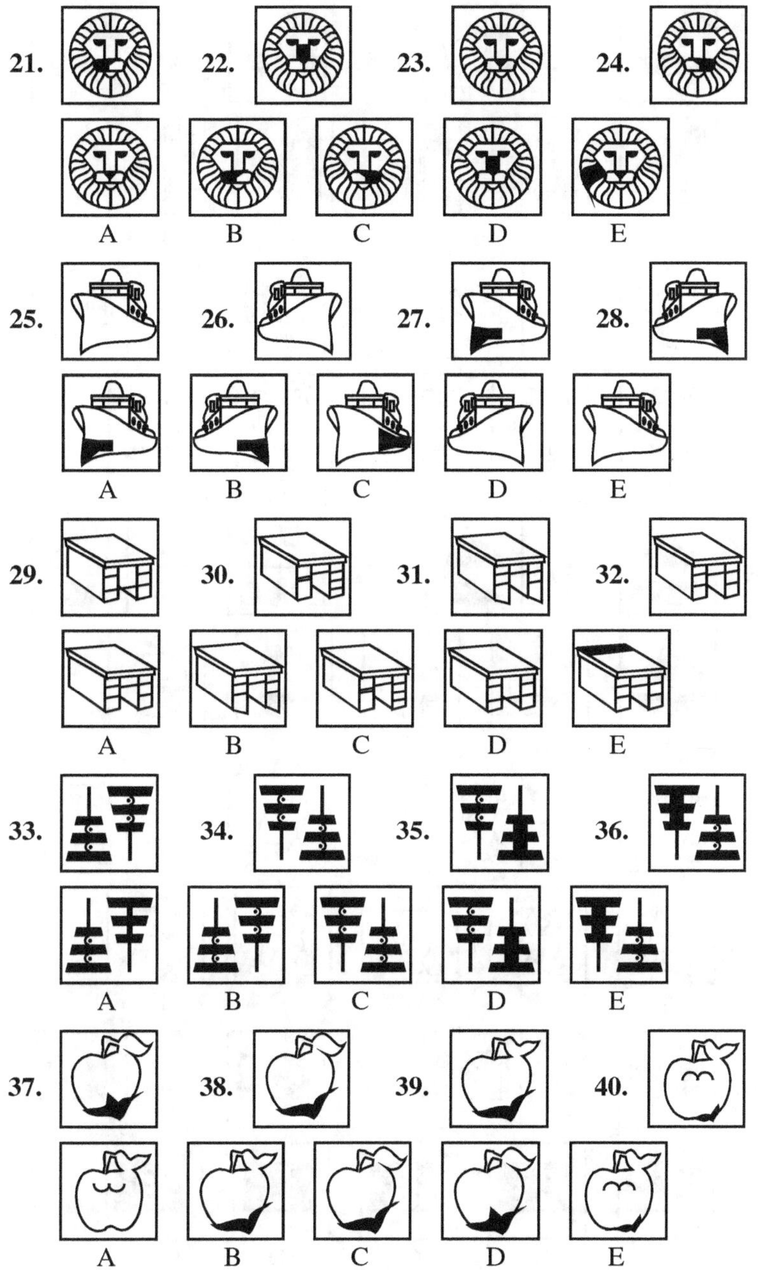

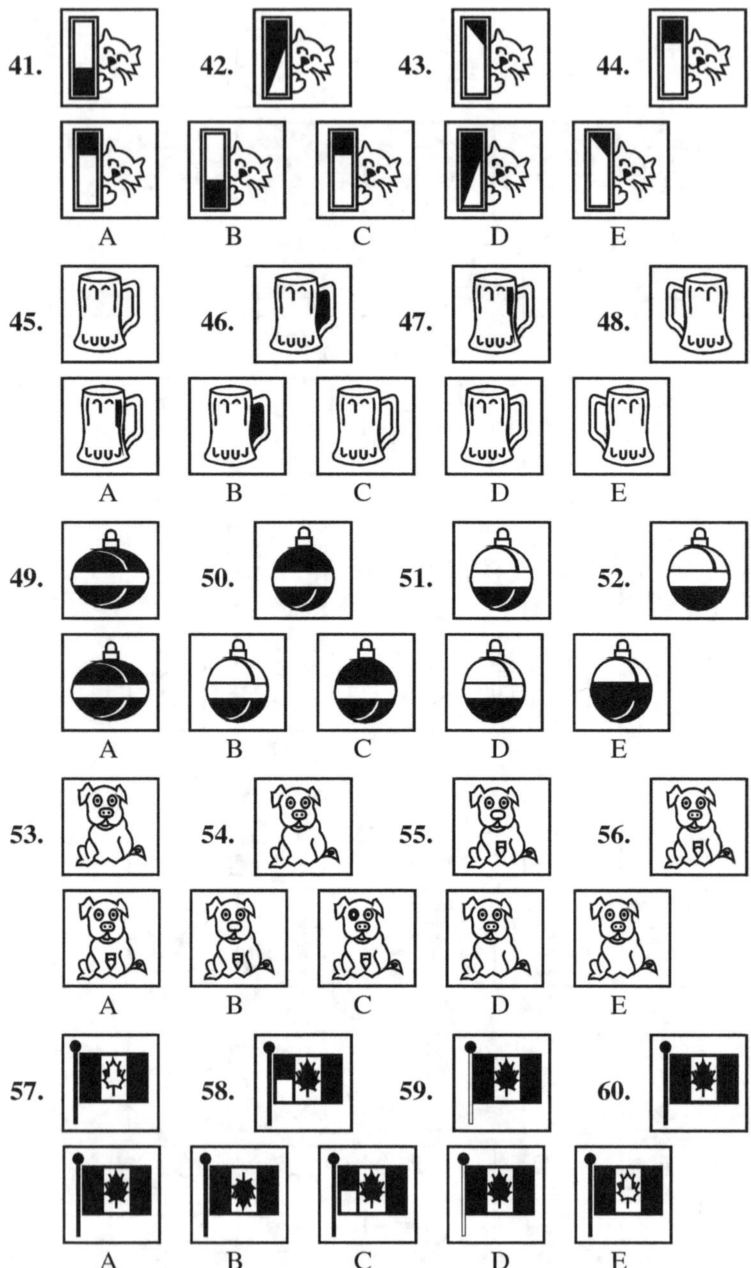

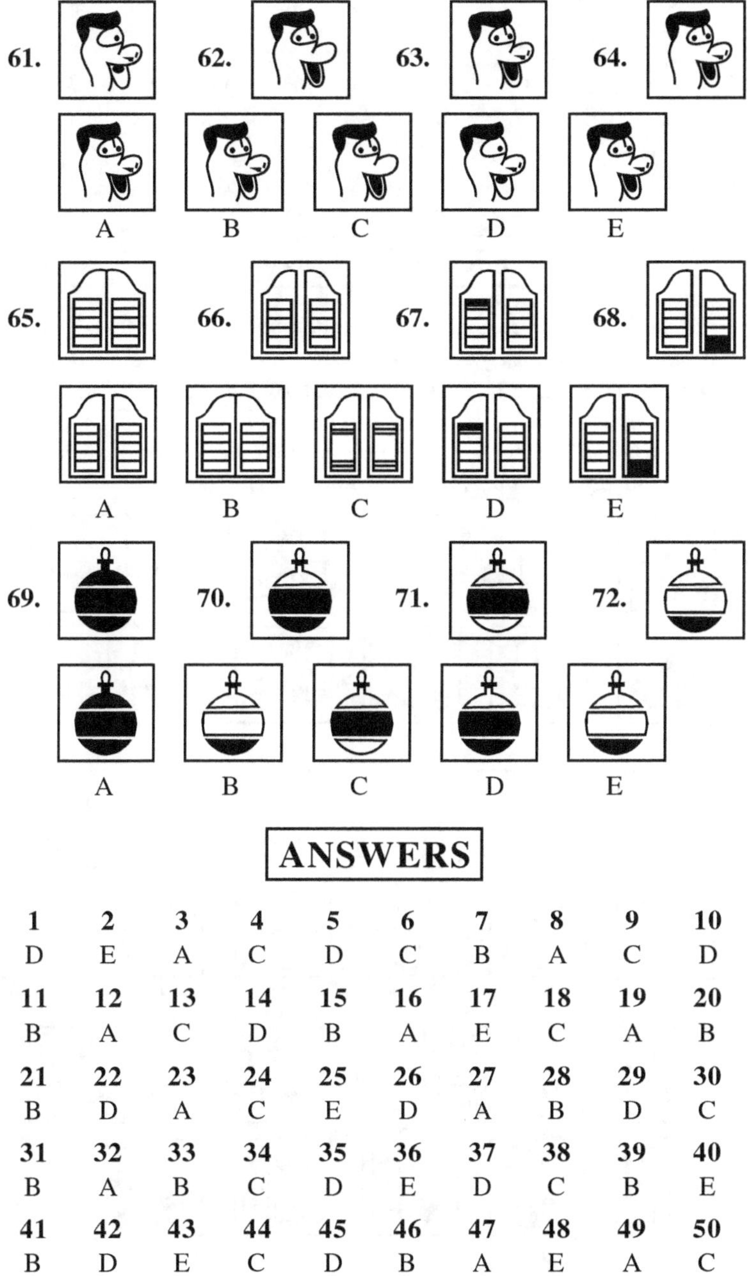

ANSWERS

1	2	3	4	5	6	7	8	9	10
D	E	A	C	D	C	B	A	C	D

11	12	13	14	15	16	17	18	19	20
B	A	C	D	B	A	E	C	A	B

21	22	23	24	25	26	27	28	29	30
B	D	A	C	E	D	A	B	D	C

31	32	33	34	35	36	37	38	39	40
B	A	B	C	D	E	D	C	B	E

41	42	43	44	45	46	47	48	49	50
B	D	E	C	D	B	A	E	A	C

51	52	53	54	55	56	57	58	59	60
B	D	E	D	B	A	E	C	D	A

61	62	63	64	65	66	67	68	69	70
D	C	B	A	B	A	D	E	A	D

71	72
C	B

EXERCISE-6

Directions (Qs. 1-72) : *In the following set similar type of figures are given on the top and these figures have been reproduced below in five boxes which are marked as A, B, C, D and E. You have to select the one figure from the five figures given below which is exact reproduction of the question figure given on the top. Indicate your answer by blackening the appropriate circle on the Answer Sheet.*

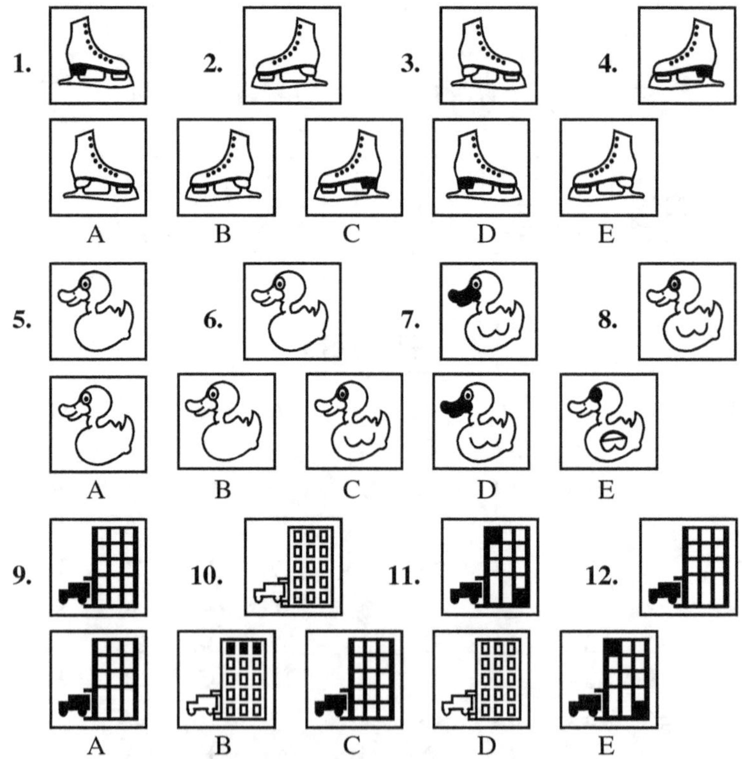

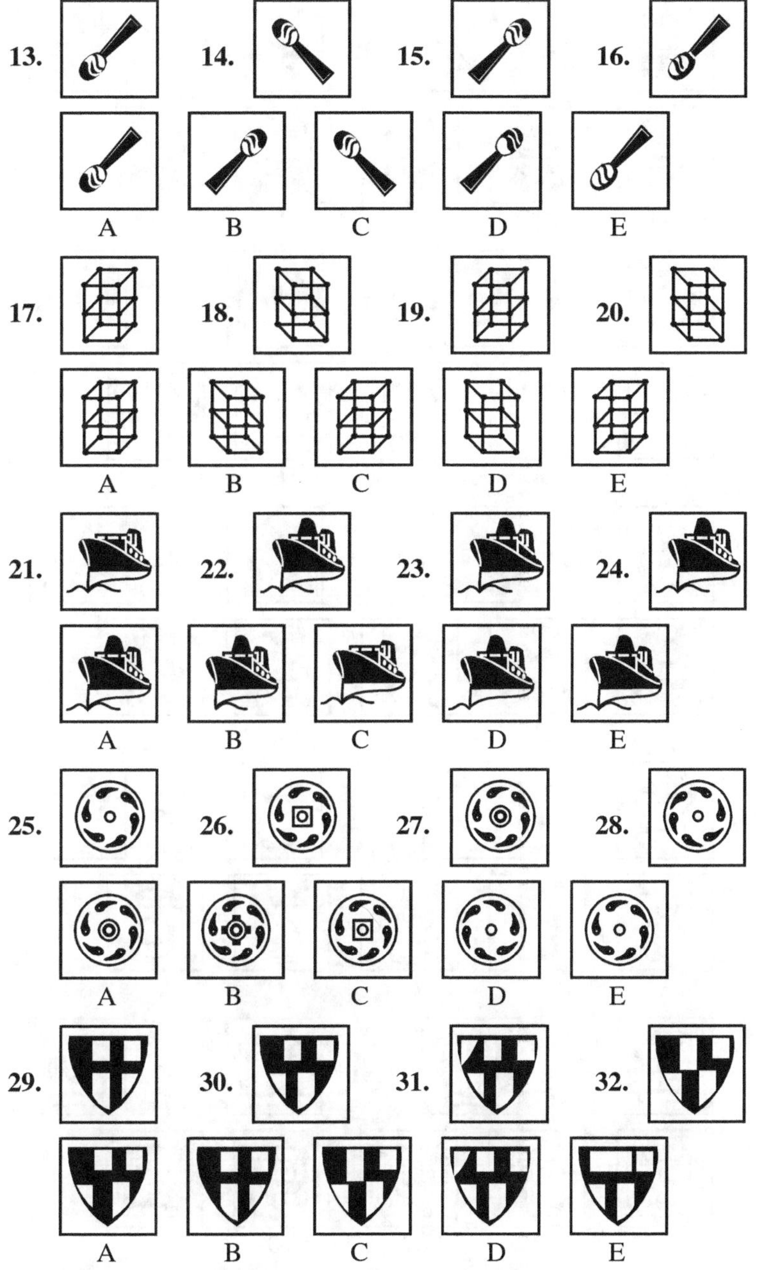

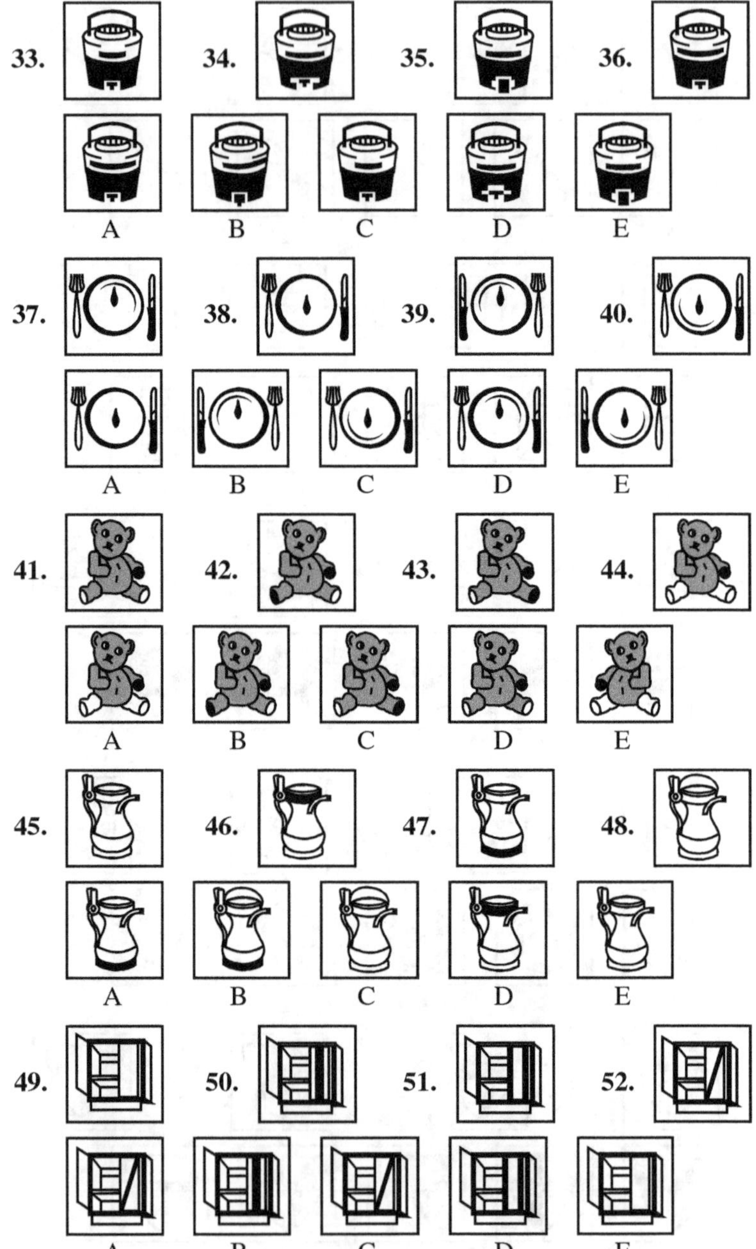

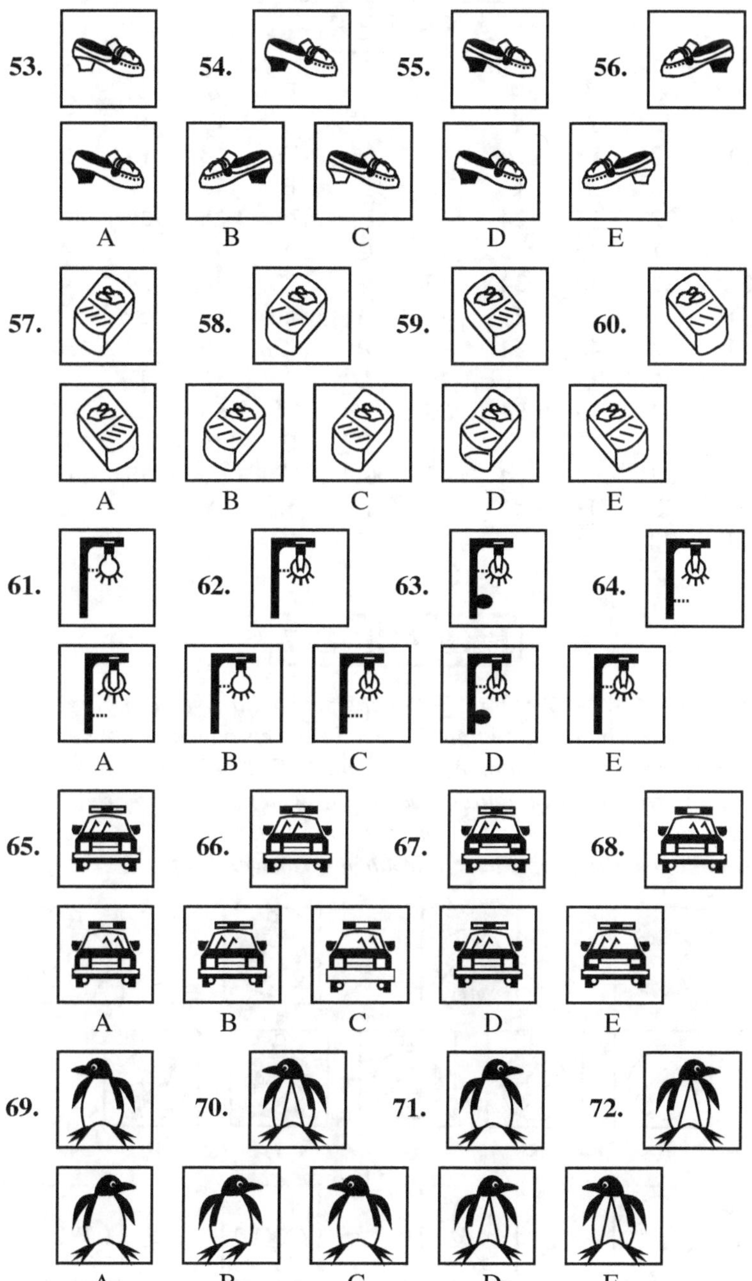

ANSWERS

1	2	3	4	5	6	7	8	9	10
D	E	A	C	B	A	D	C	C	D
11	**12**	**13**	**14**	**15**	**16**	**17**	**18**	**19**	**20**
E	A	A	C	B	E	E	D	A	B
21	**22**	**23**	**24**	**25**	**26**	**27**	**28**	**29**	**30**
C	D	E	A	E	C	A	D	B	A
31	**32**	**33**	**34**	**35**	**36**	**37**	**38**	**39**	**40**
D	C	C	D	E	A	D	A	B	C
41	**42**	**43**	**44**	**45**	**46**	**47**	**48**	**49**	**50**
D	B	C	A	E	D	A	C	E	B
51	**52**	**53**	**54**	**55**	**56**	**57**	**58**	**59**	**60**
D	A	C	D	A	B	C	B	A	E
61	**62**	**63**	**64**	**65**	**66**	**67**	**68**	**69**	**70**
B	E	D	C	B	D	E	A	C	E
71	**72**								
A	D								

EXERCISE-7

Directions (Qs. 1-72) : *In the following set similar type of figures are given on the top and these figures have been reproduced below in five boxes which are marked as A, B, C, D and E. You have to select the one figure from the five figures given below which is exact reproduction of the question figure given on the top. Indicate your answer by blackening the appropriate circle on the Answer Seet.*

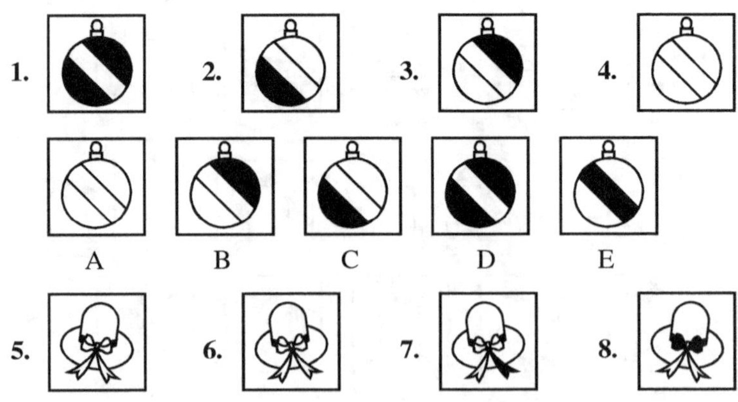

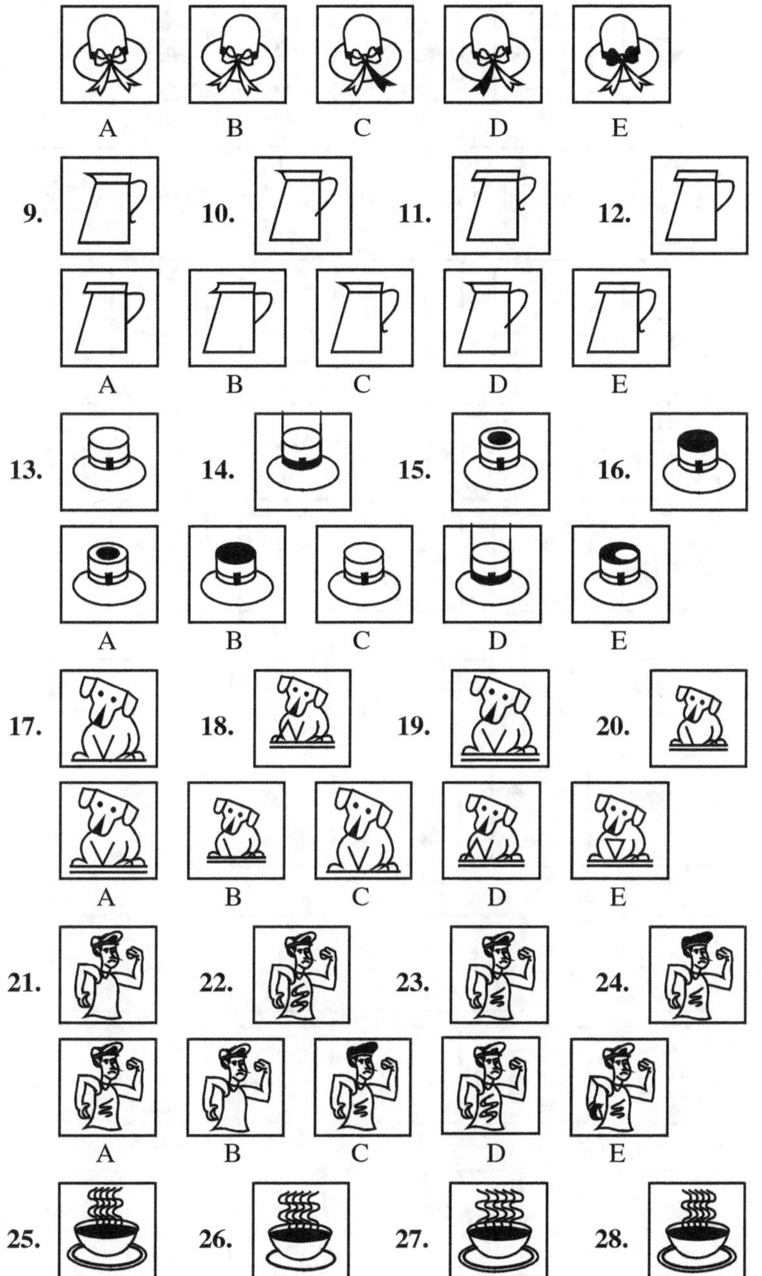

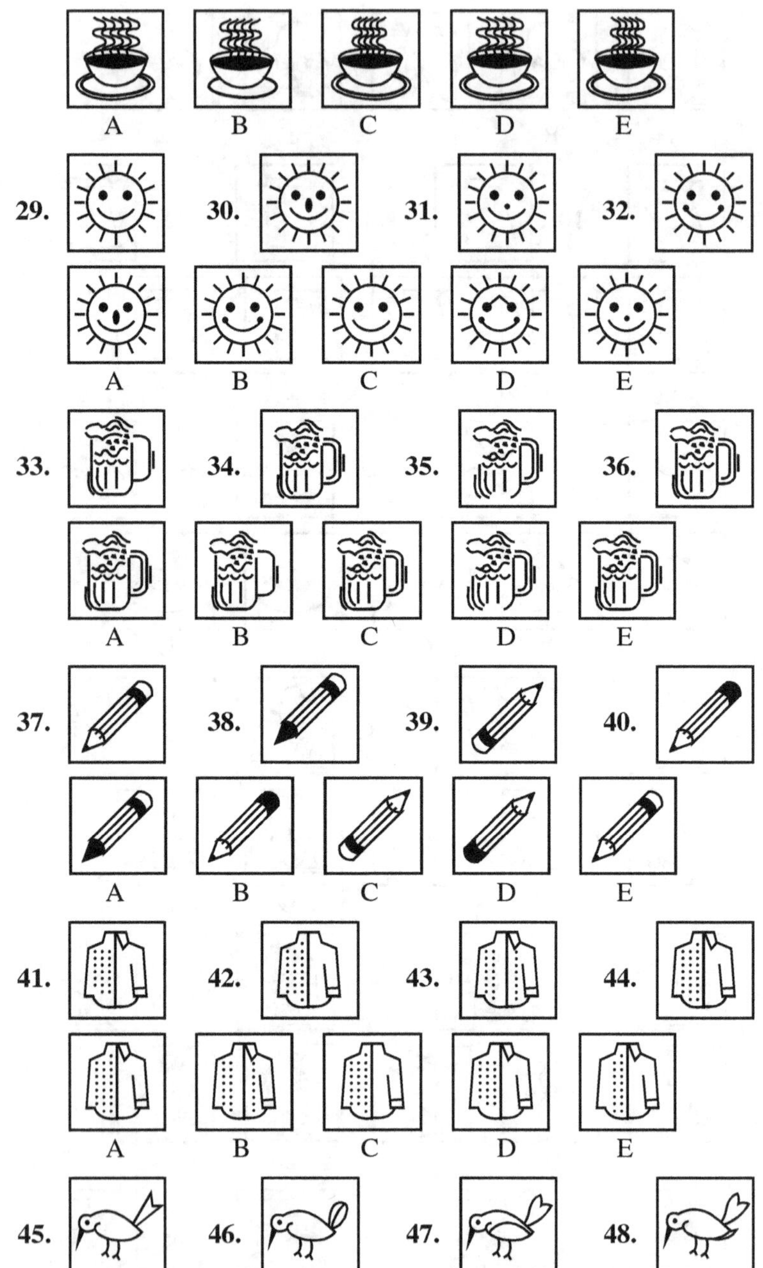

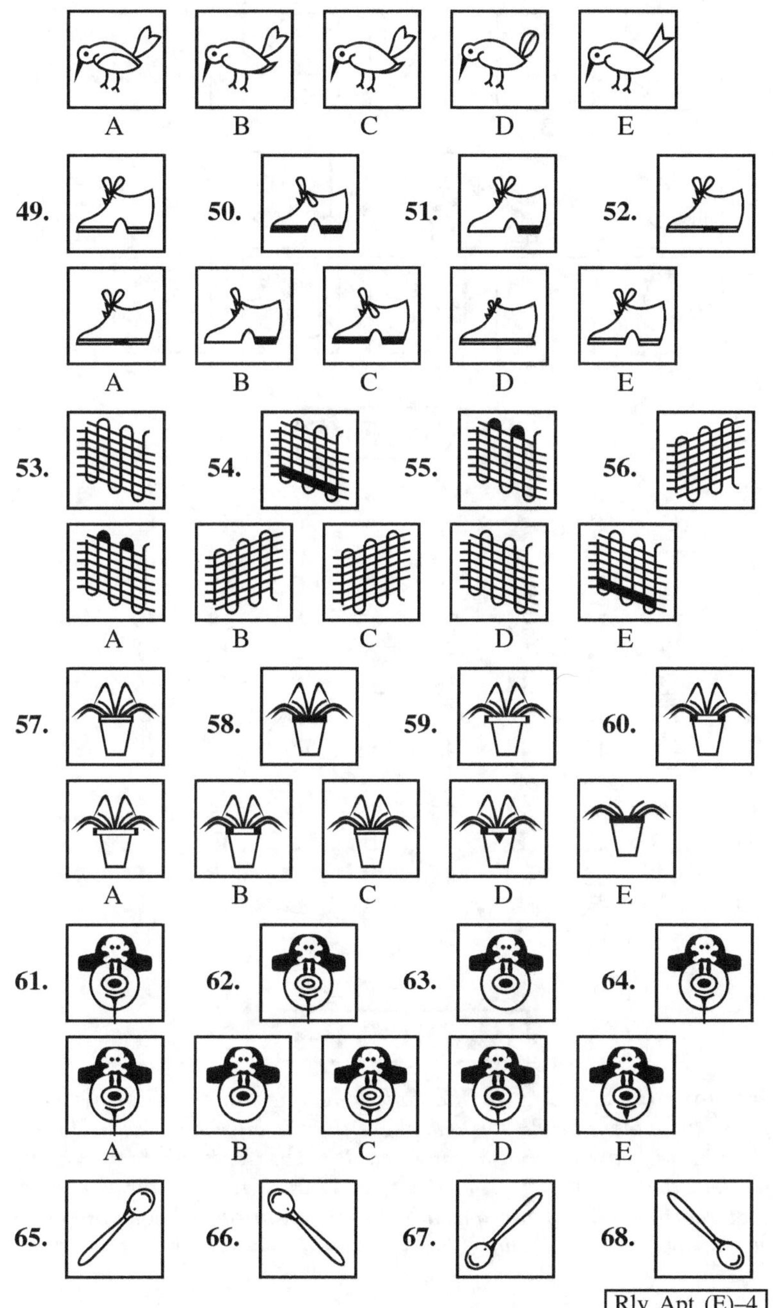

49.   50.   51.   52.

53.   54.   55.   56.

57.   58.   59.   60.

61.   62.   63.   64.

65.   66.   67.   68.

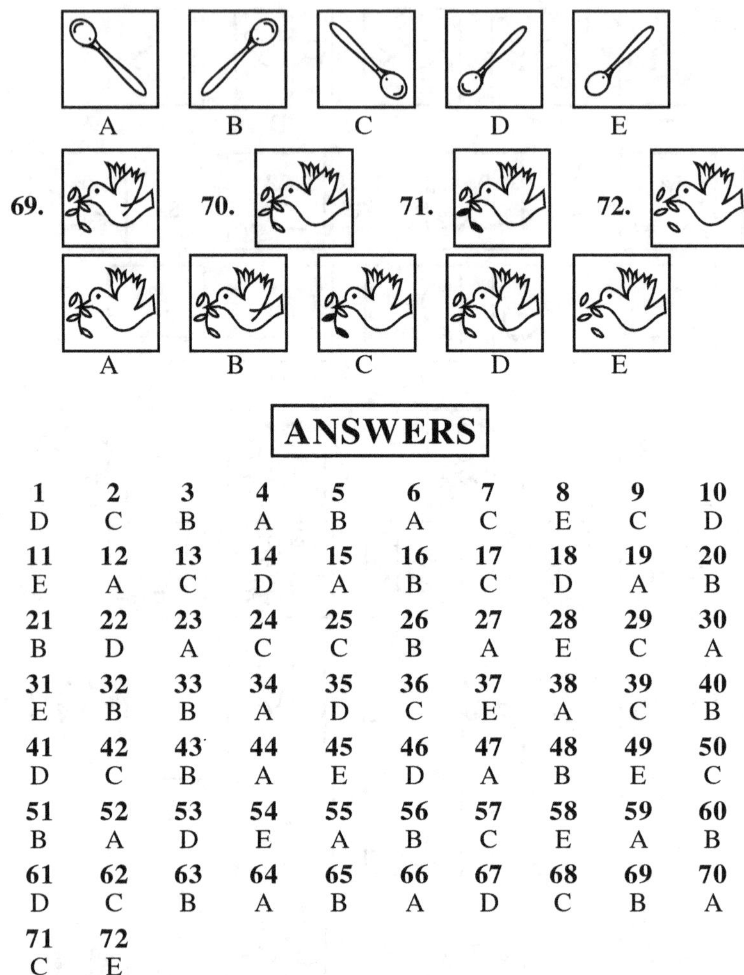

ANSWERS

1	2	3	4	5	6	7	8	9	10
D	C	B	A	B	A	C	E	C	D

11	12	13	14	15	16	17	18	19	20
E	A	C	D	A	B	C	D	A	B

21	22	23	24	25	26	27	28	29	30
B	D	A	C	C	B	A	E	C	A

31	32	33	34	35	36	37	38	39	40
E	B	B	A	D	C	E	A	C	B

41	42	43	44	45	46	47	48	49	50
D	C	B	A	E	D	A	B	E	C

51	52	53	54	55	56	57	58	59	60
B	A	D	E	A	B	C	E	A	B

61	62	63	64	65	66	67	68	69	70
D	C	B	A	B	A	D	C	B	A

71	72
C	E

EXERCISE-8

Directions (Qs. 1-72) : *In the following questions similar type of figures are given on the top and these figures have been reproduced below in five boxes which are marked as A, B, C, D and E. You have to select the one figure from the five figures given below which is exact reproduction of the question figure given on the top. Indicate your answer by blackening the appropriate circle on the Answer Sheet.*

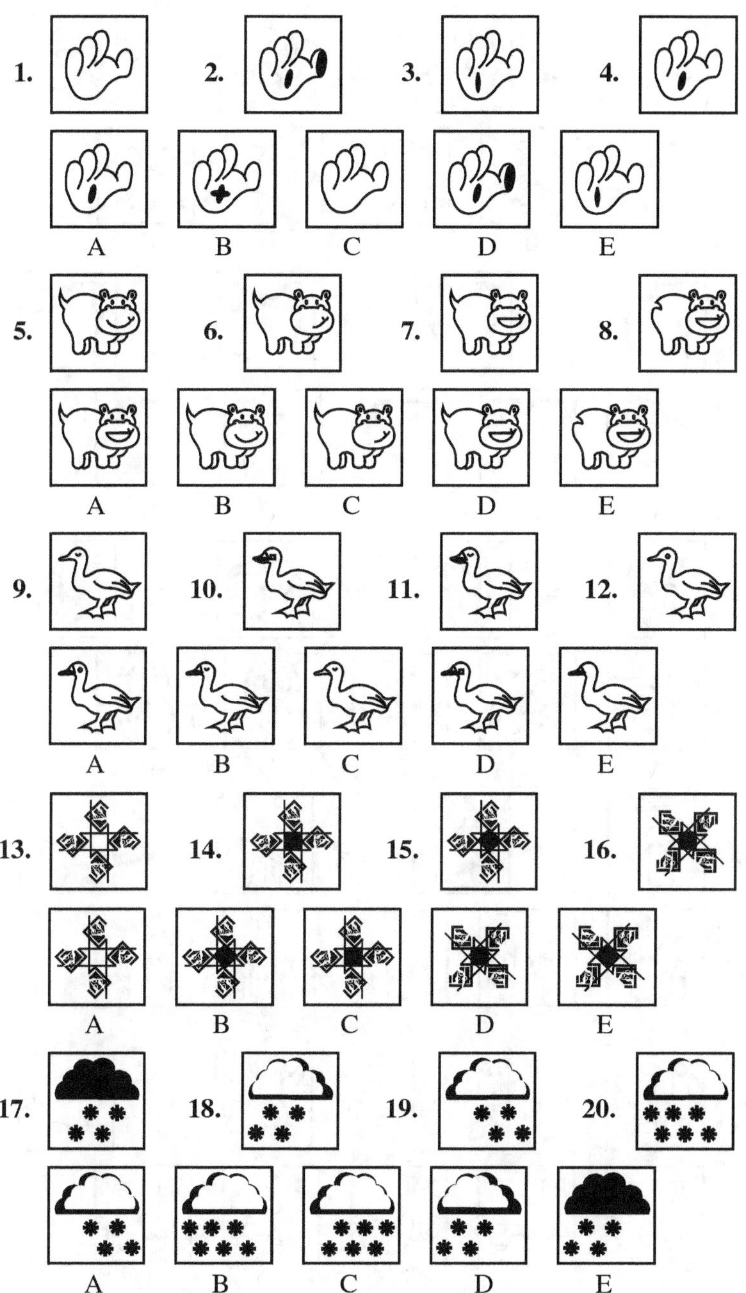

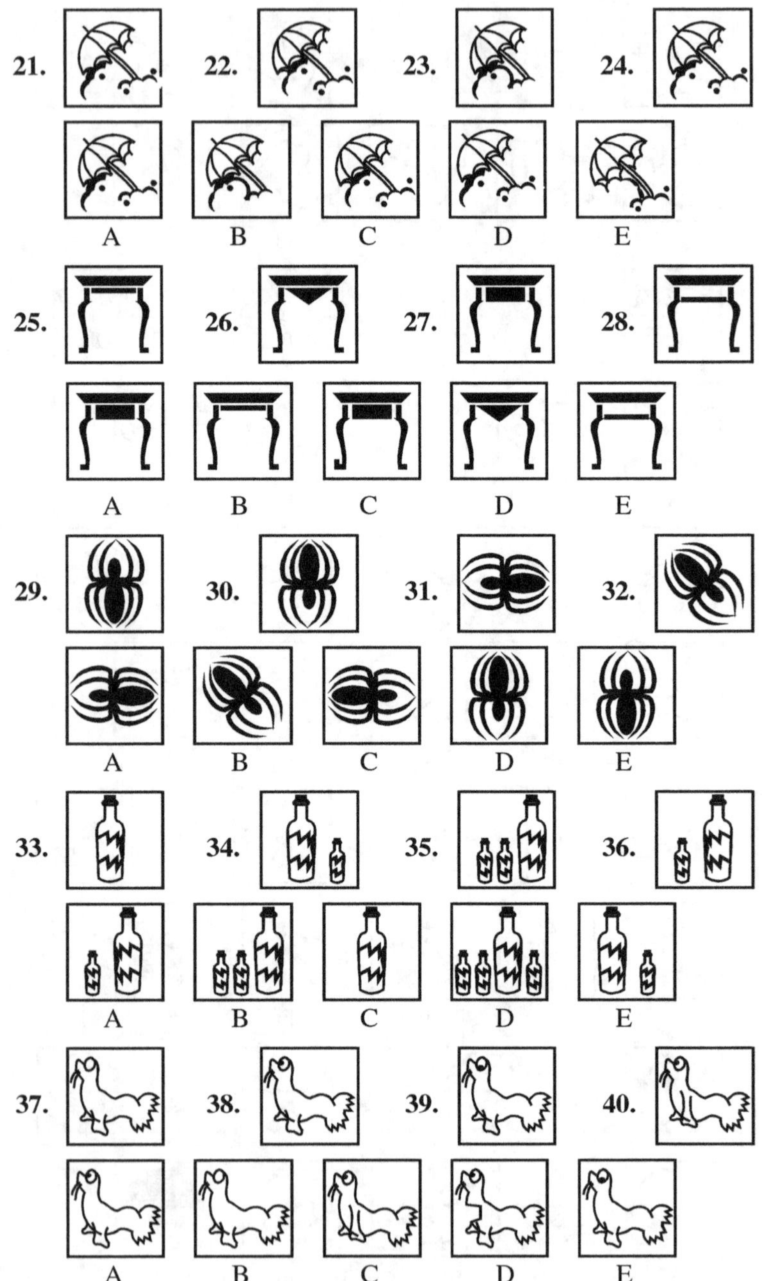

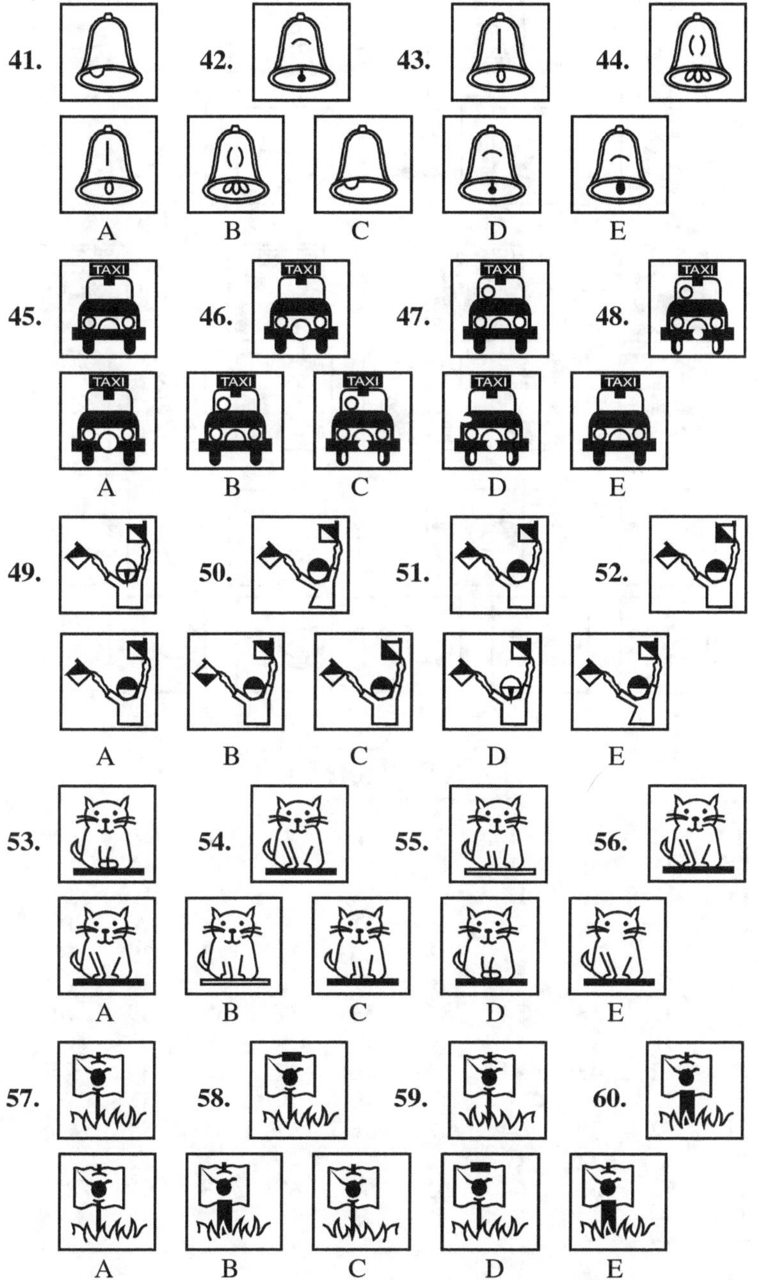

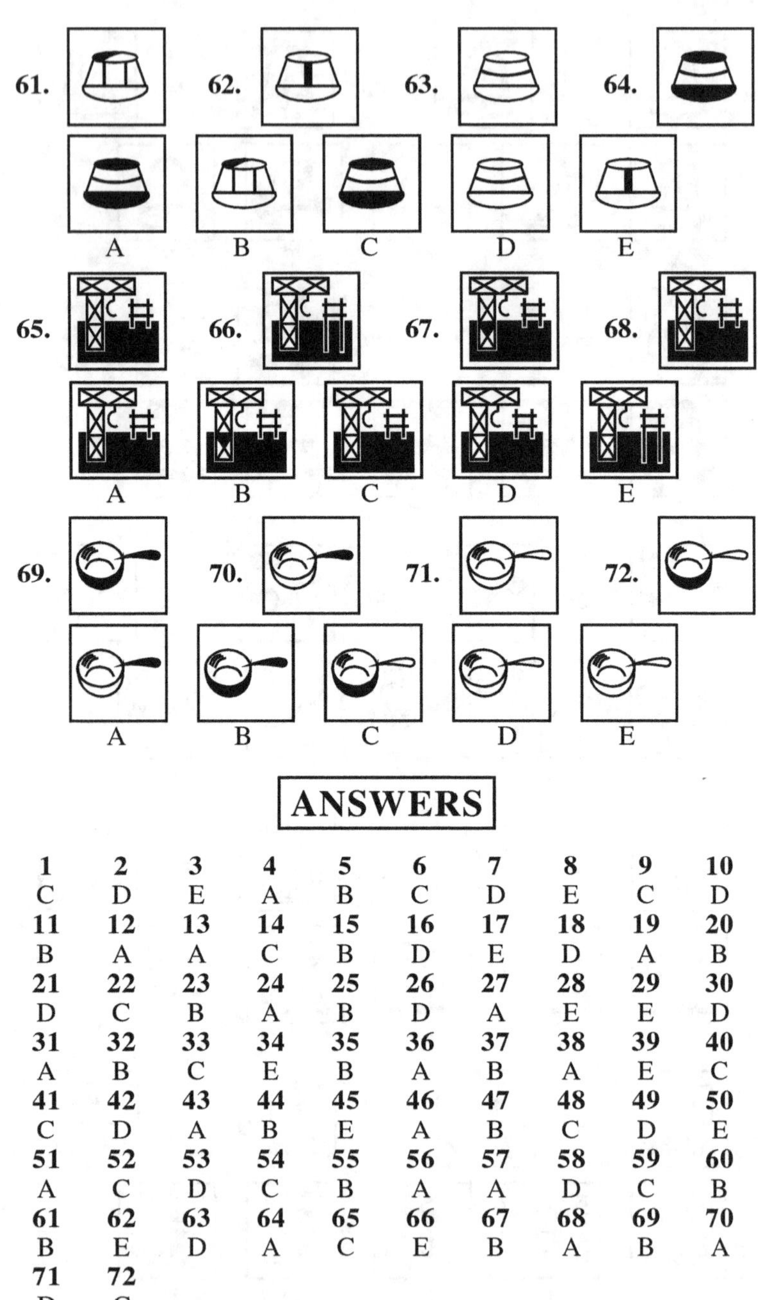

ANSWERS

1	2	3	4	5	6	7	8	9	10
C	D	E	A	B	C	D	E	C	D

11	12	13	14	15	16	17	18	19	20
B	A	A	C	B	D	E	D	A	B

21	22	23	24	25	26	27	28	29	30
D	C	B	A	B	D	A	E	E	D

31	32	33	34	35	36	37	38	39	40
A	B	C	E	B	A	B	A	E	C

41	42	43	44	45	46	47	48	49	50
C	D	A	B	E	A	B	C	D	E

51	52	53	54	55	56	57	58	59	60
A	C	D	C	B	A	A	D	C	B

61	62	63	64	65	66	67	68	69	70
B	E	D	A	C	E	B	A	B	A

71	72
D	C

EXERCISE-9

Directions (Qs. 1-72): *In the following questions, similar type of four questions are given on the left side and these figures have been reproduced on the right side. Which are named as A, B, C, D and E. You have to find the exact reproduction of the question figures from the given five answer figure A, B, C, D and E.*

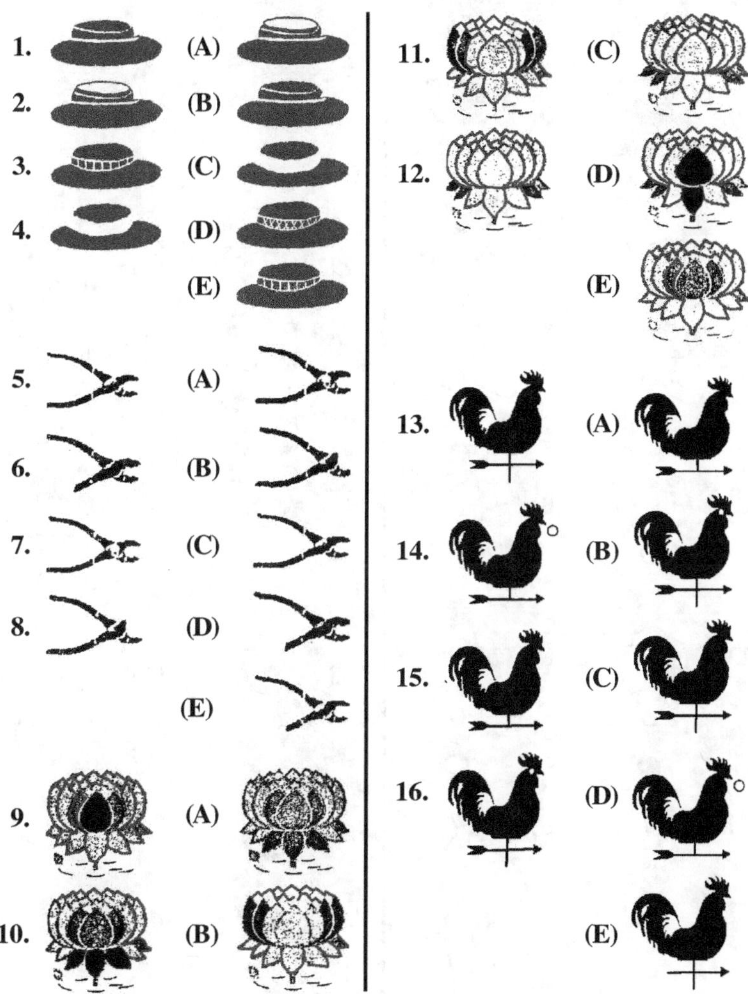

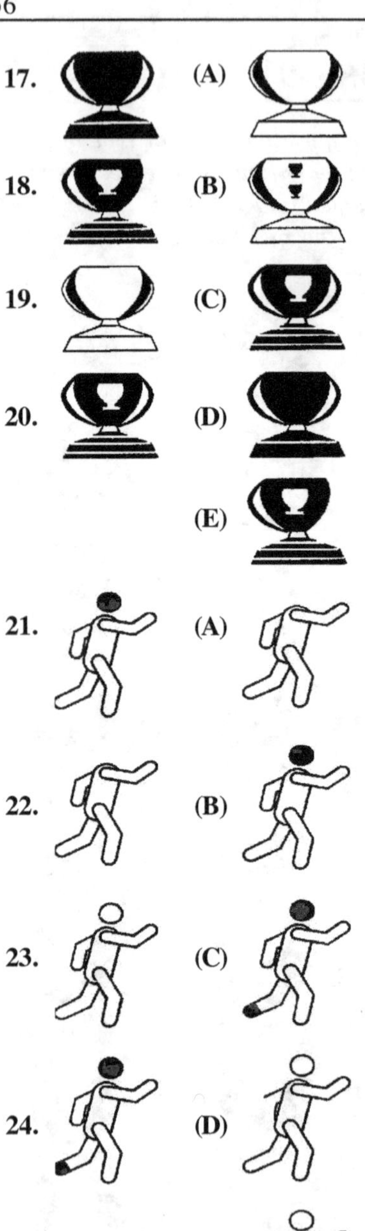

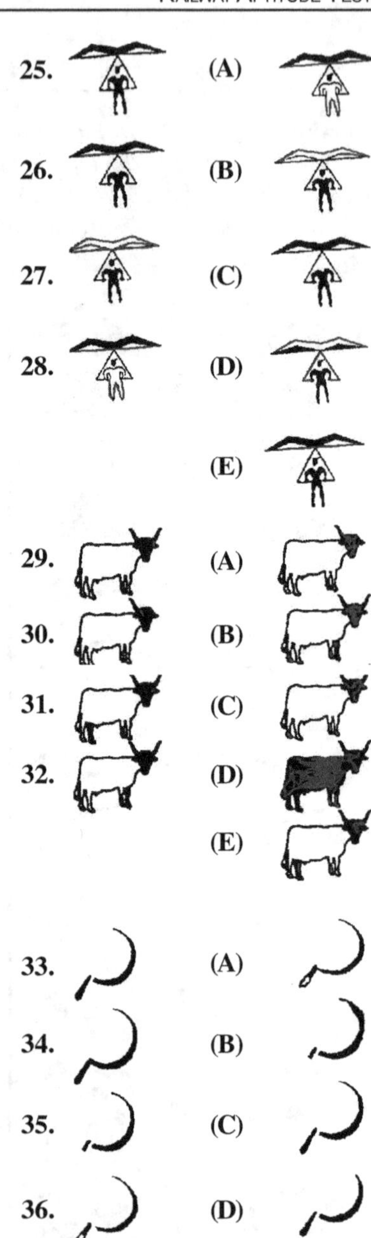

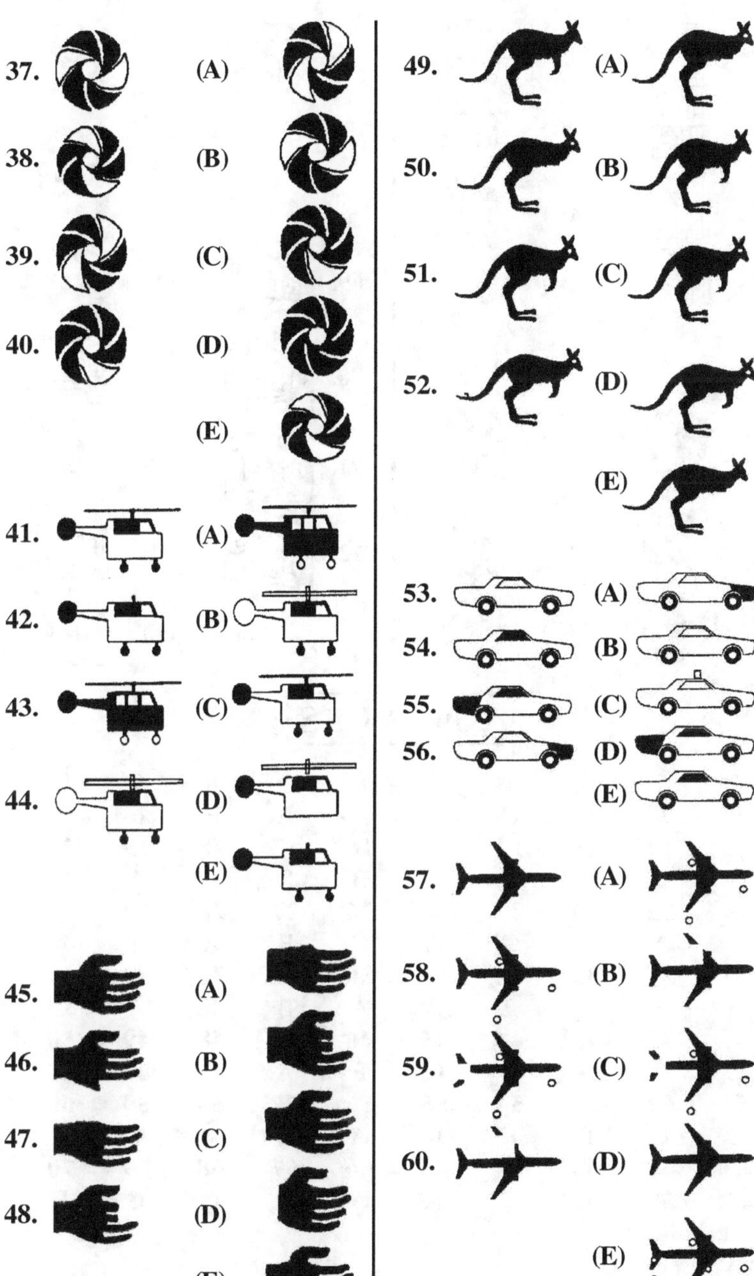

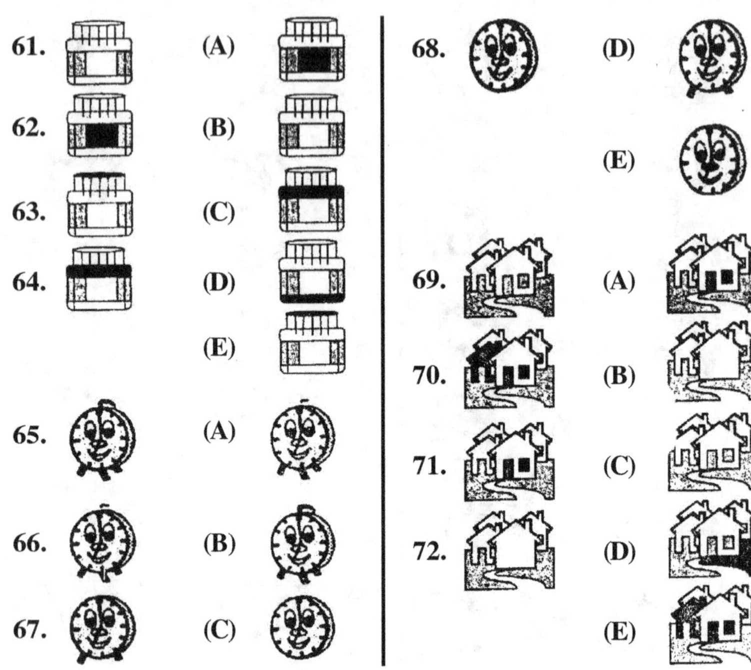

ANSWERS

1	2	3	4	5	6	7	8	9	10
B	A	E	C	C	D	A	B	E	A

11	12	13	14	15	16	17	18	19	20
B	C	C	D	A	B	D	E	A	C

21	22	23	24	25	26	27	28	29	30
B	A	E	C	E	C	B	A	C	A

31	32	33	34	35	36	37	38	39	40
E	B	C	E	B	A	B	E	A	C

41	42	43	44	45	46	47	48	49	50
C	E	A	B	C	E	A	B	B	A

51	52	53	54	55	56	57	58	59	60
D	C	B	E	D	A	D	A	C	B

61	62	63	64	65	66	67	68	69	70
B	A	E	C	A	A	D	C	C	E

71	72
A	B

MEMORY TEST

In this type of test two figures are given. In the first figure some pictures are given and in the second figure, some alphabets are given and they are arranged so as to come on the same places as those of pictures in the first figure. You have to find the correct alphabet in place of the pictures of the second figure.

EXERCISE-1

Directions : *Questions 1-12 are based on following diagram.*

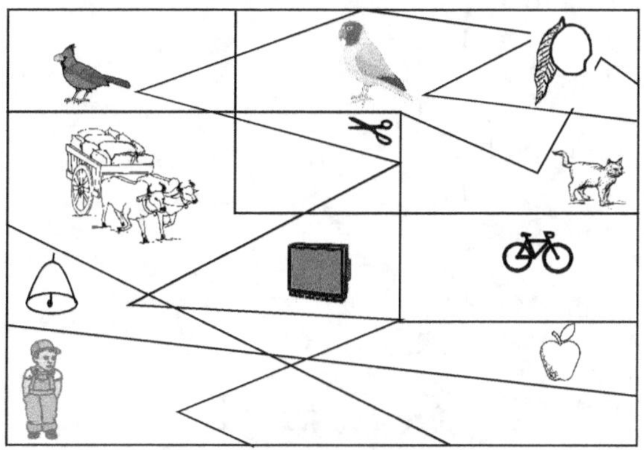

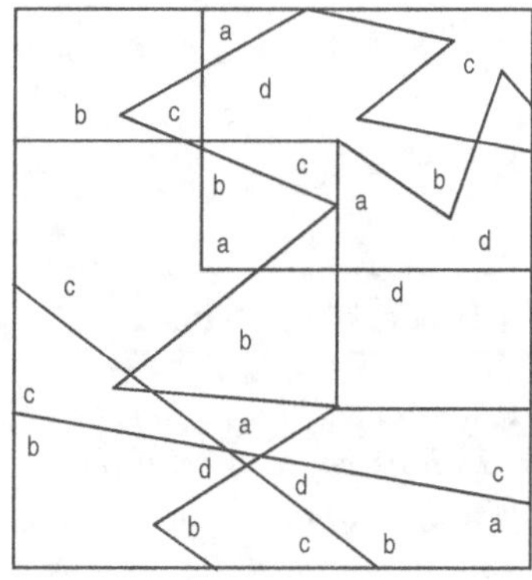

1. Where is the Cycle?

    A. a   B. b   C. c   D. d

2. Where is the Bullock Cart?

    A. a   B. b   C. c   D. d

3. Where is the Banana?

    A. a   B. b   C. c   D. d

4. Where is the Parrot?

    A. a   B. b   C. c   D. d

5. Where is the Child?

    A. a   B. b   C. c   D. d

6. Where is the Scissors?

    A. a   B. b   C. c   D. d

7. Where is the Apple?

    A. a   B. b   C. c   D. d

8. Where is the Bell?

    A. a   B. b   C. c   D. d

9. Where is the T.V.?

    A. a   B. b   C. c   D. d

10. Where is the Bird?

    A. a   B. b   C. c   D. d

11. Where is the Cat?

    A. a   B. b   C. c   D. d

12. Where is the Mango?

    A. a   B. b   C. c   D. d

ANSWERS

1	2	3	4	5	6	7	8	9	10
D	C	A	D	B	C	C	C	B	B

11	12
D	C

EXERCISE-2

Directions (Qs. 1-12) : *Answer all the 12 questions given in this part. In order to solve the questions you are required to observe carefully both the pages one by one. Within 2 Minutes try to remember the positions of all the 12 figures given on the first page. Thereafter turn over the page and try to correlate the position of figures with that of* *letters given on the second page and then blacken the appropriate circle on the Answer sheet only by HB pencil or otherwise as directed.*

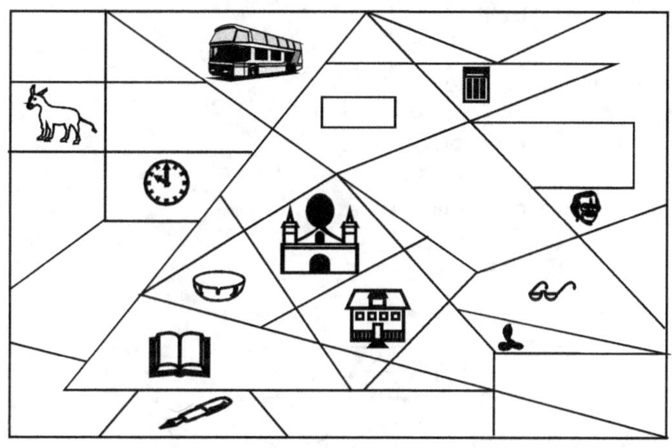

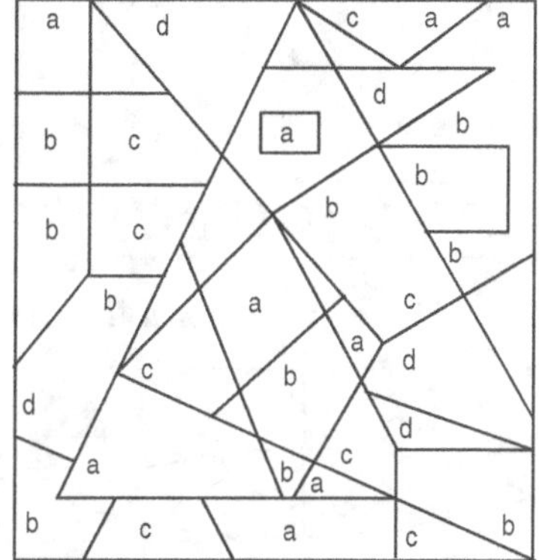

1. Which is the right place of Spectacles?
   A. a   B. b   C. c   D. d
2. Which is the right place of Clock?
   A. a   B. b   C. c   D. d
3. Which is the right place of Book?
   A. a   B. b   C. c   D. d
4. Which is the right place of Calculator?
   A. a   B. b   C. c   D. d
5. Which is the right place of House?
   A. a   B. b   C. c   D. d
6. Which is the right place of Ass?
   A. a   B. b   C. c   D. d

7. Which is the right place of Pen?

  A. a   B. b   C. c   D. d

8. Which is the right place of Snake?

  A. a   B. b   C. c   D. d

9. Which is the right place of Bus?

  A. a   B. b   C. c   D. d

10. Which is the right place of Man?

  A. a   B. b   C. c   D. d

11. Which is the right place of Bowl?

  A. a   B. b   C. c   D. d

12. Which is the right place of Temple?

  A. a   B. b   C. c   D. d

ANSWERS

1	2	3	4	5	6	7	8	9	10
D	C	A	D	B	B	C	D	D	B

11	12
C	A

EXERCISE-3

Directions : *Questions 1-12 are based on following diagram.*

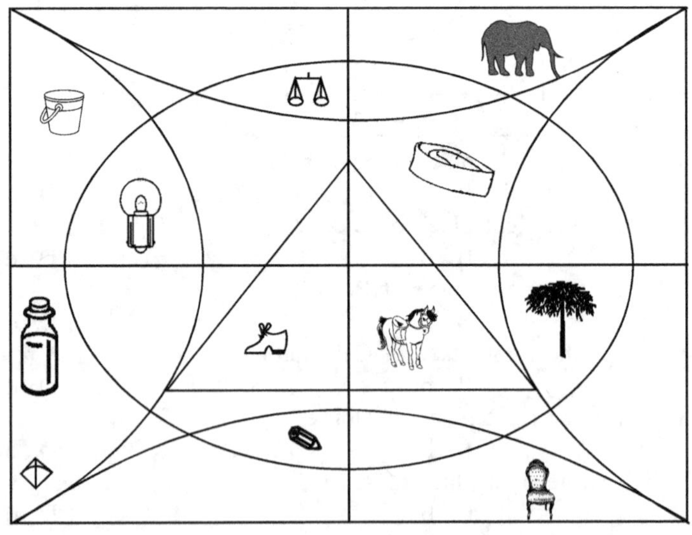

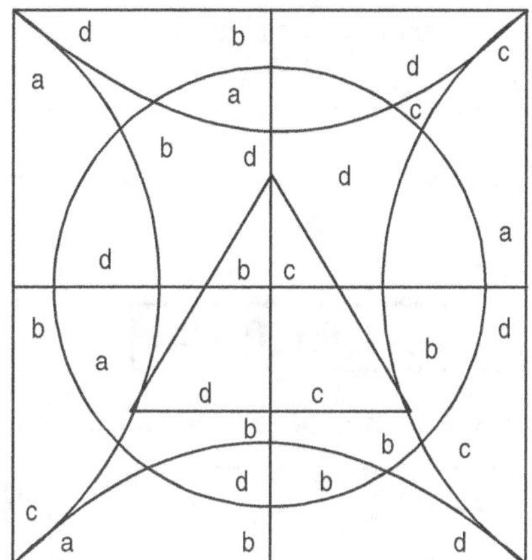

1. Where is the Bottle?
   A. a   B. b   C. c   D. d
2. Where is the Cap?
   A. a   B. b   C. c   D. d
3. Where is the Shoe?
   A. a   B. b   C. c   D. d
4. Where is the Chair?
   A. a   B. b   C. c   D. d
5. Where is the Weighing-Scale?
   A. a   B. b   C. c   D. d
6. Where is the Kite?
   A. a   B. b   C. c   D. d
7. Where is the Elephant?
   A. a   B. b   C. c   D. d
8. Where is the Tree?
   A. a   B. b   C. c   D. d
9. Where is the Bulb?
   A. a   B. b   C. c   D. d
10. Where is the Horse?
    A. a   B. b   C. c   D. d
11. Where is the Bucket?
    A. a   B. b   C. c   D. d
12. Where is the Pencil?
    A. a   B. b   C. c   D. d

ANSWERS

1	2	3	4	5	6	7	8	9	10
B	D	D	D	A	C	D	B	D	C

11	12
A	D

EXERCISE-4

Directions : *Questions 1-12 are based on following diagram.*

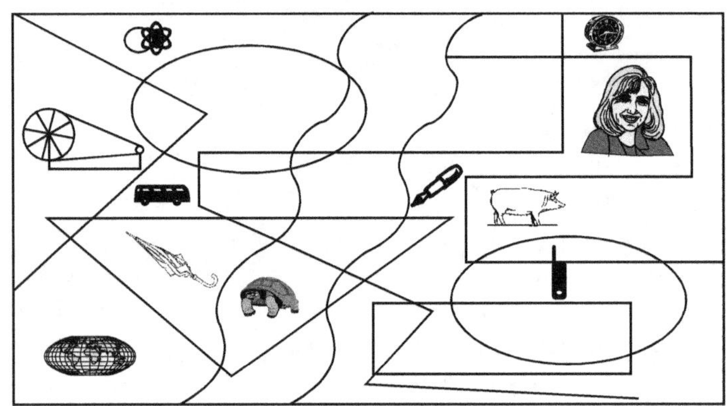

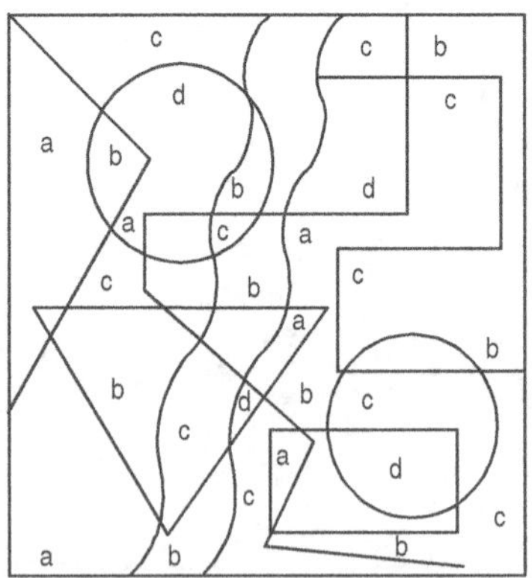

1. Where is the Tortoise?

   A. a   B. b   C. c   D. d

12. Where is the Girl?

   A. a   B. b   C. c   D. d

3. Where is the Bus?
   - A. a   B. b   C. c   D. d
4. Where is the Ring?
   - A. a   B. b   C. c   D. d
5. Where is the Mobile Phone?
   - A. a   B. b   C. c   D. d
6. Where is the Clock?
   - A a   B. b   C. c   D. d
7. Where is the Globe?
   - A. a   B. b   C. c   D. d
8. Where is the Pen?
   - A. a   B. b   C. c   D. d
9. Where is the Charkha?
   - A. a   B. b   C. c   D. d
10. Where is the Umbrella?
    - A. a   B. b   C. c   D. d
11. Where is the Pig?
    - A. a   B. b   C. c   D. d
12. Where is the Comb?
    - A. a   B. b   C. c   D. d

ANSWERS

1	2	3	4	5	6	7	8	9	10
C	C	C	C	C	B	A	A	A	B

11	12
C	D

EXERCISE-5

Directions (Qs. 1-12) : *Answer all the 12 questions given in this part. In order to solve the questions you are required to observe carefully both the pages one by one. Within 2 Minutes try to remember the positions of all the 12 figures given on the first page. Then after turn over the page and try to correlate the position of figures with that of letters given on the second page and then blacken the appropriate circle on the Answer sheet only by HB pencil or otherwise as directed.*

Rly Apt (E)–5

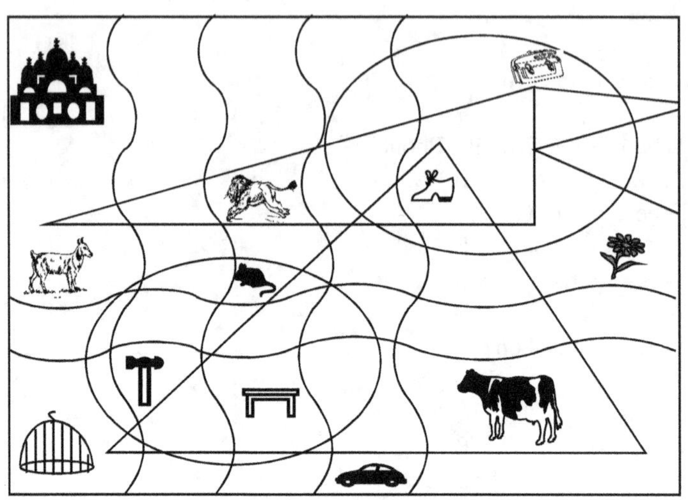

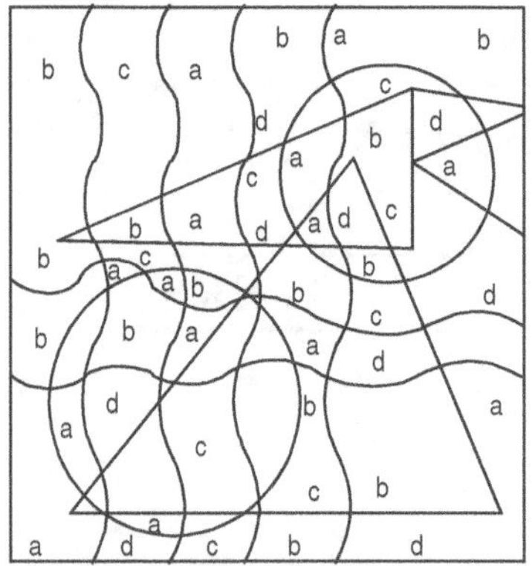

1. Which is the right place of Lion?

    A. a   B. b   C. c   D. d

2. Which is the right place of Car?

    A. a   B. b   C. c   D. d

3. Which is the right place of Flower?

    A. a   B. b   C. c   D. d

4. Which is the right place of Hammer?

    A. a   B. b   C. c   D. d

5. Which is the right place of Bag?

    A. a   B. b   C. c   D. d

6. Which is the right place of Cage?

A. a B. b C. c D. d

7. Which is the right place of Shoe?

A. a B. b C. c D. d

8. Where is the Goat located?

A. a B. b C. c D. d

9. Which is the right place of Cow?

A. a B. b C. c D. d

10. Which is the right place of Table?

A. a B. b C. c D. d

11. Which is the right place of Rat?

A. a B. b C. c D. d

12. Which is the right place of Gurudawara?

A. a B. b C. c D. d

ANSWERS

1	2	3	4	5	6	7	8	9	10
A	B	D	D	C	A	D	B	B	C

11	12
B	B

EXERCISE-6

Directions : *Questions 1-12 are based on following diagram.*

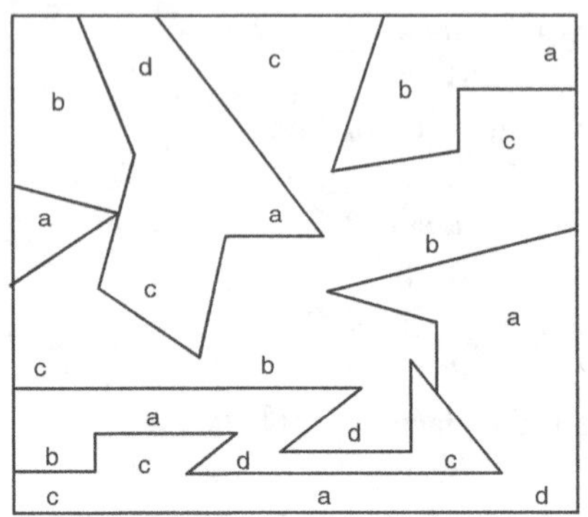

1. Where is the Church?
   A. a   B. b   C. c   D. d
2. Where is the Book?
   A. a   B. b   C. c   D. d
3. Where is the School?
   A. a   B. b   C. c   D. d
4. Where is the Owl?
   A. a   B. b   C. c   D. d
5. Where is the Rat?
   A. a   B. b   C. c   D. d
6. Where is the Telephone?
   A. a   B. b   C. c   D. d
7. Where is the Scissors?
   A. a   B. b   C. c   D. d
8. Where is the Glass?
   A. a   B. b   C. c   D. d
9. Where is the Mango?
   A. a   B. b   C. c   D. d
10. Where is the Radio?
    A. a   B. b   C. c   D. d
11. Where is the Ice-Cream?
    A. a   B. b   C. c   D. d
12. Where is the Dog?
    A. a   B. b   C. c   D. d

ANSWERS

1	2	3	4	5	6	7	8	9	10
B	A	B	B	C	C	A	A	A	B

11	12
A	A

SPATIAL SCANNING TEST
(Shortest Route Search Test)

To answer the question based on this test, the following should be kept in mind:

1. Which is the shortest path?

2. Which path contains minimum number of turning?

3. The vertical rays ($\updownarrow$) and horizontal rays ($\leftrightarrow$) denotes the paths. Obstacles (——||——) are also there in between them which cannot be crossed.

4. Small squares ☐ are also there which contain some digit inside them. These small squares are made up for walls, the two walls are connected to the paths.

5. The path you select to go from one place to another, must touch two or one walls of any square. The path which touches the square, the number of the same square will be your answer.

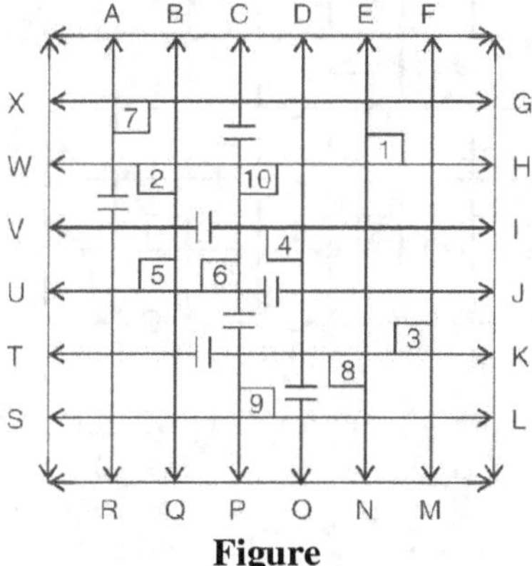

Figure

Q. Find the shortest path to reach M from A in above figure.

Ans. To reach M from A we have to touch two walls of square No. 1 and wall of square No. 3. All other paths are longer. Hence, the correct answer is 1.

EXERCISE-1

Directions (Qs. 1-40) :

- Study each diagram given below carefully and trace the shortest possible route for going one place to another.
- In each diagram vertical (↕) and horizontal (↔) line segments show routes which are intersected by barriers (—O—) which could not be crossed.
- There are small squares in the figure in which numbers 1 to 10 are written and two sides of squares touch the routes.
- The route selected by you should pass over touching the two sides of any square and the number of that square will be your route number (answer).

SECTION–1

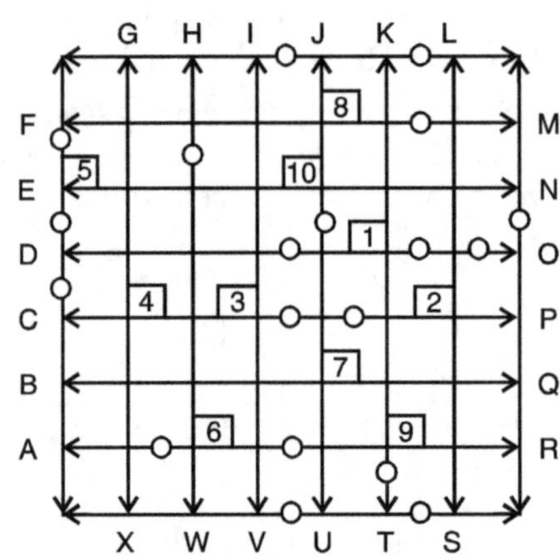

1. Which is the shortest route to reach L from B?
   A. 2   B. 3   C. 10   D. 4
2. Which is the shortest route to reach V from D?
   A. 2   B. 3   C. 5   D. 10
3. Which is the shortest route to reach from A?
   A. 2   B. 5   C. 6   D. 7
4. Which is the shortest route to reach Q from U?
   A. 4   B. 10   C. 8   D. 7
5. Which is the shortest route to reach E from T?
   A. 1   B. 2   C. 5   D. 6

6. Which is the shortest route to reach P from K?

    A. 2   B. 4   C. 10   D. 9

7. Which is the shortest route to reach J from D?

    A. 4   B. 5   C. 2   D. 8

8. Which is the shortest route to reach I from A?

    A. 3   B. 10   C. 7   D. 8

9. Which is the shortest route to reach O from A?

    A. 7   B. 9   C. 8   D. 5

10. Which is the shortest route to reach V from P?

    A. 10   B. 7   C. 2   D. 3

SECTION–2

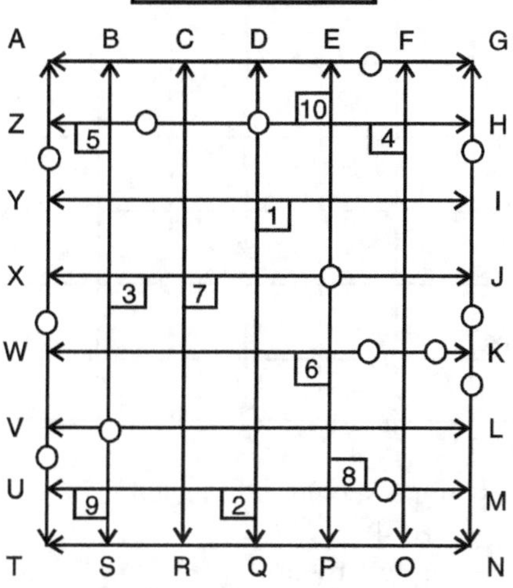

11. Which is the shortest route to reach R from A?

    A. 4   B. 7   C. 5   D. 6

12. Which is the shortest route to reach B from J?

    A. 5   B. 8   C. 1   D. 10

13. Which is the shortest route to reach O from F?

    A. 5   B. 9   C. 7   D. 4

14. Which is the shortest route to reach U from P?

    A. 9   B. 5   C. 4   D. 3

15. Which is the shortest route to reach C from Q?

    A. 4   B. 7   C. 5   D. 6

16. Which is the shortest route to reach T from H?

    A. 8   B. 5   C. 4   D. 3

17. Which is the shortest route to reach E from M
     A. 10   B. 9   C. 8   D. 6

18. Which is the shortest route to reach U from N
     A. 7   B. 9   C. 10   D. 8

19. Which is the shortest route to reach F from R?
     A. 4   B. 8   C. 9   D. 10

20. Which is the shortest route to reach O from X?
     A. 3   B. 7   C. 4   D. 5

SECTION–3

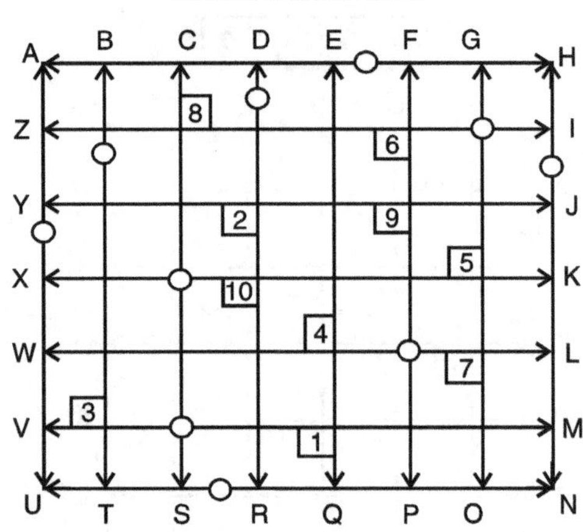

21. Which shortest route should be selected to travel from B to L?
     A. 9   B. 4   C. 5   D. 6

22. Which will be the best route to reach from D to V?
     A. 5   B. 8   C. 6   D. 7

23. Starting from A which will be the best way to reach O?
     A. 6   B. 5   C. 4   D. 7

24. Which is the best way to travel from position W to position N?
     A. 4   B. 5   C. 8   D. 9

25. Which is the most convenient route to travel from U to E?
     A. 8   B. 9   C. 4   D. 10

26. What is the number of the shortest route that connect J and P?
     A. 7   B. 6   C. 8   D. 9

27. Which is the shortest route to reach from D to J?
     A. 5   B. 8   C. 9   D. 10

28. Which will be the shortest way to travel from C to I?
     A. 2   B. 10   C. 5   D. 6

29. Which is the shortest route to reach A from N?

    A. 2   B. 6   C. 4   D. 10

30. Which is the shortest route to reach V from M?

    A. 1   B. 5   C. 10   D. 9

SECTION–4

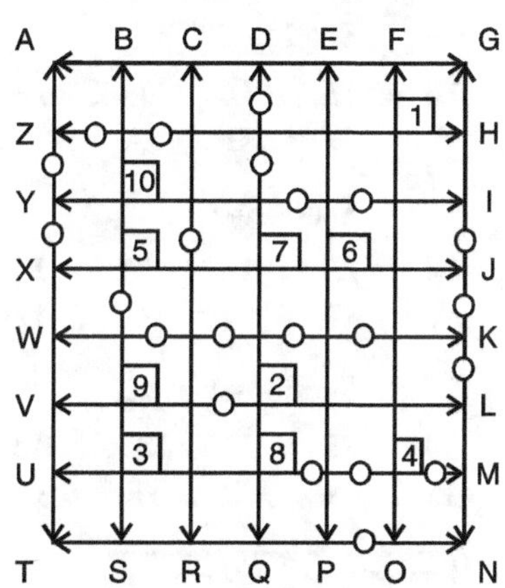

31. Which is the shortest route to reach Y from C?

    A. 2   B. 5   C. 10   D. 8

32. Which is the shortest route to reach J from F?

    A. 1   B. 3   C. 5   D. 8

33. Which is the shortest route to reach J from E?

    A. 2   B. 8   C. 6   D. 5

34. Which is the shortest route to reach L from X?

    A. 4   B. 8   C. 6   D. 2

35. Which is the shortest route to reach R from W?

    A. 9   B. 7   C. 1   D. 2

36. Which is the shortest route to reach Q from L?

    A. 5   B. 4   C. 8   D. 1

37. Which is the shortest route to reach R from V?

    A. 6   B. 3   C. 1   D. 5

38. Which is the shortest route to reach X from C?

    A. 6   B. 2   C. 5   D. 3

39. Which is the shortest route to reach M from G?

    A. 7   B. 4   C. 8   D. 5

40. Which is the shortest route to reach E from C?

    A. 2   B. 7   C. 4   D. 9

ANSWERS

Section–1

1	2	3	4	5	6	7	8	9	10
C	B	D	D	C	A	D	A	A	B

Section–2

11	12	13	14	15	16	17	18	19	20
B	C	D	A	B	C	A	B	A	A

Section–3

21	22	23	24	25	26	27	28	29	30
A	B	C	A	C	A	C	D	C	A

Section–4

31	32	33	34	35	36	37	38	39	40
C	A	C	D	A	C	B	C	B	B

EXERCISE-2

Directions (Qs. 1-40) :

- Forty questions are given which are sub-divided into four parts. Each part contains ten questions.

- See carefully each of the figures. You have to select the shortest path to reach from one place to another in each figure.

- The vertical rays (↕) and horizontal rays (↔) denotes the paths. Obstacles (—⊩—) are also there in between them which cannot be crossed.

- There are small squares in the figure in which numbers 1 to 10 are written and two sides of squares touch the routes.

- The path you select to go from one place to another, must touch two walls of any square. The path which touches the square, the number of the same square will be your answer.

- Squares are numbered from 1 to 10 and your answer sheet also contains ten alternatives. The path you select, you have blacken the answer sheet corresponding the number of the square.

SECTION–1

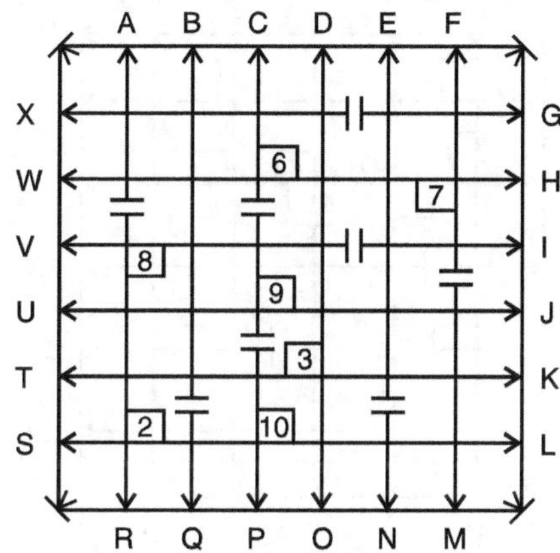

1. Which is the shortest route to go to I from C?
   A. 8   B. 7   C. 6   D. 10

2. Which is the shortest route to go to P from E?
   A. 10   B. 7   C. 8   D. 3

3. Which is the shortest route to go to C from K?
   A. 6   B. 3   C. 7   D. 2

4. Which is the shortest route to go to R from F?
   A. 10   B. 3   C. 6   D. 8

5. Which is the shortest route to go to B from Q?
   A. 2   B. 7   C. 6   D. 4

6. Which is the shortest route to go to E from T?
   A. 7   B. 6   C. 5   D. 3

7. Which is the shortest route to go to V from D?
   A. 6   B. 8   C. 3   D. 10

8. Which is the shortest route to go to X from L?
   A. 10   B. 3   C. 7   D. 2

9. Which is the shortest route to go to P from D?
   A. 7   B. 2   C. 9   D. 3

10. Which is the shortest route to go to O from A?
    A. 9   B. 2   C. 6   D. 7

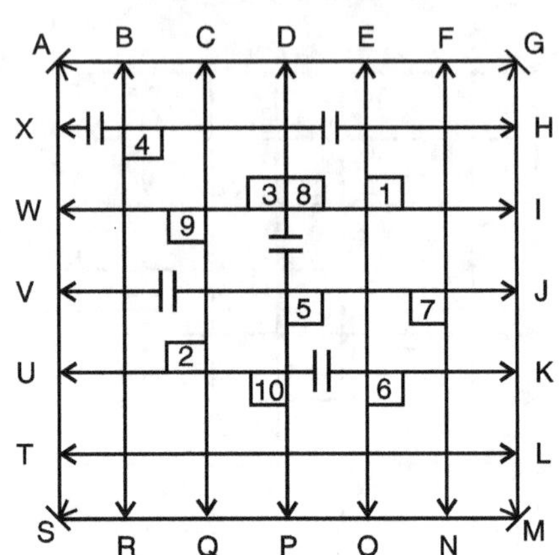

11. Which is the shortest route to go to W from C?
A. 4   B. 8   C. 6   D. 7

12. Which is the shortest route to go to U from C?
A. 3   B. 6   C. 2   D. 7

13. Which is the shortest route to go to O from K?
A. 3   B. 6   C. 2   D. 5

14. Which is the shortest route to go to N from E?
A. 7   B. 8   C. 1   D. 3

15. Which is the shortest route to go to P from J?
A. 3   B. 8   C. 2   D. 5

16. Which is the shortest route to go to E from I?
A. 1   B. 5   C. 2   D. 3

17. Which is the shortest route to go to W from J?
A. 2   B. 5   C. 9   D. 6

18. Which is the shortest route to go to D from W?
A. 2   B. 6   C. 3   D. 7

19. Which is the shortest route to go to I from D?
A. 2   B. 5   C. 7   D. 8

20. Which is the shortest route to go to V from P?
A. 10   B. 3   C. 5   D. 2

SECTION–3

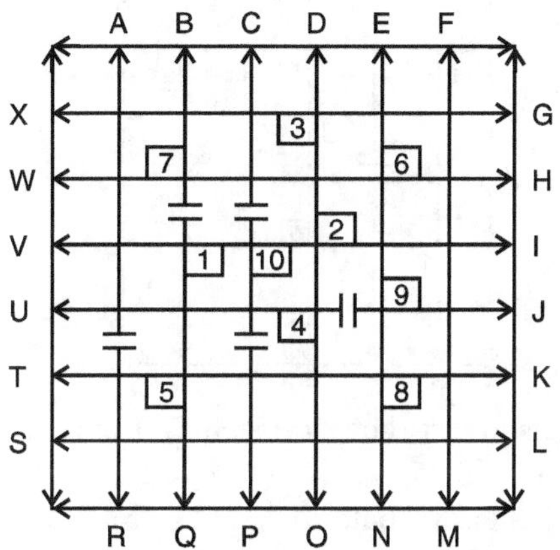

21. Which is the shortest route to reach M from A?
    A. 4   B. 3   C. 2   D. 1

22. Which is the shortest route to reach S from F?
    A. 3   B. 4   C. 2   D. 1

23. Which is the best way to travel from T to H?
    A. 1   B. 3   C. 4   D. 2

24. Which is the best way to travel from K to B?
    A. 4   B. 10   C. 9   D. 2

25. Which is the shortest route to reach L from U?
    A. 5   B. 4   C. 3   D. 2

26. Which is the shortest route to reach O from B?
    A. 10   B. 8   C. 5   D. 3

27. Which is the shortest route to reach G from R?
    A. 1   B. 2   C. 3   D. 4

28. Choose the best way from J to X.
    A. 7   B. 8   C. 9   D. 10

29. Which is the shortest route to reach G from U?
    A. 10   B. 7   C. 8   D. 1

30. Which is the best route to travel from R to D?
    A. 2   B. 4   C. 5   D. 1

SECTION–4

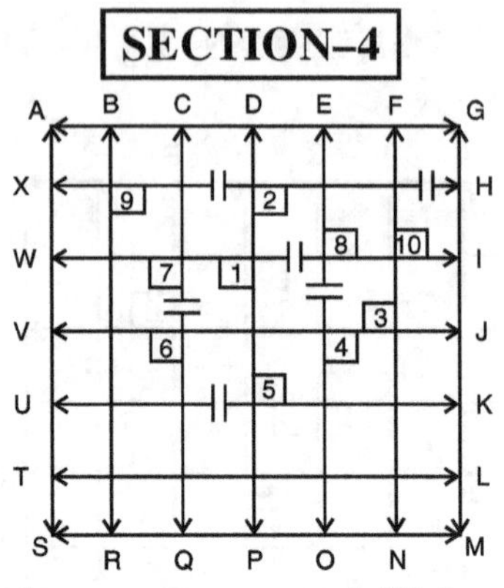

31. Which is the shortest route to reach W from C?

    A. 7   B. 5   C. 2   D. 9

32. Which is the shortest route to reach V from C?

    A. 2   B. 7   C. 1   D. 9

33. Which is the shortest route to reach Q from V?

    A. 2   B. 1   C. 6   D.3

34. Which is the shortest route to reach I from E?

    A. 4   B. 8   C. 5   D. 3

35. Which is the shortest route to reach I from O?

    A. 3   B. 2   C. 1   D. 4

36. Which is the shortest route to reach I from V?

    A. 3   B. 2   C. 8   D. 6

37. Which is the shortest route to reach O from D?

    A. 4   B. 5   C. 3   D. 2

38. Which is the shortest route to reach I from F?

    A. 8   B. 7   C. 1   D. 10

39. Which is the shortest route to reach E from W?

    A. 4   B. 2   C. 8   D. 7

40. Which is the shortest route to reach F from C?

    A. 1   B. 8   C. 7   D. 2

ANSWERS

Section–1

1	2	3	4	5	6	7	8	9	10
C	D	A	B	A	D	B	A	D	C

Section–2

11	12	13	14	15	16	17	18	19	20
A	C	B	A	D	A	C	C	D	A

Section–3

21	22	23	24	25	26	27	28	29	30
A	D	A	D	B	D	A	C	A	D

Section–4

31	32	33	34	35	36	37	38	39	40
D	D	C	B	D	A	B	D	B	A

EXERCISE-3

Directions (Qs. 1-40) : *In the following figure every vertical ($\updownarrow$) and horizontal line ($\leftrightarrow$) denote the route. Between these lines there are some disturbances (—⊣⊢—), in which you cannot go on. A number is indicated in the corner of same boxes. Choose the shortest route number :*

SECTION–1

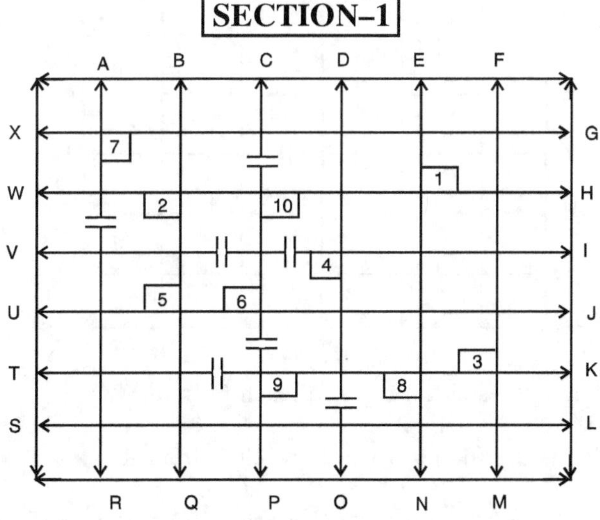

1. Which is the shortest route to reach A from M?

   A. 2   B. 6   C. 1   D. 5

2. Which is the shortest route to reach G from P?

    A. 3   B. 4   C. 6   D. 5

3. Which is the shortest route to reach C from K?

    A. 2   B. 1   C. 5   D. 6

4. Which is the shortest route to reach Q from W?

    A. 1   B. 2   C. 5   D. 6

5. Which is the shortest route to reach N from J?

    A. 3   B. 5   C. 7   D. 4

6. Which is the shortest route to reach D from U?

    A. 7   B. 6   C. 5   D. 8

7. Which is the shortest route to reach I from O?

    A. 2   B. 3   C. 5   D. 8

8. Which is the shortest route to reach D from N?

    A. 7   B. 6   C. 8   D. 5

9. Which is the shortest route to reach B from U?

    A. 5   B. 6   C. 8   D. 7

10. Which is the shortest route to reach E from H?

    A. 1   B. 2   C. 8   D. 5

SECTION–2

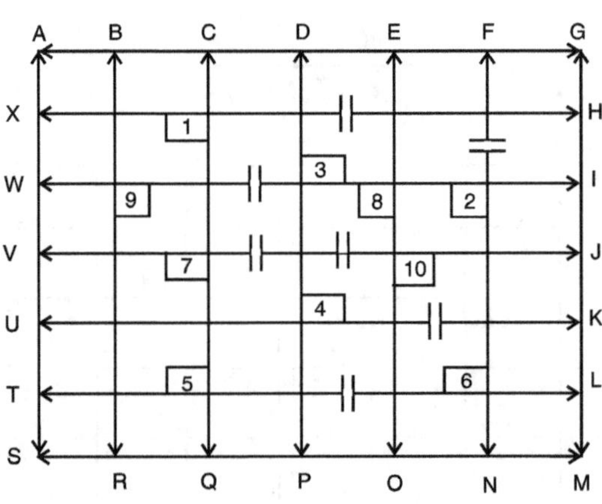

11. Which is the shortest route to reach D from S?

    A. 3   B. 2   C. 4   D. 5

12. Which is the shortest route to reach C from R?

    A. 4   B. 10   C. 5   D. 9

13. Which is the shortest route to reach O from I?

    A. 6   B. 8   C. 10   D. 4

14. Which is the shortest route to reach E from U?
    A. 10   B. 8   C. 6   D. 9

15. Which is the shortest route to reach V from Q?
    A. 2   B. 3   C. 7   D. 9

16. Which is the shortest route to reach C from V?
    A. 9   B. 5   C. 8   D. 6

17. Which is the shortest route to reach O from K?
    A. 5   B. 2   C. 6   D. 3

18. Which is the shortest route to reach D from I?
    A. 3   B. 2   C. 4   D. 1

19. Which is the shortest route to reach O from P?
    A. 5   B. 2   C. 7   D. 4

20. Which is the shortest route to reach V from P?
    A. 3   B. 7   C. 2   D. 8

SECTION–3

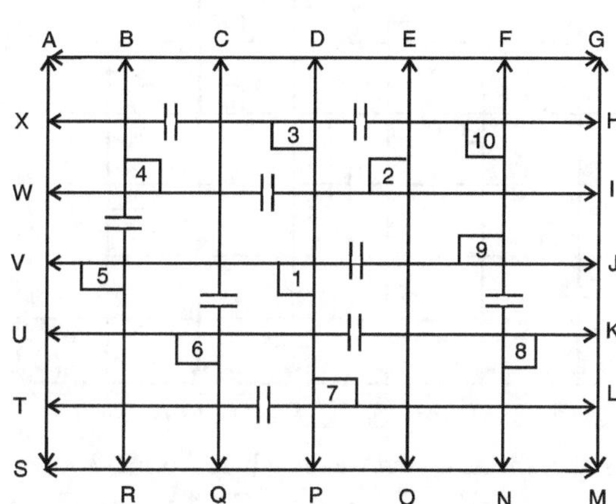

21. Which is the shortest route to reach A from I?
    A. 9   B. 10   C. 8   D. 2

22. Which is the shortest route to reach R from V?
    A. 5   B. 6   C. 1   D. 4

23. Which is the shortest route to reach O from I?
    A. 1   B. 2   C. 9   D. 4

24. Which is the shortest route to reach E from V?
    A. 2   B. 4   C. 8   D. 6

25. Which is the shortest route to reach C from I?
    A. 3   B. 5   C. 8   D. 7

26. Which is the shortest route to reach Q from U?
  A. 3   B. 2   C. 6   D. 4

27. Which is the shortest route to reach O from I?
  A. 2   B. 9   C. 3   D. 4

28. Which is the shortest route to reach J from N?
  A. 7   B. 4   C. 8   D. 5

29. Which is the shortest route to reach D from L?
  A. 7   B. 4   C. 5   D. 3

30. Which is the shortest route to reach H from N?
  A. 4   B. 8   C. 5   D. 7

SECTION–4

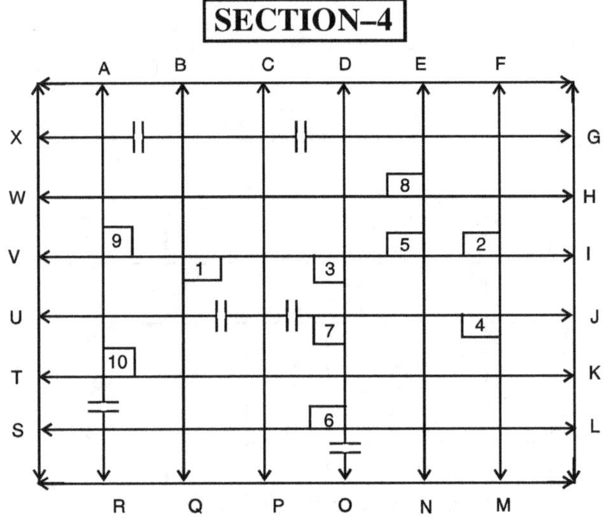

31. Which is the shortest route to reach L from B?
  A. 3   B. 4   C. 5   D. 6

32. Which is the shortest route to reach Q from D?
  A. 2   B. 1   C. 3   D. 4

33. Which is the shortest route to reach G from W?
  A. 8   B. 9   C. 10   D. 5

34. Which is the shortest route to reach D from M?
  A. 5   B. 4   C. 6   D. 8

35. Which is the shortest route to reach E from W?
  A. 3   B. 5   C. 8   D. 4

36. Which is the shortest route to reach C from S?
  A. 2   B. 1   C. 3   D. 4

37. Which is the shortest route to reach M from V?
    A. 3   B. 2   C. 4   D. 5

38. Which is the shortest route to go to P from E?
    A. 4   B. 5   C. 6   D. 8

39. Which is the shortest route to go to P from A?
    A. 9   B. 1   C. 3   D. 4

40. Which is the best route to go to A from M?
    A. 9   B. 10   C. 8   D. 5

ANSWERS

SECTION–1

1	2	3	4	5	6	7	8	9	10
C	A	B	B	A	C	B	C	A	A

SECTION–2

11	12	13	14	15	16	17	18	19	20
D	C	C	D	C	A	C	A	D	B

SECTION–3

21	22	23	24	25	26	27	28	29	30
B	A	C	A	A	C	B	C	A	B

SECTION–4

31	32	33	34	35	36	37	38	39	40
A	B	A	B	C	B	A	D	A	B

BRICK TEST

In this test, you will see a pile of bricks with some bricks numbered A, B, C etc. Your task is to count the number of bricks that are touching bricks of the pile that has a letter on it. All bricks are of same size and shape.

Example:

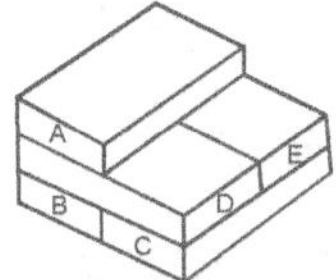

Ans. 1. Two bricks (D, E) are touched by brick A.

    2. Three bricks (C, D, E) are touched by brick B.

    3. Three bricks (B, D, E) are touched by brick C.

    4. Four bricks (C, B, A, E) are touched by brick D.

EXERCISE-1

Directions (Qs. 1-50) : *In this set 10 arrangements of bricks in the form of cuboids are given. There are five questions each on every diagram. In the given diagrams some of the bricks have been marked A, B, C, D and E. You are required to count the number of bricks which are in contact with the particular brick.*

SECTION–1

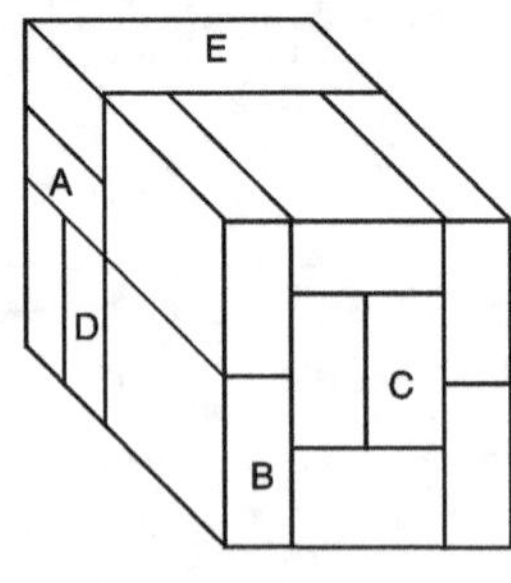

1. How many bricks are touched by brick A?
   A. 7   B. 4
   C. 5   D. 8

2. How many bricks are touched by brick B?
   A. 3   B. 4
   C. 2   D. 7

3. How many bricks are touched by brick C?
   A. 8   B. 5
   C. 2   D. 7

4. How many bricks are touched by brick D?
   A. 7   B. 2
   C. 3   D. 5

5. How many bricks are touched by brick E?
   A. 7   B. 8
   C. 6   D. 4

SECTION–2

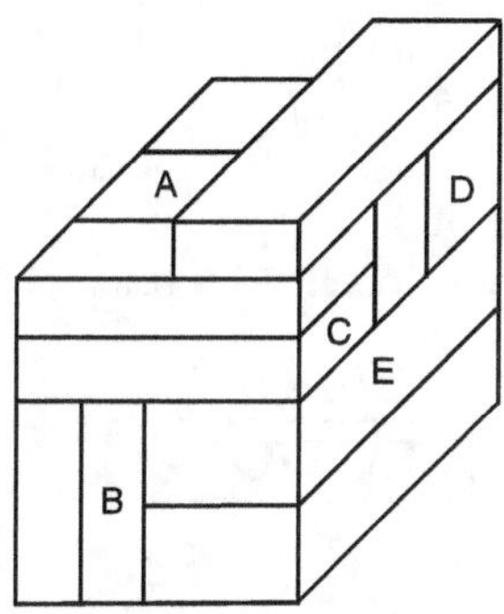

6. How many bricks are touched by brick A?
   A. 5   B. 7   C. 8   D. 6

7. How many bricks are touched by brick B?
   A. 6   B. 3   C. 4   D. 5

8. How many bricks are touched by brick C?
   A. 4   B. 5   C. 8   D. 9

9. How many bricks are touched by brick D?
   A. 7   B. 6   C. 3   D. 5

10. How many bricks are touched by brick E?
    A. 6   B. 3   C. 9   D. 5

SECTION–3

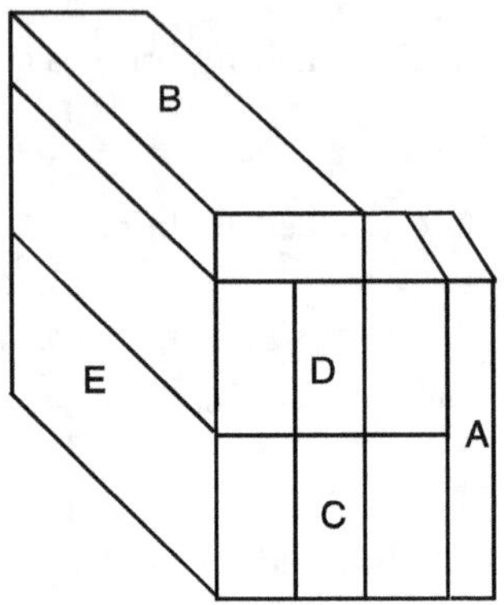

11. How many bricks are touched by brick A?
   A. 1   B. 2   C. 5   D. 6
12. How many bricks are touched by brick B?
   A. 3   B. 2   C. 8   D. 6
13. How many bricks are touched by brick C?
   A. 3   B. 5   C. 2   D. 1
14. How many bricks are touched by brick D?
   A. 6   B. 4   C. 7   D. 8
15. How many bricks are touched by brick E?
   A. 9   B. 2   C. 7   D. 6

SECTION–4

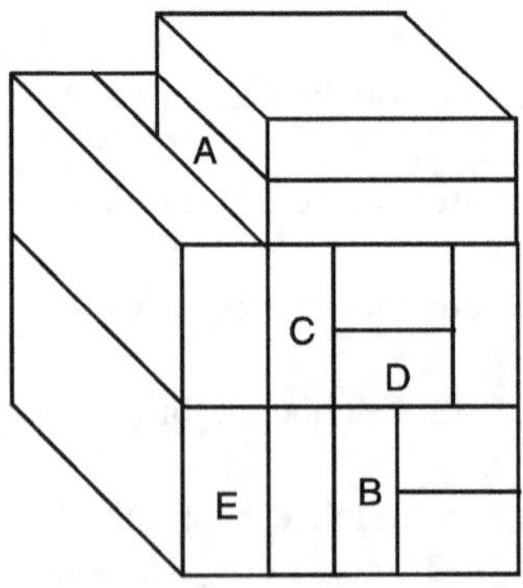

16. How many bricks are touched by brick A?

    A. 6   B. 5

    C. 4   D. 7

17. How many bricks are touched by brick B?

    A. 8   B. 6

    C. 5   D. 4

18. How many bricks are touched by brick C?

    A. 3   B. 5

    C. 8   D. 1

19. How many bricks are touched by brick D?

    A. 6   B. 4

    C. 3   D. 5

20. How many bricks are touched by brick E?

    A. 2   B. 6

    C. 9   D. 7

SECTION–5

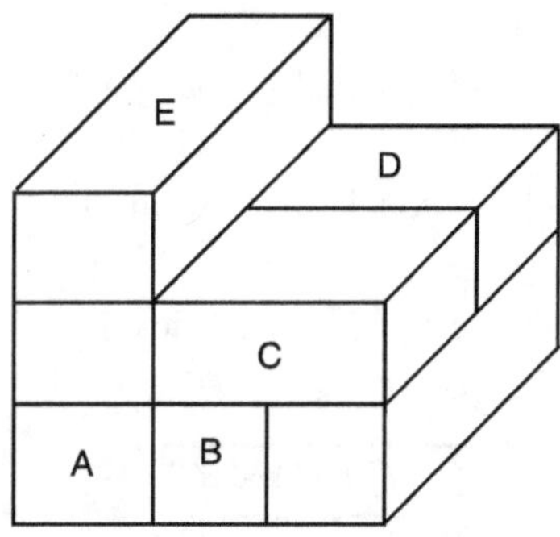

21. How many bricks are touched by brick A?

    A. 7   B. 5   C. 2   D. 3

22. How many bricks are touched by brick B?

    A. 4   B. 6   C. 5   D. 2

23. How many bricks are touched by brick C?

    A. 4   B. 5   C. 7   D. 6

24. How many bricks are touched by brick D?

    A. 9   B. 4   C. 6   D. 8

25. How many bricks are touched by brick E?

    A. 1   B. 3   C. 5   D. 4

SECTION–6

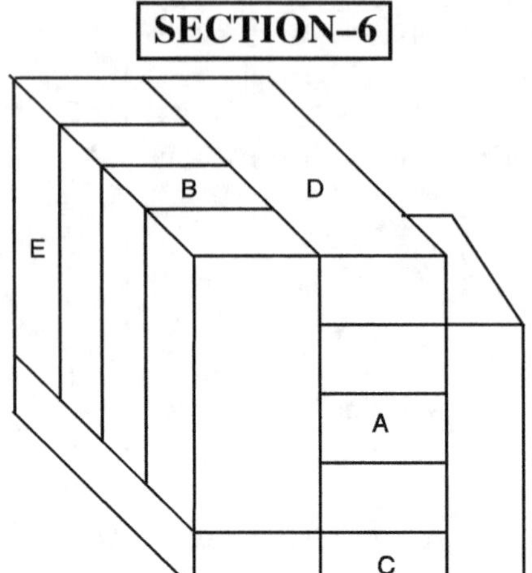

26. How many bricks are touched by brick A?

    A. 7   B. 5   C. 3   D. 2

27. How many bricks are touched by brick B?

    A. 7   B. 8   C. 4   D. 6

28. How many bricks are touched by brick C?

    A. 1   B. 5   C. 3   D. 2

29. How many bricks are touched by brich D?

    A. 5   B. 3   C. 8   D. 7

30. How many bricks are touched by brick E?

    A. 7   B. 6   C. 9   D. 5

SECTION–7

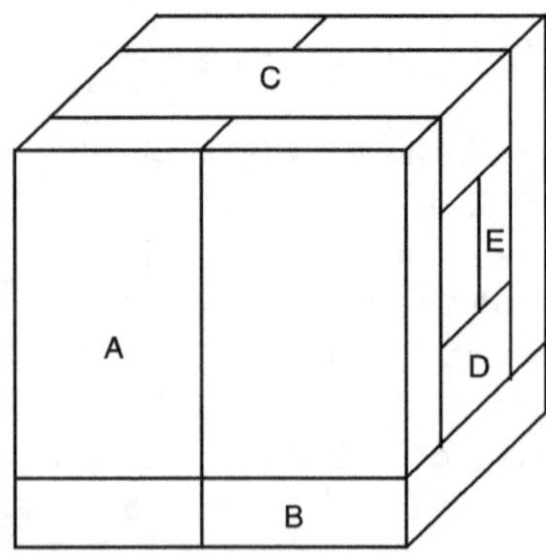

31. How many bricks are touched by brick A?

    A. 8   B. 5   C. 7   D. 6

32. How many bricks are touched by brick B?

    A. 1   B. 2   C. 4   D. 5

33. How many bricks are touched by brick C?

    A. 4   B. 3   C. 6   D. 8

34. How many bricks are touched by brick D?

    A. 4   B. 8   C. 6   D. 7

35. How many bricks are touched by brick E?

    A. 2   B. 3   C. 4   D. 5

SECTION–8

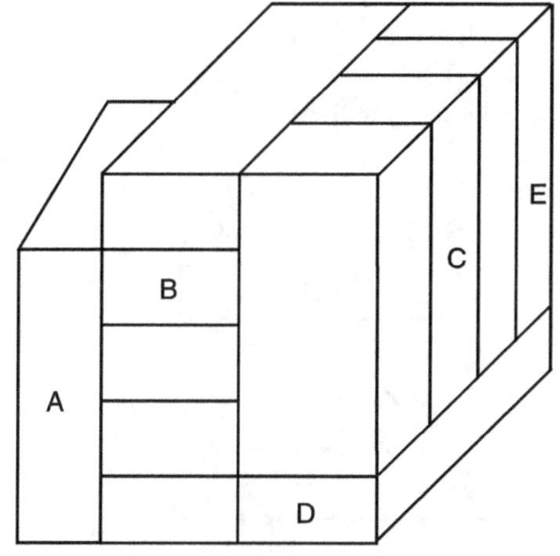

36. How many bricks are touched by brick A?

    A. 4   B. 5   C. 6   D. 7

37. How many bricks are touched by brick B?

    A. 8   B. 7   C. 9   D. 6

38. How many bricks are touched by brick C?

    A. 5   B. 6   C. 4   D. 7

39. How many bricks are touched by brick D?

    A. 7   B. 5   C. 3   D. 2

40. How many bricks are touched by brick E?

    A. 6   B. 3   C. 8   D. 4

SECTION–9

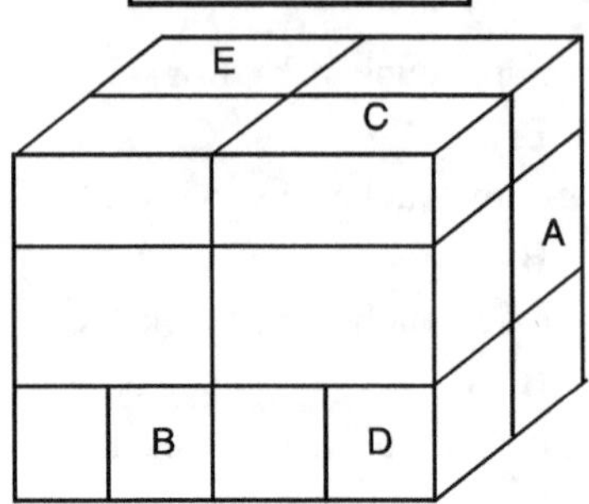

41. How many bricks are touched by brick A?
    A. 7   B. 5   C. 9   D. 4

42. How many bricks are touched by brick B?
    A. 6   B. 5   C. 4   C. 3

43. How many bricks are touched by brick C?
    A. 3   B. 6   C. 7   D. 8

44. How many bricks are touched by brick D?
    A. 5   B. 3   C. 2   D. 1

45. How many bricks are touched by brick E?
    A. 5   B. 8   C. 9   D. 3

SECTION–10

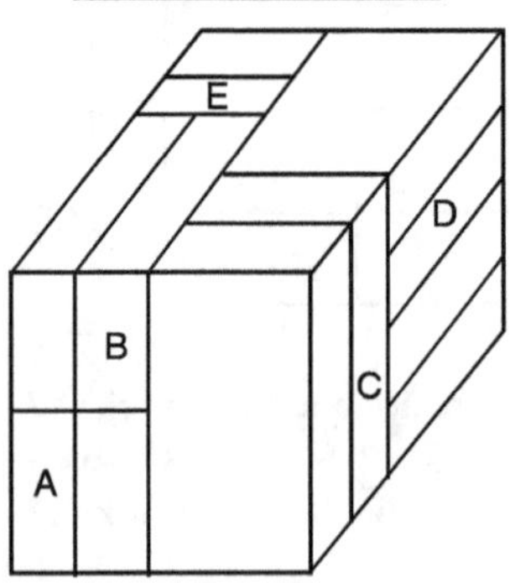

46. How many bricks are touched by brick A?
    A. 5   B. 7   C. 8   D. 3

47. How many bricks are touched by brick B?
    A. 7   B. 3   C. 4   D. 6

48. How many bricks are touched by brick C?
    A. 5   B. 7   C. 6   D. 8

49. How many bricks are touched by brick D?
    A. 1   B. 9   C. 6   D. 8

50. How many bricks are touched by brick E?
    A. 7   B. 8   C. 9   D. 10

ANSWERS

SECTION–1

1	2	3	4	5
A	B	D	A	D

SECTION–2

6	7	8	9	10
B	A	B	D	D

SECTION–3

11	12	13	14	15
A	B	A	B	B

SECTION–4

16	17	18	19	20
C	D	B	D	A

SECTION–5

21	22	23	24	25
C	A	A	B	A

SECTION–6

26	27	28	29	30
A	A	C	A	B

SECTION–7

31	32	33	34	35
B	C	C	B	D

SECTION–8

36	37	38	39	40
A	B	D	B	A

SECTION–9

41	42	43	44	45
B	C	A	B	D

SECTION–10

46	47	48	49	50
D	A	B	C	C

EXERCISE-2

Directions (Qs. 1-50) : *In this set 10 arrangements of bricks in the form of cuboids are given. There are five questions each on every diagram. In the given diagrams some of the bricks have been marked A, B, C, D and E. You are required to count the number of bricks which are in contact with the particular brick.*

SECTION–1

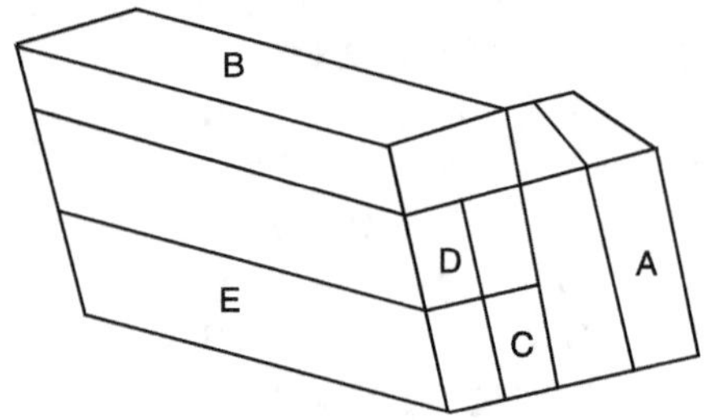

1. How many bricks are touched by brick A?
   A. 1   B. 5   C. 6   D. 7
2. How many bricks are touched by brick B?
   A. 2   B. 3   C. 4   D. 9
3. How many bricks are touched by brick C?
   A. 8   B. 7   C. 4   D. 3
4. How many bricks are touched by brick D?
   A. 3   B. 5   C. 6   D. 8
5. How many bricks are touched by brick E?
   A. 8   B. 7   C. 2   D. 1

SECTION–2

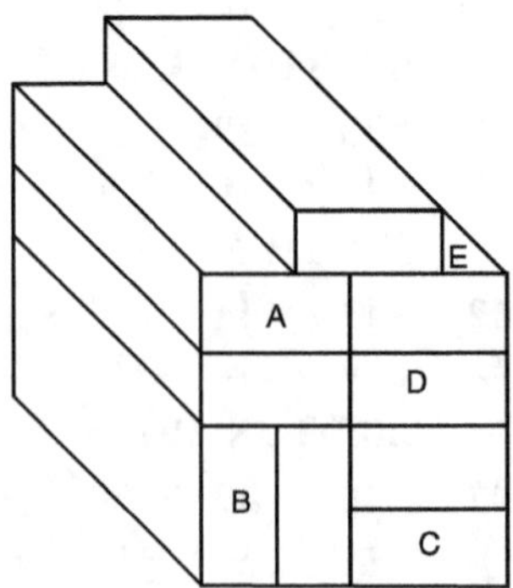

6. How many bricks are touched by brick A?

    A. 3   B. 4   C. 5   D. 6

7. How many bricks are touched by brick B?

    A. 6   B. 2   C. 5   D. 4

8. How many bricks are touched by brick C?

    A. 3   B. 4   C. 2   D. 8

9. How many bricks are touched by brick D?

    A. 3   B. 5   C. 8   D. 9

10. How many bricks are touched by brick E?

    A. 7   B. 5   C. 3   D. 10

SECTION–3

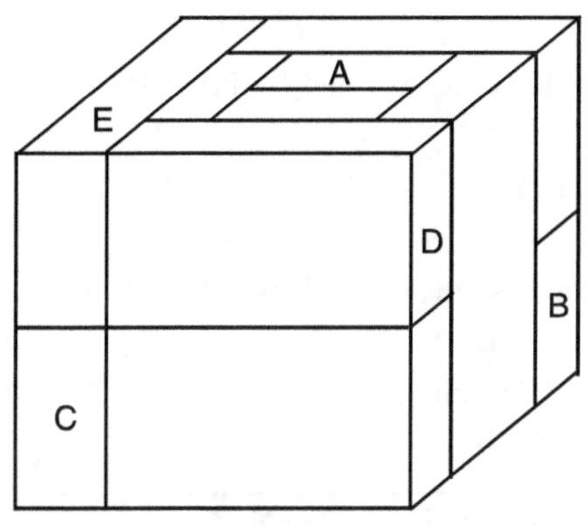

11. How many bricks are touched by brick A?

    A. 3   B. 4   C. 5   D. 6

12. How many bricks are touched by brick B?

    A. 5   B. 2   C. 6   D. 9

13. How many bricks are touched by brick C?

    A. 6   B. 7   C. 3   D. 4

14. How many bricks are touched by brick D?

    A. 5   B. 4   C. 6   D. 8

15. How many bricks are touched by brick E?

    A. 4   B. 3   C. 7   D. 5

SECTION–4

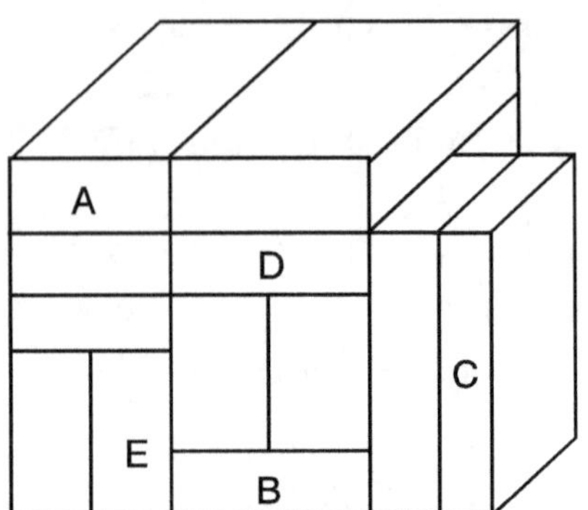

16. How many bricks are touched by brick A?
   A. 6   B. 5   C. 4   D. 2

17. How many bricks are touched by brick B?
   A. 4   B. 5   C. 7   D. 6

18. How many bricks are touched by brick C?
   A. 6   B. 5   C. 7   D. 1

19. How many bricks are touched by brick D?
   A. 2   B. 5   C. 8   D. 4

20. How many bricks are touched by brick E?
   A. 9   B. 8   C. 6   D. 4

SECTION–5

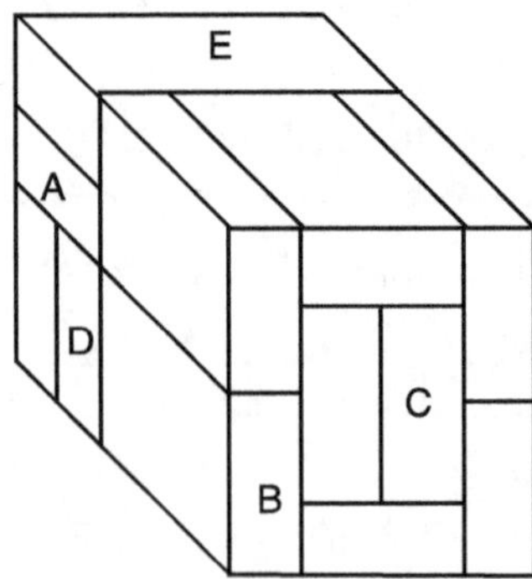

21. How many bricks are touched by brick A?
    A. 7   B. 5   C. 4   D. 3

22. How many bricks are touched by brick B?
    A. 4   B. 8   C. 7   D. 6

23. How many bricks are touched by brick C?
    A. 4   B. 5   C. 7   D. 8

24. How many bricks are touched by brick D?
    A. 4   B. 2   C. 3   D. 7

25. How many bricks are touched by brick E?
    A. 4   B. 5   C. 7   D. 8

SECTION–6

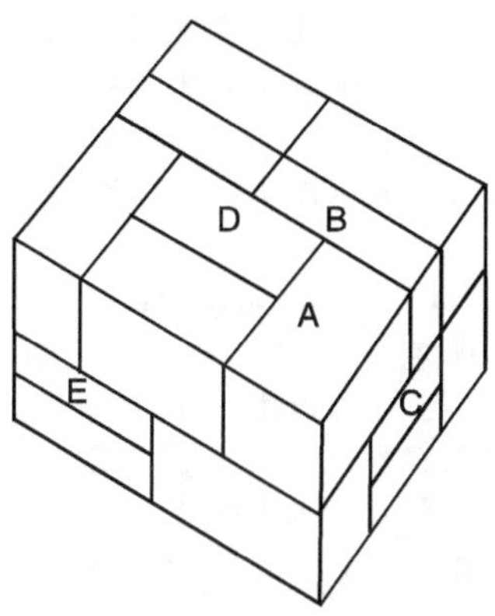

26. How many bricks are touched by brick A?
    A. 5   B. 6   C. 7   D. 4

27. How many bricks are touched by brick B?
    A. 7   B. 8   C. 9   D. 5

28. How many bricks are touched by brick C?
    A. 5   B. 4   C. 8   D. 6

29. How many bricks are touched by brick D?
    A. 7   B. 4   C. 5   D. 8

30. How many bricks are touched by brick E?
    A. 7   B. 3   C. 5   D. 6

SECTION–7

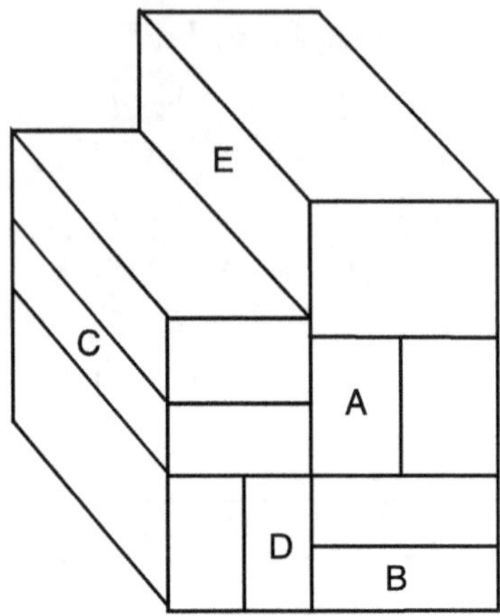

31. How many bricks are touched by brick A?
    A. 3   B. 4   C. 5   D. 6

32. How many bricks are touched by brick B?
    A. 4   B. 5   C. 2   D. 8

33. How many bricks are touched by brick C?
    A. 3   B. 4   C. 8   D. 7

34. How many bricks are touched by brick D?
    A. 5   B. 7   C. 2   D. 4

35. How many bricks are touched by brick E?
    A. 2   B. 3   C. 4   D. 1

SECTION–8

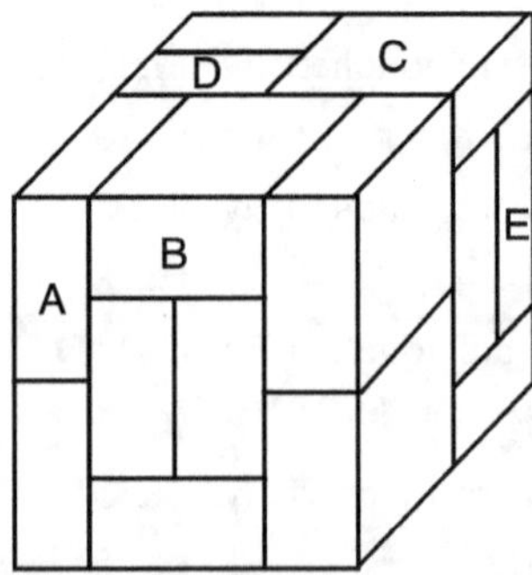

36. How many bricks are touched by brick A?

    A. 5   B. 6   C. 4   D. 3

37. How many bricks are touched by brick B?

    A. 7   B. 9   C. 6   D. 8

38. How many bricks are touched by brick C?

    A. 4   B. 5   C. 6   D. 7

39. How many bricks are touched by brick D?

    A. 2   B. 7   C. 5   D. 4

40. How many bricks are touched by brick E?

    A. 9   B. 8   C. 4   D. 3

SECTION–9

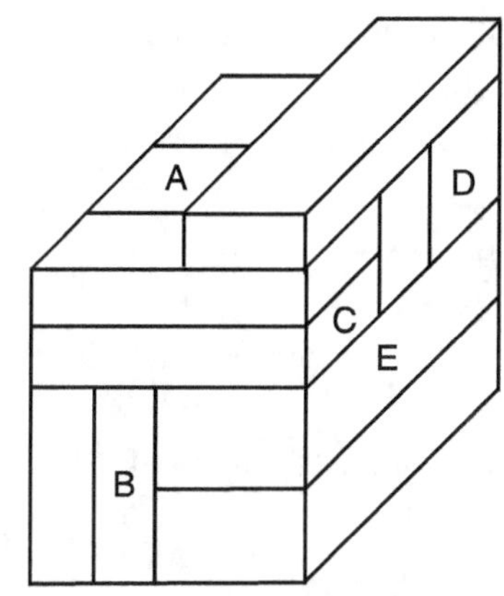

41. How many bricks are touched by brick A?

    A. 4   B. 7   C. 8   D. 9

42. How many bricks are touched by brick B?

    A. 6   B. 3   C. 4   D. 5

43. How many bricks are touched by brick C?

    A. 5   B. 6   C. 7   D. 3

44. How many bricks are touched by brick D?

    A. 6   B. 5   C. 3   D. 4

45. How many bricks are touched by brick E?

    A. 4   B. 5   C. 6   D. 7

SECTION–10

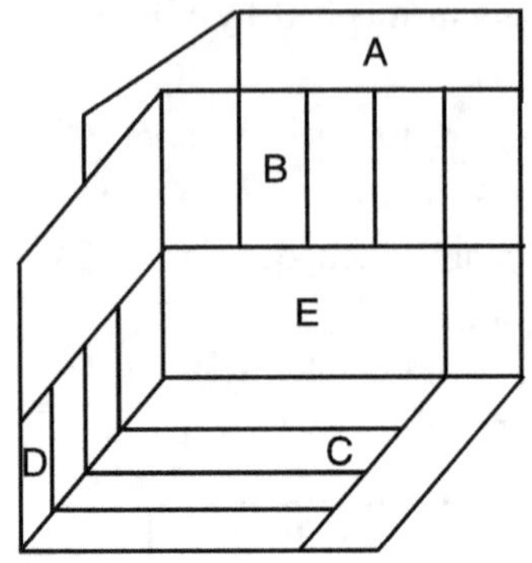

46. How many bricks are touched by brick A?

    A. 1   B. 9   C. 7   D. 4

47. How many bricks are touched by brick B?

    A. 5   B. 4   C. 8   D. 7

48. How many bricks are touched by brick C?

    A. 3   B. 7   C. 6   D. 5

49. How many bricks are touched by brick D?

    A. 2   B. 6   C. 8   D. 7

50. How many bricks are touched by brick E?

    A. 2   B. 5   C. 6   D. 4

ANSWERS

SECTION–1

1	2	3	4	5
A	A	D	A	C

SECTION–2

6	7	8	9	10
A	B	C	A	C

SECTION–3

11	12	13	14	15
C	C	D	A	A

SECTION–4

16	17	18	19	20
D	A	D	B	D

SECTION–5

21	22	23	24	25
A	A	C	D	A

SECTION–6

26	27	28	29	30
A	D	C	A	A

SECTION–7

31	32	33	34	35
C	C	B	D	A

SECTION–8

36	37	38	39	40
C	C	C	B	D

SECTION–9

41	42	43	44	45
B	A	A	B	B

SECTION–10

46	47	48	49	50
D	D	B	B	C

EXERCISE-3

Directions (Qs. 1-50) :

- There are 10 sections in this part of Psychological Test. There are five questions in each section.
- Some bricks are arranged in the form of a cube or cuboid in each section. Some of the bricks are marked A, B, C, D and E in each section.
- You are required to ascertain the number of such bricks which are neighbours of a specified brick or how many bricks are being touched by a specified bricks.

SECTION–1

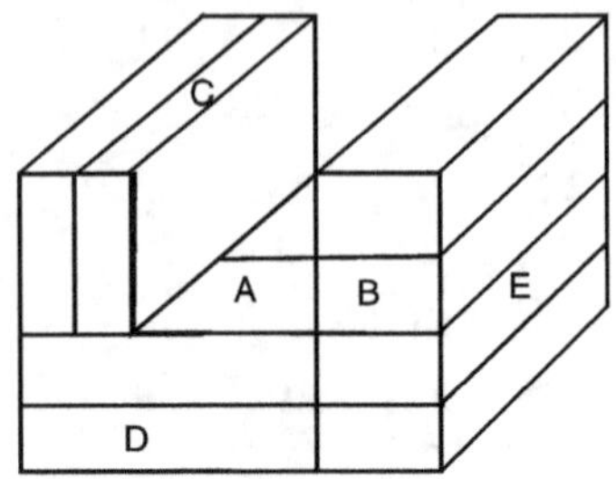

1. How many bricks are touched by brick A?
   - A. 4
   - B. 6
   - C. 5
   - D. 2
2. How many bricks are touched by brick B?
   - A. 1
   - B. 2
   - C. 7
   - D. 8
3. How many bricks are touched by brick C?
   - A. 4
   - B. 3
   - C. 5
   - D. 2
4. How many bricks are touched by brick D?
   - A. 5
   - B. 4
   - C. 3
   - D. 2
5. How many bricks are touched by brick E?
   - A. 4
   - B. 2
   - C. 3
   - D. 8

SECTION–2

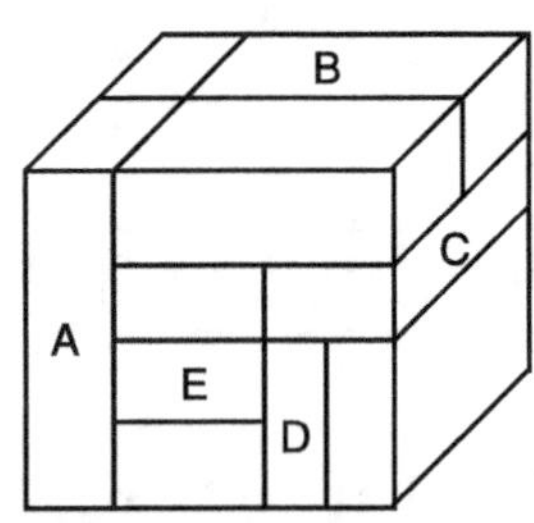

6. How many bricks are touched by brick A?
   - A. 4
   - B. 2
   - C. 5
   - D. 8
7. How many bricks are touched by brick B?
   - A. 8
   - B. 4
   - C. 9
   - D. 5
8. How many bricks are touched by brick C?
   - A. 7
   - B. 5
   - C. 6
   - D. 9
9. How many bricks are touched by brick D?
   - A. 5
   - B. 4
   - C. 6
   - D. 9
10. How many bricks are touched by brick E?
    - A. 9
    - B. 2
    - C. 4
    - D. 5

SECTION–3

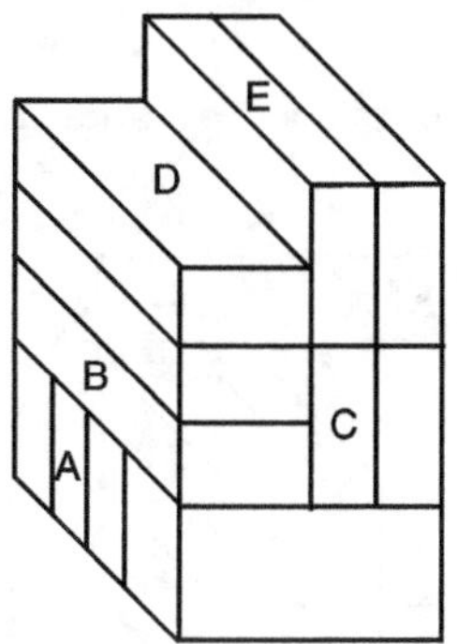

11. How many bricks are touched by brick A?
    A. 5   B. 2   C. 4   D. 9

12. How many bricks are touched by brick B?
    A. 4   B. 6   C. 3   D. 2

13. How many bricks are touched by brick C?
    A. 2   B. 4   C. 8   D. 9

14. How many bricks are touched by brick D?
    A. 8   B. 7   C. 1   D. 2

15. How many bricks are touched by brick E?
    A. 3   B. 4   C. 7   D. 6

SECTION– 4

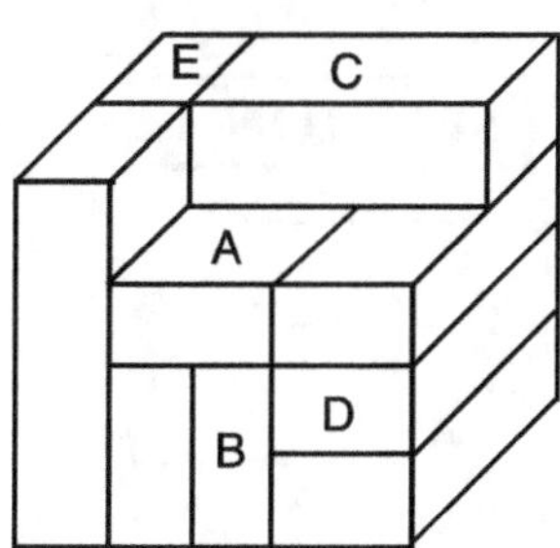

16. How many bricks are touched by brick A?
    A. 5   B. 6   C. 4   D. 7

17. How many bricks are touched by brick B?
    A. 3   B. 2   C. 4   D. 9

18. How many bricks are touched by brick C?
   A. 12   B. 3   C. 8   D. 9
19. How many bricks are touched by brick D?
   A. 3   B. 6   C. 8   D. 9
20. How many bricks are touched by brick E?
   A. 5   B. 4   C. 3   D. 2

SECTION–5

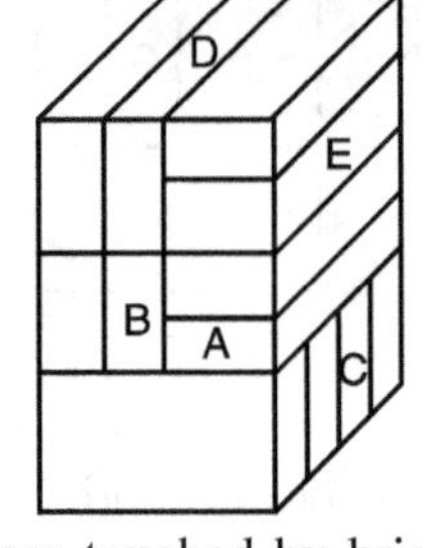

21. How many bricks are touched by brick A?
   A. 5   B. 6   C. 7   D. 8
22. How many bricks are touched by brick B?
   A. 8   B. 7   C. 9   D. 10
23. How many bricks are touched by brick C?
   A. 3   B. 4   C. 2   D. 5
24. How many bricks are touched by brick D?
   A. 1   B. 4   C. 9   D. 10
25. How many bricks are touched by brick E?
   A. 3   B. 9   C. 10   D. 11

SECTION–6

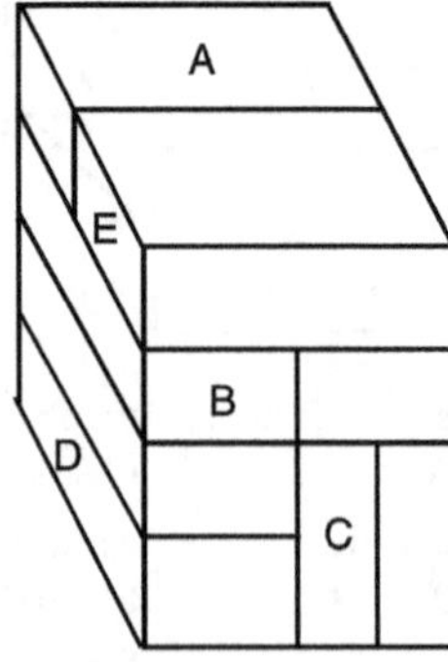

26. How many bricks are touched by brick A?

    A. 5   B. 4   C. 3   D. 2

27. How many bricks are touched by brick B?

    A. 8   B. 9   C. 2   D. 4

28. How many bricks are touched by brick C?

    A. 4   B. 8   C. 7   D. 2

29. How many bricks are touched by brick D?

    A. 4   B. 2   C. 6   D. 8

30. How many bricks are touched by brick E?

    A. 7   B. 3   C. 1   D. 2

SECTION–7

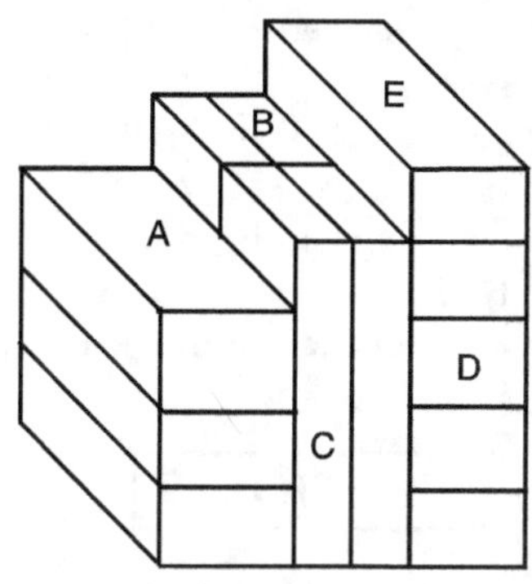

31. How many bricks are touched by brick A?

    A. 6   B. 3   C. 5   D. 4

32. How many bricks are touched by brick B?

    A. 6   B. 5   C. 4   D. 3

33. How many bricks are touched by brick C?

    A. 4   B. 5   C. 8   D. 9

34. How many bricks are touched by brick D?

    A. 6   B. 4   C. 3   D. 10

35. How many bricks are touched by brick E?

    A. 1   B. 2   C. 9   D. 11

SECTION–8

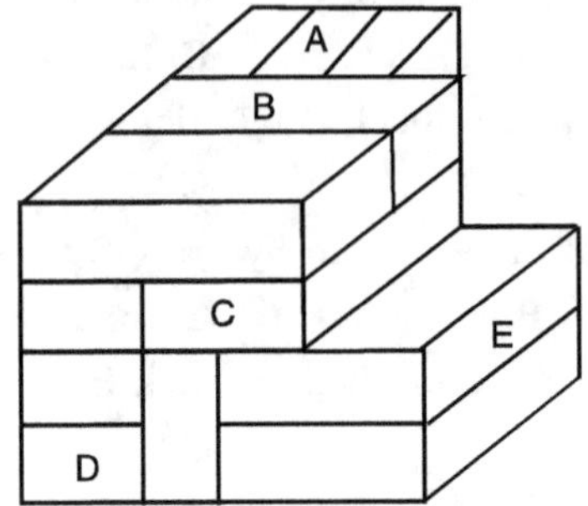

36. How many bricks are touched by brick A?
   A. 7   B. 8   C. 6   D. 5
37. How many bricks are touched by brick B?
   A. 3   B. 4   C. 6   D. 5
38. How many bricks are touched by brick C?
   A. 6   B. 4   C. 9   D. 11
39. How many bricks are touched by brick D?
   A. 8   B. 2   C. 4   D. 9
40. How many bricks are touched by brick E?
   A. 5   B. 4   C. 3   D. 2

SECTION–9

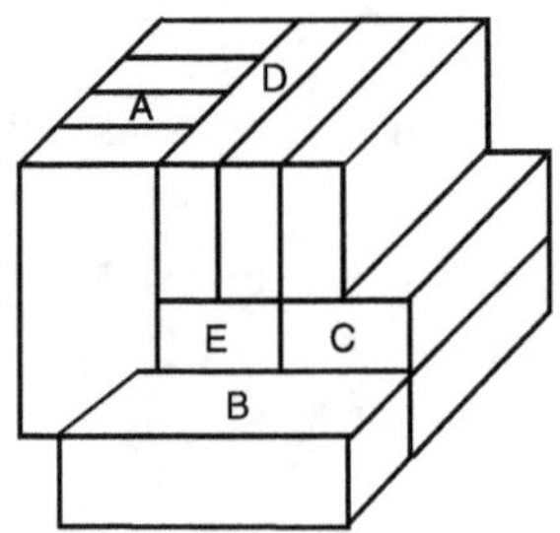

41. How many bricks are touched by brick A?
   A. 4   B. 3   C. 1   D. 5
42. How many bricks are touched by brick B?
   A. 2   B. 4   C. 3   D. 2
43. How many bricks are touched by brick C?
   A. 10   B. 7   C. 8   D. 3

44. How many bricks are touched by brick D?
   A. 6   B. 5   C. 7   D. 8

45. How many bricks are touched by brick E?
   A. 8   B. 7   C. 6   D. 2

SECTION–10

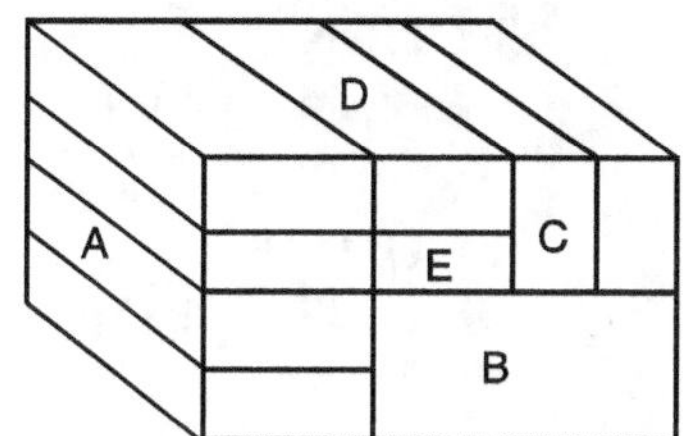

46. How many bricks are touched by brick A?
   A. 6   B. 7   C. 8   D. 5

47. How many bricks are touched by brick B?
   A. 1   B. 6   C. 4   D. 5

48. How many bricks are touched by brick C?
   A. 3   B. 4   C. 7   D. 8

49. How many bricks are touched by brick D?
   A. 3   B. 4   C. 5   D. 7

50. How many bricks are touched by brick E?
   A. 4   B. 8   C. 7   D. 9

ANSWERS

SECTION–1

1	2	3	4	5
C	B	B	C	A

SECTION–2

6	7	8	9	10
C	B	B	B	D

SECTION–3

11	12	13	14	15
A	B	C	D	A

SECTION–4

16	17	18	19	20
B	C	B	A	B

SECTION–5

21	22	23	24	25
B	A	D	B	A

SECTION–6

26	27	28	29	30
C	D	A	B	B

SECTION–7

31	32	33	34	35
B	A	B	B	A

SECTION–8

36	37	38	39	40
C	C	A	B	C

SECTION–9

41	42	43	44	45
D	A	D	A	A

SECTION–10

46	47	48	49	50
A	B	C	A	C

EXERCISE-4

Directions (Qs. 1-50) : *In the following questions 10 arrangements of bricks in the form of cuboids are given and five questions have been asked on each figure. Study the diagram carefully and mark your answer on the Answer Sheet according to the number of bricks touched by specified bricks marked as A, B, C, D and E.*

SECTION–1

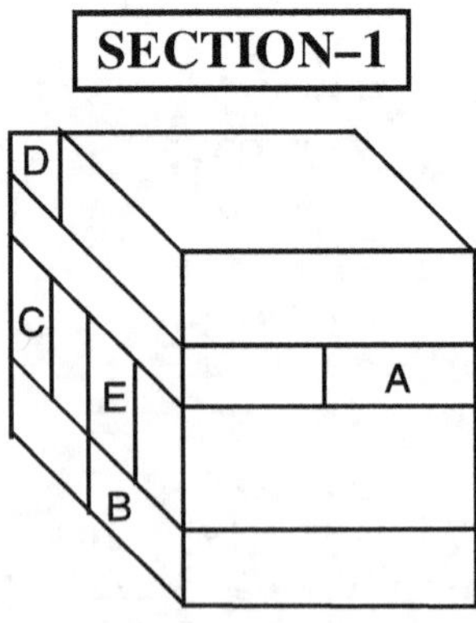

1. How many bricks are touched by brick A?
   A. 7   B. 8   C. 6   D. 5
2. How many bricks are touched by brick B?
   A. 1   B. 2   C. 4   D. 3
3. How many bricks are touched by brick C?
   A. 5   B. 4   C. 3   D. 2
4. How many bricks are touched by brick D?
   A. 8   B. 7   C. 6   D. 9
5. How many bricks are touched by brick E?
   A. 4   B. 5   C. 8   D. 9

SECTION–2

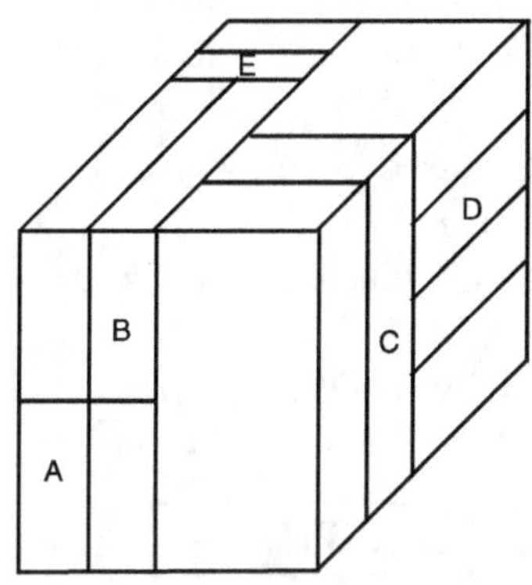

6. How many bricks are touched by brick A?
   A. 3   B. 4   C. 5   D. 8
7. How many bricks are touched by brick B?
   A. 9   B. 8   C. 2   D. 7
8. How many bricks are touched by brick C?
   A. 10   B. 7   C. 8   D. 9
9. How many bricks are touched by brick D?
   A. 6   B. 4   C. 3   D. 1
10. How many bricks are touched by brick E?
   A. 2   B. 8   C. 9   D. 7

SECTION–3

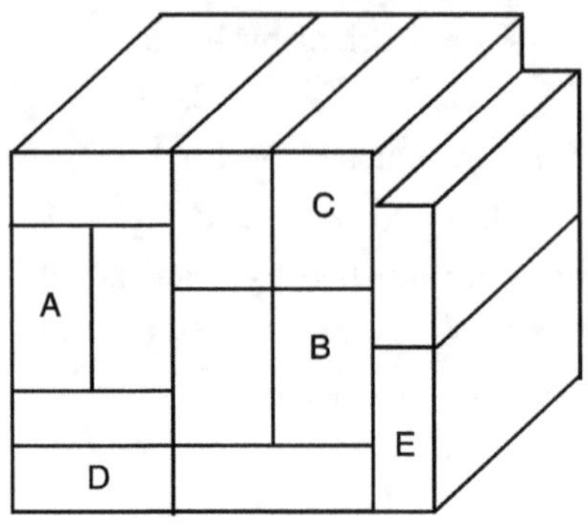

11. How many bricks are touched by brick A?

    A. 2   B. 5   C. 3   D. 8

12. How many bricks are touched by brick B?

    A. 3   B. 5   C. 8   D. 9

13. How many bricks are touched by brick C?

    A. 1   B. 8   C. 3   D. 7

14. How many bricks are touched by brick D?

    A. 8   B. 4   C. 5   D. 2

15. How many bricks are touched by brick E?

    A. 3   B. 8   C. 7   D. 6

SECTION–4

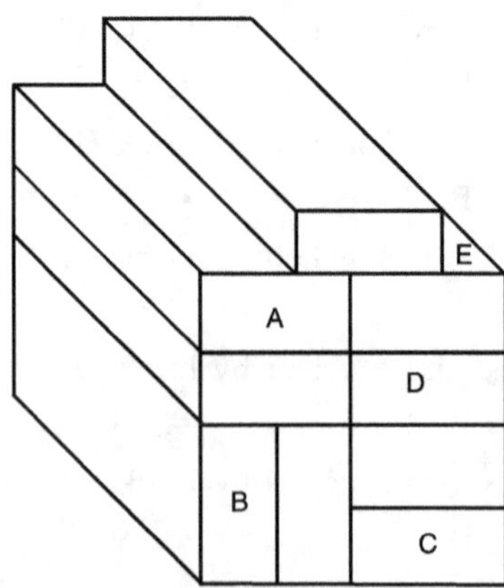

16. How many bricks an touched by brick A?

    A. 7   B. 8   C. 3   D. 4

17. How many bricks an touched by brick B?

    A. 5   B. 2   C. 8   D. 10

18. How many bricks are touched by brick C?

    A. 2   B. 4   C. 9   D. 7

19. How many bricks are touched by brick D?

    A. 3   B. 6   C. 8   D. 4

20. How many bricks are touched by brick E?

    A. 3   B. 4   C. 6   D. 8

SECTION–5

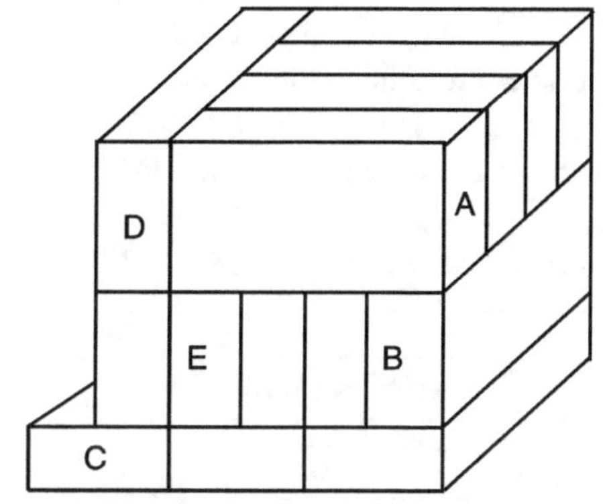

21. How many bricks are touhced by brick A?

    A. 6   B. 4   C. 8   D. 7

22. How many bricks are touched by brick B?

    A. 7   B. 6   C. 3   D. 8

23. How many bricks are touched by brick C?

    A. 2   B. 5   C. 4   D. 6

24. How many bricks are touched by brick D?

    A. 5   B. 4   C. 3   D. 2

25. How many bricks are touched by brick E?

    A. 7   B. 5   C. 8   D. 9

SECTION–6

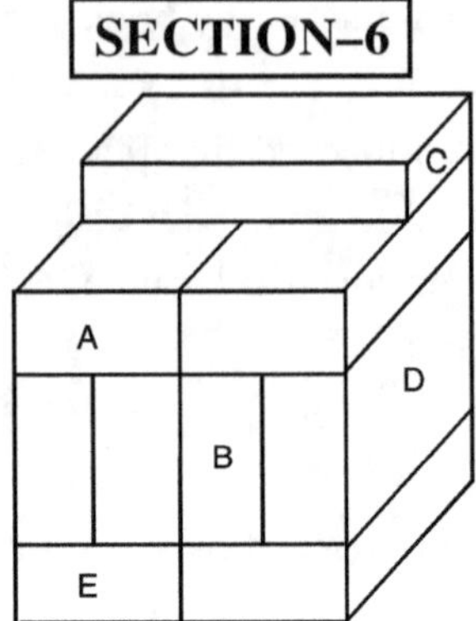

26. How many bricks are touched by brick A?
    A. 6   B. 5   C. 4   D. 7

27. How many bricks are touched by brick B?
    A. 5   B. 4   C. 3   D. 2

28. How many bricks are touched by brick C?
    A. 7   B. 8   C. 2   D. 6

29. How many bricks are touched by brick D?
    A. 5   B. 3   C. 8   D. 7

30. How many bricks are touched by brick E?
    A. 8   B. 3   C. 5   D. 6

SECTION–7

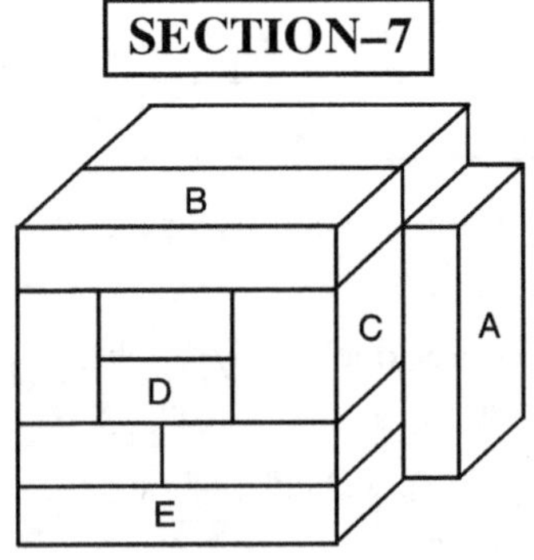

31. How many bricks are touched by brick A?
    A. 3   B. 5   C. 6   D. 7

32. How many bricks are touched by brick B?
    A. 9   B. 7   C. 8   D. 4

33. How many bricks are touched by brick C?
    A. 6   B. 5   C. 3   D. 4

34. How many bricks are touched by brick D?

    A. 2   B. 1   C. 5   D. 6

35. How many bricks are touched by brick E?

    A. 4   B. 2   C. 7   D. 6

SECTION–8

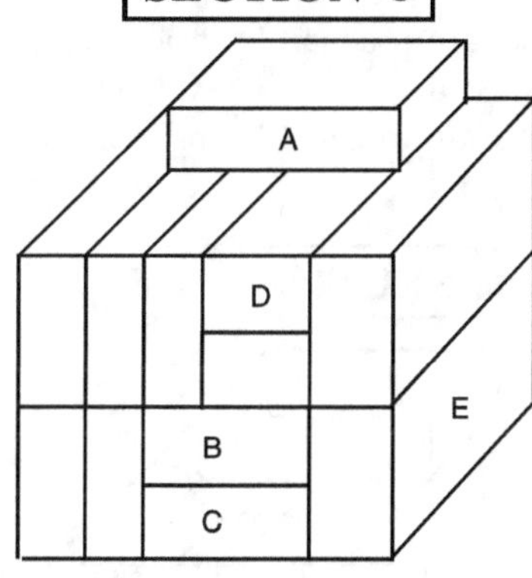

36. How many bricks are touched by brick A?

    A. 3   B. 4   C. 6   D. 5

37. How many bricks are touched by brick B?

    A. 9   B. 7   C. 2   D. 5

38. How many bricks are touched by brick C?

    A. 2   B. 4   C. 3   D. 8

39. How many bricks are touched by brick D?

    A. 5   B. 6   C. 4   D. 7

40. How many bricks are touched by brick E?

    A. 6   B. 7   C. 2   D. 10

SECTION–9

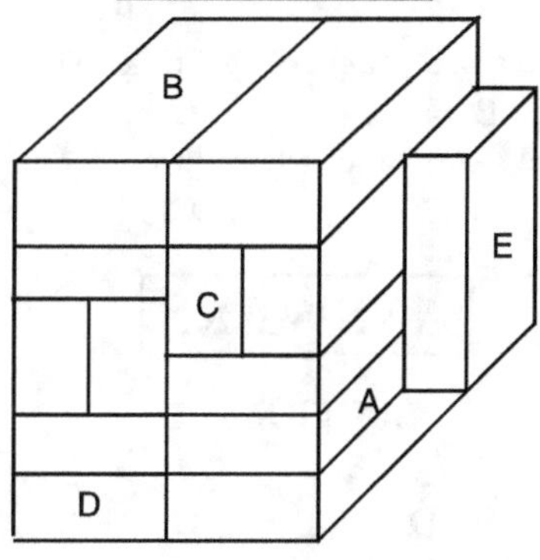

41. How many bricks are touched by brick A?
   A. 5   B. 6   C. 4   D. 3
42. How many bricks are touched by brick B?
   A. 1   B. 2   C. 3   D. 5
43. How many bricks are touched by brick C?
   A. 5   B. 4   C. 4   D. 3
44. How many bricks are touched by brick D?
   A. 3   B. 4   C. 6   D. 2
45. How many bricks are touched by brick E?
   A. 5   B. 4   C. 3   D. 2

SECTION–10

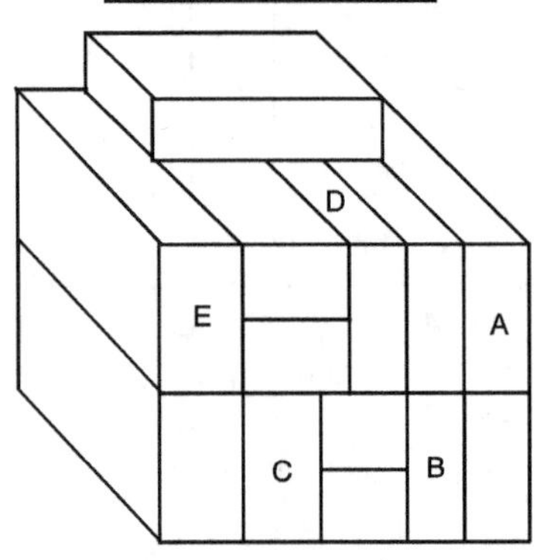

46. How many bricks are touched by brick A?
   A. 6   B. 4   C. 2   D. 1
47. How many bricks are touched by brick B?
   A. 6   B. 8   C. 4   D. 3
48. How many bricks are touched by brick C?
   A. 4   B. 8   C. 9   D. 10
49. How many bricks are touched by brick D?
   A. 2   B. 4   C. 5   D. 8
50. How many bricks are touched by brick E?
   A. 3   B. 2   C. 1   D. 4

ANSWERS

SECTION–1

1	2	3	4	5
C	D	B	C	B

SECTION–2

6	7	8	9	10
A	D	B	A	C

SECTION–3

11	12	13	14	15
C	B	C	D	A

SECTION–4

16	17	18	19	20
C	B	A	A	A

SECTION–5

21	22	23	24	25
A	B	A	A	A

SECTION–6

26	27	28	29	30
C	B	C	B	B

SECTION 7

31	32	33	34	35
A	D	A	C	B

SECTION–8

36	37	38	39	40
A	D	C	C	C

SECTION–9

41	42	43	44	45
C	B	A	D	C

SECTION–10

46	47	48	49	50
C	C	A	C	A

EXERCISE-5

Directions (Qs. 1-50) : *In the following questions 10 arrangements of bricks in the form of cuboids are given. There are five questions each on every diagram. In the given diagrams some of the bricks have been marked A, B, C, D and E. You are required to count the number of bricks which are in contact with the particular brick.*

Rly Apt (E)–8

SECTION–1

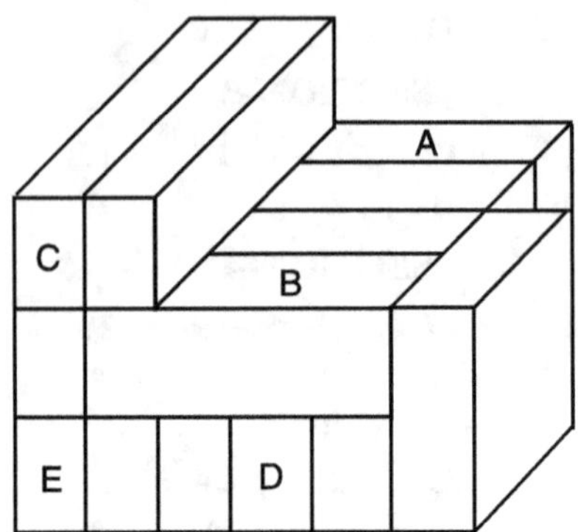

1. How many bricks are touched by brick A?
   A. 7   B. 4   C. 8   D. 9
2. How many bricks are touched by brick B?
   A. 4   B. 2   C. 8   D. 6
3. How many bricks are touched by brick C?
   A. 5   B. 6   C. 7   D. 2
4. How many bricks are touched by brick D?
   A. 4   B. 5   C. 6   D. 7
5. How many bricks are touched by brick E?
   A. 6   B. 5   C. 1   D. 2

SECTION–2

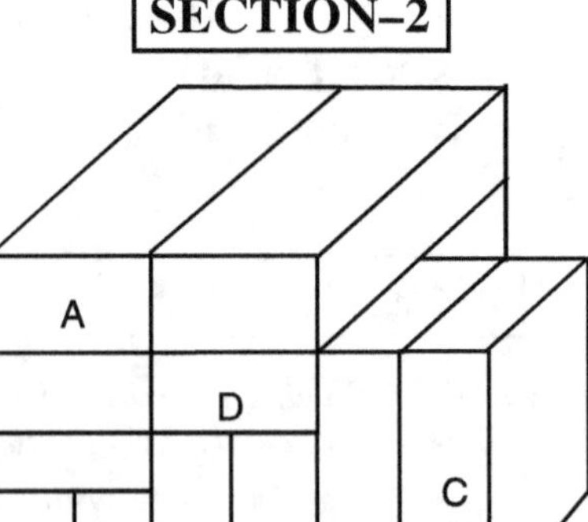

6. How many bricks are touched by brick A?

    A. 8   B. 9   C. 2   D. 6

7. How many bricks are touched by brick B?

    A. 4   B. 3   C. 2   D. 8

8. How many bricks are touched by brick C?

    A. 8   B. 9   C. 10   D. 1

9. How many bricks are touched by brick D?

    A. 5   B. 7   C. 8   D. 6

10. How many bricks are touched by brick E?

    A. 3   B. 2   C. 4   D. 6

SECTION–3

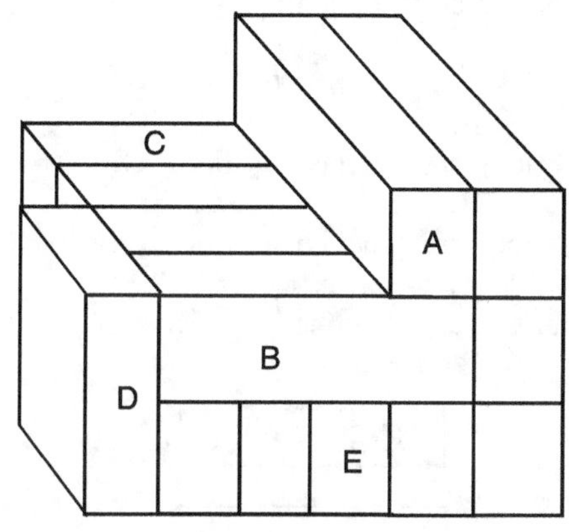

11. How many bricks are touched by brick A?

    A. 1   B. 2   C. 3   D. 5

12. How many bricks are touched by brick B?

    A. 5   B. 8   C. 7   D. 6

13. How many bricks are touched by brick C?

    A. 7   B. 8   C. 5   D. 9

14. How many bricks are touched by brick D?

    A. 7   B. 6   C. 4   D. 3

15. How many bricks are touched by brick E?

    A. 3   B. 4   C. 9   D. 6

SECTION–4

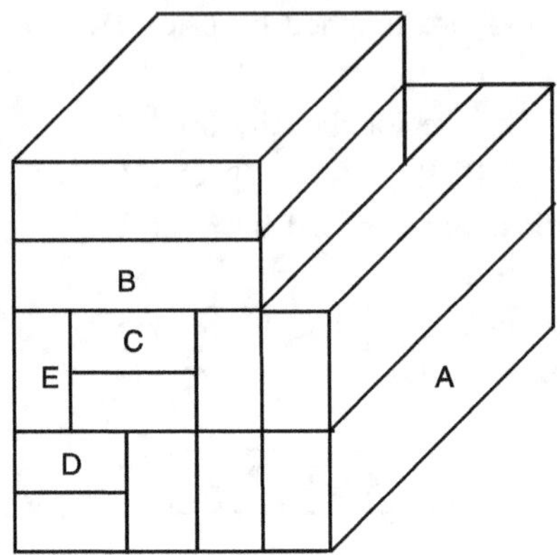

16. How many bricks are touched by brick A?
A. 2   B. 8   C. 9   D. 7

17. How many bricks are touched by brick B?
A. 8   B. 4   C. 7   D. 6

18. How many bricks are touched by brick C?
A. 8   B. 4   C. 3   D. 2

19. How many bricks are touched by brick D?
A. 4   B. 8   C. 9   D. 10

20. How many bricks are thouched by brick E?
A. 2   B. 3   C. 4   D. 5

SECTION–5

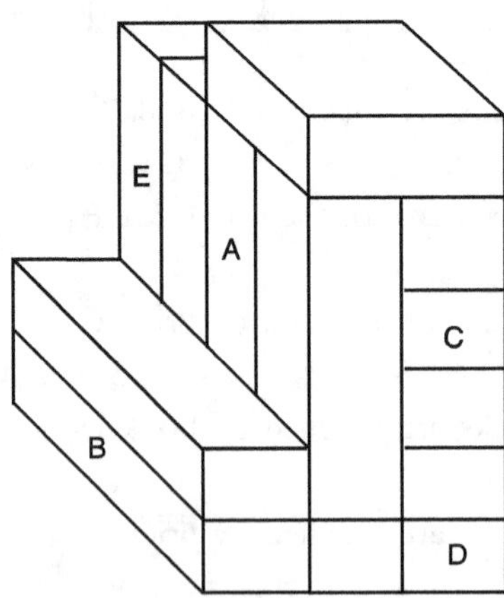

21. How many bricks are touched by brick A?

    A. 9   B. 6   C. 5   D. 4

22. How many bricks are touched by brick B?

    A. 6   B. 9   C. 8   D. 2

23. How many bricks are touched by brick C?

    A. 3   B. 6   C. 4   D. 8

24. How many bricks are touched by brick D?

    A. 7   B. 2   C. 4   D. 8

25. How many bricks are touched by brick E?

    A. 7   B. 8   C. 9   D. 10

SECTION–6

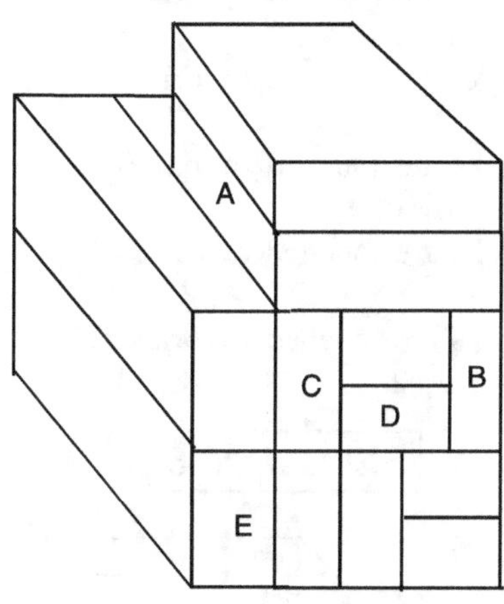

26. How many bricks are touched by brick A?

    A. 4   B. 6   C. 7   D. 10

27. How many bricks are touched by brick B?

    A. 7   B. 4   C. 2   D. 1

28. How many bricks are touched by brick C?

    A. 6   B. 5   C. 3   D. 4

29. How nany bricks are touched by brick D?

    A. 8   B. 9   C. 4   D. 5

30. How many bricks are touched by brick E?

    A. 6   B. 4   C. 3   D. 2

<h2 style="text-align:center">SECTION–7</h2>

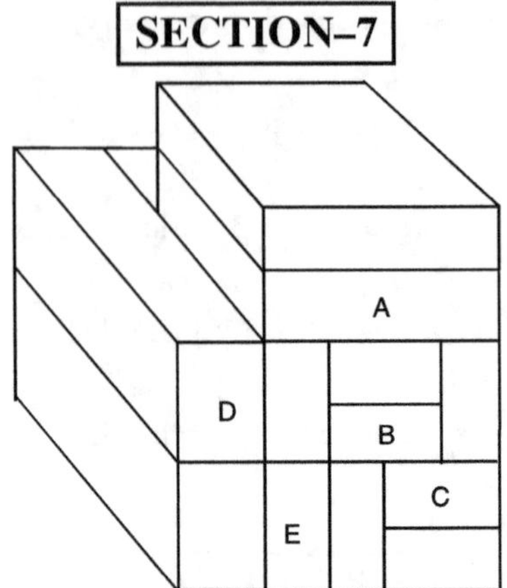

31. How many bricks are touched by brick A?

    A. 8   B. 4   C. 5   D. 7

32. How many bricks are touched by brick B?

    A. 7   B. 8   C. 5   D. 9

33. How many bricks are touched by brick C?

    A. 8   B. 1   C. 4   D. 6

34. How many bricks are touched by bricks D?

    A. 2   B. 8   C. 5   D. 4

35. How many bricks are touched by brick E?

    A. 10   B. 2   C. 3   D. 8

<h2 style="text-align:center">SECTION–8</h2>

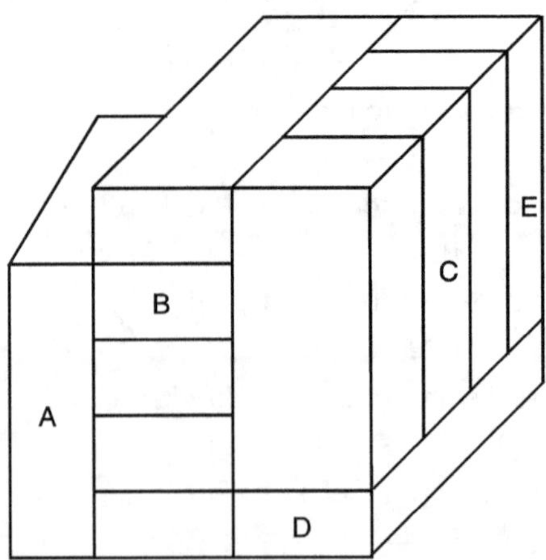

36. How many bricks are touched by brick A?

    A. 3   B. 4   C. 8   D. 9

37. How many bricks are touched by brick B?

    A. 7   B. 4   C. 1   D. 2

38. How many bricks are touched by brick C?

    A. 2   B. 9   C. 7   D. 6

39. How many bricks are touched by brick D?

    A. 4   B. 5   C. 8   D. 9

40. How many bricks are touched by brick E?

    A. 3   B. 4   C. 5   D. 6

SECTION–9

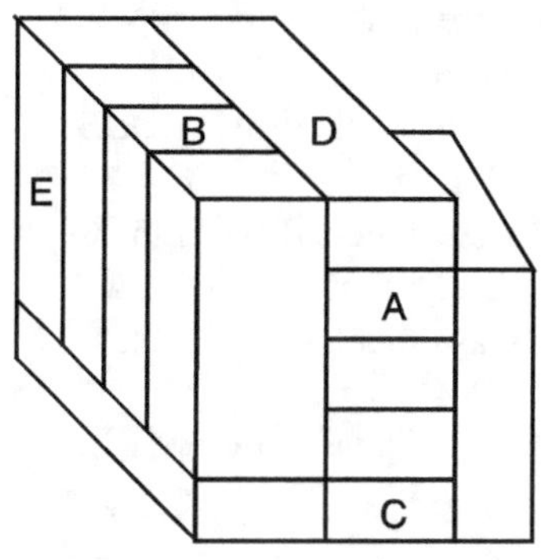

41. How many bricks are touched by brick A?

    A. 5   B. 8   C. 7   D. 2

42. How many bricks are touched by brick B?

    A. 7   B. 6   C. 5   D. 4

43. How many bricks are touched by brick C?

    A. 8   B. 1   C. 2   D. 3

44. How many bricks are touched by brick D?

    A. 5   B. 8   C. 6   D. 10

45. How many bricks are touched by brick E?

    A. 6   B. 5   C. 4   D. 3

SECTION–10

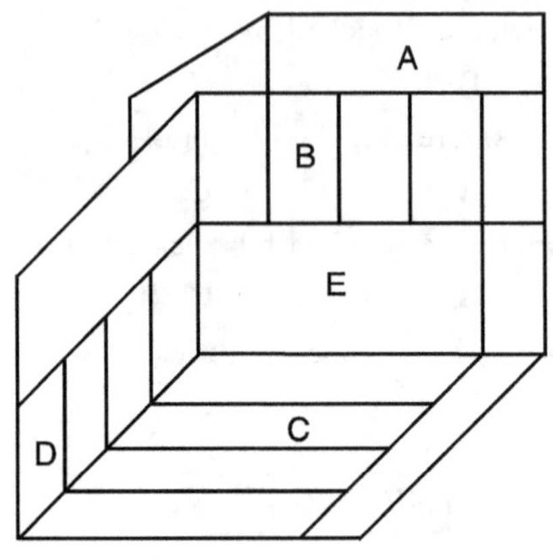

46. How many bricks are touched by brick A?
   A. 4   B. 6   C. 7   D. 8
47. How many bricks are touched by brick B?
   A. 2   B. 3   C. 4   D. 7
48. How many bricks are touched by brick C?
   A. 8   B. 7   C. 2   D. 1
49. How many bricks are touched by brick D?
   A. 3   B. 4   C. 6   D. 2
50. How many bricks are touched by brick E?
   A. 8   B. 6   C. 4   D. 2

ANSWERS

SECTION–1

1	2	3	4	5
A	C	D	C	D

SECTION–2

6	7	8	9	10
C	A	D	A	C

SECTION–3

11	12	13	14	15
D	B	A	D	D

SECTION–4

16	17	18	19	20
A	B	B	A	C

SECTION–5

21	22	23	24	25
A	D	B	B	A

SECTION–6

26	27	28	29	30
A	B	B	D	D

SECTION–7

31	32	33	34	35
B	C	C	A	C

SECTION–8

36	37	38	39	40
B	A	C	B	D

SECTION–9

41	42	43	44	45
C	A	D	A	A

SECTION–10

46	47	48	49	50
A	D	B	C	B

This is a test to find out how quickly you can compare two numbers and decide whether they are same or not. If the numbers are the same, darken the circle 'Yes' otherwise darken 'No' on your answer sheet. Do not makes any marks on the booklet. Try to solve following problems.

Example:

1.	589	=	589	**Yes**	No
2.	2768	=	2786	Yes	**No**
3.	36463	=	36462	Yes	**No**
4.	712963	=	712963	**Yes**	No
5.	487562	=	487652	Yes	**No**

EXERCISE-1

Directions (Qs. 1-96) : *In each of the following questions there are two sets of numbers. The question is : Is the number same or not? If the number is similar write 'Yes' otherwise write 'No'.*

1.	246212561	=	246212516	Yes	No
2.	872510052	=	872510052	Yes	No
3.	628561892	=	628561892	Yes	No
4.	756187251	=	756187151	Yes	No
5.	487561562	=	487561562	Yes	No
6.	926125612	=	926125621	Yes	No
7.	156800254	=	156800251	Yes	No
8.	6125612651	=	6125612654	Yes	No
9.	546125612	=	546125612	Yes	No
10.	925617516	=	925617561	Yes	No
11.	61515615165	=	61515615165	Yes	No
12.	18965126125	=	18965126125	Yes	No
13.	285613856	=	285613865	Yes	No
14.	465166255	=	465166255	Yes	No

15.	671561256	=	675161256	Yes	No
16.	865964256	=	865964265	Yes	No
17.	148625961	=	148625961	Yes	No
18.	516152615	=	516152615	Yes	No
19.	256192612	=	256192621	Yes	No
20.	896522615	=	896523615	Yes	No
21.	95997272	=	95977272	Yes	No
22.	615921596	=	615921596	Yes	No
23.	87195961201	=	87915961201	Yes	No
24.	64891256	=	64891256	Yes	No
25.	5610050051	=	5610050051	Yes	No
26.	95251615	=	95251625	Yes	No
27.	38282589	=	38282589	Yes	No
28.	72516126125	=	72516126115	Yes	No
29.	861528172	=	861528173	Yes	No
30.	672815675	=	672815657	Yes	No
31.	15961050505	=	15961050505	Yes	No
32.	852596123	=	852596123	Yes	No
33.	259612325	=	259612352	Yes	No
34.	956128752	=	956128752	Yes	No
35.	28752341	=	287525341	Yes	No
36.	759253215	=	759235215	Yes	No
37.	705050205	=	705050205	Yes	No
38.	869725932	=	869725932	Yes	No
39.	359230507	=	359230506	Yes	No
40.	532935298	=	532932598	Yes	No
41.	651832005	=	651832005	Yes	No
42.	8161521161	=	8661521161	Yes	No
43.	379256125	=	379256125	Yes	No
44.	100005005	=	100005005	Yes	No
45.	465923751	=	465923751	Yes	No
46.	387259615	=	387259651	Yes	No
47.	995566612	=	995566612	Yes	No
48.	2596127526	=	2596127562	Yes	No

49.	872596127	=	872569127	Yes	No
50.	682925613	=	927156127	Yes	No
51.	927156127	=	927156127	Yes	No
52.	759127592	=	759127592	Yes	No
53.	615912725	=	615912752	Yes	No
54.	6189665616	=	6189665616	Yes	No
55.	1869596729	=	1869596727	Yes	No
56.	1596123005	=	1596123006	Yes	No
57.	97156127	=	97156127	Yes	No
58.	729252625	=	729252525	Yes	No
59.	681596761	=	6815696751	Yes	No
60.	189561589	=	189561589	Yes	No
61.	496189615	=	496189615	Yes	No
62.	387256121	=	387256123	Yes	No
63.	897256159	=	897256159	Yes	No
64.	7565872523	=	7565872532	Yes	No
65.	4815612759	=	4815612759	Yes	No
66.	96456275	=	96456275	Yes	No
67.	498725619	=	498726519	Yes	No
68.	2975617598	=	2975617589	Yes	No
69.	505060505	=	505060565	Yes	No
70.	897278927	=	897287927	Yes	No
71.	486962759	=	486962759	Yes	No
72.	7872757677	=	7872757577	Yes	No
73.	3896156127	=	3896156217	Yes	No
74.	872596672	=	872596672	Yes	No
75.	429567156	=	429567165	Yes	No
76.	859615279	=	859615179	Yes	No
77.	7561556278	=	7561556278	Yes	No
78.	9627156959	=	9627156995	Yes	No
79.	496325275	=	496325275	Yes	No
80.	879629272	=	879629273	Yes	No
81.	34956287	=	34956287	Yes	No
82.	28615987	=	28615978	Yes	No

83.	932561789	=	932561789	Yes	No
84.	786156119	=	786156119	Yes	No
85.	987295615	=	987295651	Yes	No
86.	3561591972	=	3561591927	Yes	No
87.	92359159	=	92359159	Yes	No
88.	781927761	=	781927716	Yes	No
89.	6159159215	=	6159152915	Yes	No
90.	9616259799	=	9616529799	Yes	No
91.	848618756	=	848618756	Yes	No
92.	981867594	=	981867549	Yes	No
93.	681596156	=	681596158	Yes	No
94.	8596159872	=	5896158972	Yes	No
95.	387615927	=	387615927	Yes	No
96.	286597586	=	286597586	Yes	No

ANSWERS

1	2	3	4	5	6	7	8	9	10
No	Yes	Yes	No	Yes	No	No	No	Yes	No

11	12	13	14	15	16	17	18	19	20
Yes	Yes	No	Yes	No	No	Yes	Yes	No	No

21	22	23	24	25	26	27	28	29	30
No	Yes	No	Yes	Yes	No	Yes	No	No	No

31	32	33	34	35	36	37	38	39	40
Yes	Yes	No	Yes	No	No	Yes	Yes	No	No

41	42	43	44	45	46	47	48	49	50
Yes	No	Yes	Yes	Yes	No	Yes	No	No	Yes

51	52	53	54	55	56	57	58	59	60
Yes	Yes	No	Yes	No	No	Yes	No	No	Yes

61	62	63	64	65	66	67	68	69	70
Yes	No	Yes	No	Yes	Yes	No	No	No	No

71	72	73	74	75	76	77	78	79	80
Yes	No	No	Yes	No	Yes	Yes	No	Yes	No

81	82	83	84	85	86	87	88	89	90
Yes	No	Yes	Yes	No	No	Yes	No	No	No

91	92	93	94	95	96
Yes	No	No	No	Yes	Yes

EXERCISE-2

Directions (Qs. 1-96) : *In each of the following questions there are two sets of numbers. The question is : Is the number same or not? If the number is similar write 'Yes' otherwise write 'No'.*

1.	486253005	=	486253005	Yes	No
2.	625211523	=	625211523	Yes	No
3.	547826153	=	547826153	Yes	No
4.	235861125	=	235861126	Yes	No
5.	6725983251	=	6752983251	Yes	No
6.	528652866	=	528652866	Yes	No
7.	956278725	=	956278275	Yes	No
8.	6587256151	=	6587256151	Yes	No
9.	8659526156	=	8659562156	Yes	No
10.	5965261725	=	5965261275	Yes	No
11.	465929275	=	465929275	Yes	No
12.	8625961271	=	8625961272	Yes	No
13.	8726597524	=	8726597534	Yes	No
14.	659275872	=	659275872	Yes	No
15.	46875985612	=	46879595612	Yes	No
16.	9865265972	=	9865265962	Yes	No
17.	5865962758	=	5865962758	Yes	No
18.	4565962787	=	4565962987	Yes	No
19.	7562872596	=	7562872596	Yes	No
20.	4658987258	=	4658987258	Yes	No
21.	5467598726	=	5467598726	Yes	No
22.	8465859625	=	8466859625	Yes	No
23.	35659872561	=	35659872561	Yes	No
24.	2562658725	=	2562658735	Yes	No
25.	11662234325	=	11662234325	Yes	No
26.	58556625235	=	58886625225	Yes	No
27.	32532552332	=	32532552332	Yes	No
28.	65872561756	=	65872561756	Yes	No
29.	4687256178	=	4687256187	Yes	No

30.	5962562596	=	5962562596	Yes	No
31.	87265972561	=	87265972561	Yes	No
32.	486590005006	=	486590005606	Yes	No
33.	8562561597	=	8562561597	Yes	No
34.	9596979792	=	9596977992	Yes	No
35.	8765972567	=	8765972557	Yes	No
36.	488662526	=	488662526	Yes	No
37.	5659872725	=	5659872735	Yes	No
38.	689625872	=	689625872	Yes	No
39.	356259725	=	356257925	Yes	No
40.	82659275612	=	82659275512	Yes	No
41.	235923465	=	235923465	Yes	No
42.	562759256	=	562759266	Yes	No
43.	2659275876	=	2659275876	Yes	No
44.	7592765865	=	7592765855	Yes	No
45.	435587526	=	435587528	Yes	No
46.	652728685	=	652728585	Yes	No
47.	482650567	=	482650567	Yes	No
48.	350259235	=	350259255	Yes	No
49.	156592757	=	156592757	Yes	No
50.	896258752	=	896258752	Yes	No
51.	786527592	=	786527592	Yes	No
52.	2561755238	=	2561755238	Yes	No
53.	487265875	=	487265855	Yes	No
54.	9275615962	=	9275615962	Yes	No
55.	18652752615	=	18652752645	Yes	No
56.	3565561556	=	3565564556	Yes	No
57.	7256156125	=	7265156125	Yes	No
58.	2565275285	=	2565275285	Yes	No
59.	3256359275	=	3256359265	Yes	No
60.	9265872596	=	9265872596	Yes	No
61.	73562875901	=	73562876901	Yes	No
62.	3575678727	=	3575678737	Yes	No
63.	9562235927	=	9562235927	Yes	No

64.	3256152752	=	3256152752	Yes	No
65.	4972561752	=	4972561652	Yes	No
66.	8725527523	=	8725527533	Yes	No
67.	42356565655	=	42356565655	Yes	No
68.	6258725615	=	6258725645	Yes	No
69.	75612359723	=	75612359723	Yes	No
70.	92356156155	=	92356156155	Yes	No
71.	56233256	=	562353266	Yes	No
72.	4965238561	=	4965238561	Yes	No
73.	2565927872	=	2565927872	Yes	No
74.	91256156756	=	91256156756	Yes	No
75.	756562759	=	756562769	Yes	No
76.	926587289	=	926587289	Yes	No
77.	3468592701	=	3468592701	Yes	No
78.	865275872	=	865275772	Yes	No
79.	3965962561	=	3965962561	Yes	No
80.	8562756927	=	8562759637	Yes	No
81.	265987256	=	265987256	Yes	No
82.	1659696265	=	1659696265	Yes	No
83.	9725615615	=	9725625165	Yes	No
84.	492765725	=	492765725	Yes	No
85.	25965275	=	25965265	Yes	No
86.	526597256	=	526597266	Yes	No
87.	261575925	=	261575925	Yes	No
88.	832659275	=	832659275	Yes	No
89.	328526525	=	328526525	Yes	No
90.	327561275	=	327561265	Yes	No
91.	6561626152	=	6561626152	Yes	No
92.	625646256	=	625646266	Yes	No
93.	4235615615	=	4235615615	Yes	No
94.	435615872	=	435615872	Yes	No
95.	36256125625	=	36256125525	Yes	No
96.	40050060005	=	4005060005	Yes	No

ANSWERS

1	2	3	4	5	6	7	8	9	10
Yes	Yes	Yes	No	No	Yes	No	Yes	No	No
11	**12**	**13**	**14**	**15**	**16**	**17**	**18**	**19**	**20**
Yes	No	No	Yes	No	No	Yes	No	Yes	Yes
21	**22**	**23**	**24**	**25**	**26**	**27**	**28**	**29**	**30**
Yes	No	Yes	No	Yes	No	Yes	Yes	No	Yes
31	**32**	**33**	**34**	**35**	**36**	**37**	**38**	**39**	**40**
Yes	No	Yes	No	No	Yes	No	Yes	No	No
41	**42**	**43**	**44**	**45**	**46**	**47**	**48**	**49**	**50**
Yes	No	Yes	No	No	No	Yes	No	Yes	Yes
51	**52**	**53**	**54**	**55**	**56**	**57**	**58**	**59**	**60**
Yes	Yes	No	Yes	No	No	Yes	Yes	No	Yes
61	**62**	**63**	**64**	**65**	**66**	**67**	**68**	**69**	**70**
No	No	Yes	Yes	No	No	Yes	No	Yes	Yes
71	**72**	**73**	**74**	**75**	**76**	**77**	**78**	**79**	**80**
No	Yes	Yes	Yes	No	Yes	Yes	No	Yes	No
81	**82**	**83**	**84**	**85**	**86**	**87**	**88**	**89**	**90**
Yes	Yes	No	Yes	No	No	Yes	Yes	Yes	No
91	**92**	**93**	**94**	**95**	**96**				
Yes	No	Yes	Yes	No	No				

EXERCISE-3

Directions (Qs. 1-96) : *In each of the following questions there are two sets of numbers. The question is: Is the number same or not? If the number is similar write* **'Yes'** *otherwise write* **'No'**.

1.	3601200	=	3601200	Yes	No
2.	18413645	=	18413645	Yes	No
3.	4124023552121	=	4224023552121	Yes	No
4.	30402022119813	=	30402022116813	Yes	No
5.	543636	=	543636	Yes	No
6.	84106034	=	84107034	Yes	No
7.	965211	=	965211	Yes	No
8.	3696216	=	3696216	Yes	No
9.	220320132145675	=	220320123145675	Yes	No
10.	78954367	=	78954467	Yes	No

Rly Apt (E)–9

11.	6703020300308	=	6703020306308	Yes	No
12.	123456987865	=	123456789865	Yes	No
13.	145494	=	145494	Yes	No
14.	4321579	=	4321579	Yes	No
15.	8491578	=	8491578	Yes	No
16.	13574628	=	13574528	Yes	No
17.	57649218	=	57649718	Yes	No
18.	14962854	=	14962854	Yes	No
19.	69142	=	69742	Yes	No
20.	469198	=	469198	Yes	No
21.	593218	=	543218	Yes	No
22.	76512894	=	76512984	Yes	No
23.	62579841	=	62579891	Yes	No
24.	1237	=	1234	Yes	No
25.	79241	=	79241	Yes	No
26.	924321	=	924321	Yes	No
27.	1784325	=	1784375	Yes	No
28.	5633217	=	5633217	Yes	No
29.	46325	=	46325	Yes	No
30.	168820141219495	=	168820141219495	Yes	No
31.	22456983	=	22456983	Yes	No
32.	666145223546	=	66614523546	Yes	No
33.	5800666233223654	=	5800666233223654	Yes	No
34.	226121228789	=	226121228879	Yes	No
35.	7878788889999	=	78787888889899	Yes	No
36.	543211118000	=	543211180600	Yes	No
37.	1234567890006	=	123456789006	Yes	No
38.	444444444444	=	444444 444 44	Yes	No
39.	743251876900	=	743251879800	Yes	No
40.	43000145672	=	4300145372	Yes	No
41.	8798543221	=	8798543221	Yes	No
42.	9877755544422	=	987775544422	Yes	No
43.	432156	=	432156	Yes	No
44.	789056	=	7890567	Yes	No

45.	1000001111	=	1000001111	Yes	No
46.	77777777777	=	7777777777	Yes	No
47.	6868789854	=	6878689854	Yes	No
48.	4450002212	=	4450002212	Yes	No
49.	1234789868	=	1234786898	Yes	No
50.	555555879863	=	555555879863	Yes	No
51.	4321456789	=	4321546798	Yes	No
52.	201245879	=	201254879	Yes	No
53.	636464666	=	636464666	Yes	No
54.	777788888	=	77778888	Yes	No
55.	1224262728	=	122426272828	Yes	No
56.	13456789021	=	13456789012	Yes	No
57.	98999924241	=	98999924242	Yes	No
58.	654897324156	=	654898324156	Yes	No
59.	56789	=	56789	Yes	No
60.	45879	=	45789	Yes	No
61.	22462122	=	22462122	Yes	No
62.	48567892	=	4856892	Yes	No
63.	424803	=	424603	Yes	No
64.	2245606	=	2245606	Yes	No
65.	94226122	=	9426122	Yes	No
66.	132124	=	132124	Yes	No
67.	4724422	=	4724422	Yes	No
68.	21312291	=	2132391	Yes	No
69.	4366506	=	4366506	Yes	No
70.	7220230	=	7220230	YES	No
71.	237965	=	237695	Yes	No
72.	3659489	=	3659489	Yes	No
73.	812235	=	814435	Yes	No
74.	121561314	=	121561314	Yes	No
75.	5734254	=	5734754	Yes	No
76.	48755597	=	4875567	Yes	No
77.	7510352	=	7510352	Yes	No
78.	65145658	=	65145658	Yes	No

79.	2231999	=	223199	Yes	No
80.	3511080	=	3511080	Yes	No
81.	3731225	=	3731225	Yes	No
82.	34502423	=	34502423	Yes	No
83.	22120047	=	2212047	Yes	No
84.	35032033	=	35637033	Yes	No
85.	6500132	=	6500432	Yes	No
86.	8792999	=	872999	Yes	No
87.	131133	=	137733	Yes	No
88.	8842221236565971	=	8842221326565971	Yes	No
89.	1461412244588116	=	1461412244588116	Yes	No
90.	4588851234	=	4588857234	Yes	No
91.	76586002314569	=	76586002314569	Yes	No
92.	8020100123	=	8020100123	Yes	No
93.	7012090123456	=	7012060123456	Yes	No
94.	17010012323143	=	17010012323143	Yes	No
95.	8009	=	8099	Yes	No
96.	904816	=	904816	Yes	No

ANSWERS

1	2	3	4	5	6	7	8	9	10
Yes	Yes	No	No	Yes	No	Yes	Yes	No	No

11	12	13	14	15	16	17	18	19	20
No	No	Yes	Yes	Yes	No	No	Yes	No	Yes

21	22	23	24	25	26	27	28	29	30
No	No	No	No	Yes	Yes	No	Yes	Yes	Yes

31	32	33	34	35	36	37	38	39	40
Yes	No	Yes	No	No	No	No	No	No	No

41	42	43	44	45	46	47	48	49	50
Yes	No	Yes	No	Yes	Yes	No	Yes	No	Yes

51	52	53	54	55	56	57	58	59	60
No	No	Yes	No	No	No	No	No	Yes	No

61	62	63	64	65	66	67	68	69	70
Yes	No	No	Yes	No	Yes	Yes	No	Yes	Yes

71	72	73	74	75	76	77	78	79	80
No	Yes	No	Yes	No	No	Yes	Yes	No	Yes

81	82	83	84	85	86	87	88	89	90
Yes	Yes	No	No	No	No	No	No	Yes	No

91	92	93	94	95	96
Yes	Yes	No	Yes	No	Yes

DIGIT SEARCH TEST

This type of test contains four large numbers under the columns A, B, C and D. You are required to find out the certain digit in the given options A, B, C and D and option containing that digit will be your answer.

Example: Find out the digit '7' in the given option.

    A. 2895432   B. 1596843   C. 4321578   D. 2083860

Ans. It is clear from the above that option 'C' contains digit 7. Hence, answer will be option C.

EXERCISE-1

Directions (Qs. 1-100): *Each question consists four large numbers under the columns A, B, C and D. Find out the digit '6' in the given options A, B, C and D and the option containing '6' digit will be your answer. Indicate your answer E if digit '6' does not appear in any option or it appears in more than one option.*

	A	B	C	D
1.	4329872	5463214	7134298	9754317
2.	2527183	2274318	9143578	3497683
3.	7531486	4319758	5726943	5763482
4.	1834729	4789132	5918637	3847219
5.	3281426	4835479	7428854	4152942
6.	8282147	8293447	6194531	7029813
7.	3367975	3892725	7293825	7298391
8.	3228597	4218243	8597261	8274591
9.	4738512	5985431	9142458	2137489
10.	2794358	7682123	8375431	4318973
11.	8151453	9248324	8124352	4871654
12.	2451789	3729451	5837984	4628731
13.	1975342	2381659	4183597	7284913
14.	4391372	2417935	2874613	3185947
15.	3614829	3584179	3728541	9245731

	A.	B.	C.	D.
16.	8193742	7195426	2158493	7442358
17.	2859417	9345172	2938754	3689714
18.	7634912	9183275	7531924	3872451
19.	2395741	4523791	6124879	7854239
20.	7953842	3164897	5498723	3891475
21.	2597813	7835542	9842531	2063860
22.	3925784	15968432	7845123	4178523
23.	2121346	2459543	5283014	4589273
24.	7941781	2487513	3162587	5932417
25.	3578431	1821714	8479753	6276348
26.	3459732	2887235	40503197	3234713
27.	2159042	8452327	8724513	5467938
28.	4248796	3751234	9457183	5312894
29.	1278903	3124587	4673218	8723459
30.	5819754	7285146	89157437	4502504
31.	8247351	2357810	2184506	7294132
32.	149865	587401	758032	890128
33.	347890	894563	187548	288017
34.	874012	379801	578946	745789
35.	4437870	4851367	2584017	098763
36.	3784711	2579801	2939041	8749687
37.	102579	3342678	7388711	124783
38.	8758103	554875	258746	5078973
39.	152735	4500326	2411587	8901137
40.	455672	7900576	8271841	282715
41.	719897	6743589	1150734	546671
42.	7285710	7820140	2897621	1831296
43.	5879081	8740167	3487971	0178547
44.	81400743	2481589	5432760	9875321
45.	2978431	2400549	7481953	6815794
46.	4691238	2470501	2854582	21232425
47.	4181731	2725827	2876903	2031547
48.	5753798	7236398	2359754	3421357
49.	75213421	2135987	3782514	5260401
50.	9864517	2835174	8723234	7521482
51.	7268543	48752152	1576834	4282543
52.	3313215	3267892	4387125	4157839

53. A. 4142598	B. 2148137	C. 6727109	D. 4281753
54. A. 5621397	B. 4517823	C. 9182735	D. 4285734
55. A. 7154239	B. 8135792	C. 2428237	D. 9651432
56. A. 31457821	B. 24832159	C. 7236485	D. 5173942
57. A. 41632811	B. 2824223	C. 34375971	D. 2587993
58. A. 9147872	B. 2456193	C. 51024782	D. 4352719
59. A. 4593271	B. 8759213	C. 20830749	D. 76192543
60. A. 4613921	B. 5432134	C. 4117328	D. 9546027
61. A. 55442283	B. 7198562	C. 8752143	D. 4978036
62. A. 54932613	B. 54982139	C. 32148578	D. 24901735
63. A. 8431752	B. 9143213	C. 8136452	D. 8188903
64. A. 7843821	B. 4531679	C. 91832401	D. 3504383
65. A. 9343218	B. 5981342	C. 5981235	D. 4630850
66. A. 3216078	B. 987034	C. 3832434	D. 2895713
67. A. 2409817	B. 71348031	C. 34596102	D. 54398173
68. A. 2819785	B. 3015034	C. 3418039	D. 57810324
69. A. 5413987	B. 78231243	C. 39686124	D. 45931278
70. A. 2810357	B. 9432105	C. 27054157	D. 2561975
71. A. 51480728	B. 25481520	C. 2708012	D. 457121
72. A. 2509081	B. 2546890	C. 8450745	D. 4410752
73. A. 1478501	B. 2320329	C. 10018580	D. 1250102
74. A. 1207405	B. 15370321	C. 3271291	D. 1517805
75. A. 1294578	B. 1575149	C. 14170521	D. 1450278
76. A. 1297854	B. 4501232	C. 4786750	D. 1570348
77. A. 4510121	B. 1571524	C. 1208719	D. 1571075
78. A. 1051472	B. 25014975	C. 14879047	D. 5401289
79. A. 1901524	B. 1419867	C. 14708508	D. 15204709
80. A. 7500402	B. 1403081	C. 1451020	D. 45796831
81. A. 8070623	B. 41023457	C. 15797806	D. 8574740
82. A. 2502873	B. 12732402	C. 78217041	D. 7396142
83. A. 1407230	B. 1470252	C. 12781609	D. 7824581
84. A. 35102345	B. 2301902	C. 5915203	D. 871258
85. A. 1789587	B. 1909547	C. 3046545	D. 5148740
86. A. 878218	B. 458372	C. 877841	D. 873014
87. A. 586073	B. 5801873	C. 470389	D. 512683
88. A. 4513621	B. 1510148	C. 4597509	D. 720587
89. A. 1573102	B. 2541706	C. 52539710	D. 18758960

90. A. 78291421   B. 98678120   C. 12041789   D. 7410821
91. A. 12478596   B. 7901208   C. 2304790   D. 3021349
92. A. 254376   B. 73202102   C. 14093587   D. 4703714
93. A. 7312904   B. 84310178   C. 15382987   D. 14717827
94. A. 4581372   B. 9801704   C. 479621   D. 435582
95. A. 1485430   B. 9547214   C. 457098   D. 1580386
96. A. 154382   B. 1512429   C. 1409073   D. 15266984
97. A. 14161531   B. 14571420   C. 1478371   D. 4219121
98. A. 2152109   B. 5423080   C. 983521   D. 54603130
99. A. 2507897   B. 14057381   C. 213701321   D. 70332507
100. A. 3543102   B. 1045230   C. 2589721   D. 87603714

ANSWERS

1	2	3	4	5	6	7	8	9	10
B	D	E	C	A	C	A	C	E	B
11	12	13	14	15	16	17	18	19	20
D	D	B	C	A	B	D	A	C	B
21	22	23	24	25	26	27	28	29	30
D	B	A	C	D	E	D	A	C	B
31	32	33	34	35	36	37	38	39	40
C	A	B	C	E	D	B	C	B	B
41	42	43	44	45	46	47	48	49	50
E	E	B	C	D	A	C	B	D	A
51	52	53	54	55	56	57	58	59	60
E	B	C	A	D	C	A	B	D	E
61	62	63	64	65	66	67	68	69	70
D	A	C	B	D	A	C	E	C	D
71	72	73	74	75	76	77	78	79	80
E	B	E	E	E	C	E	E	B	D
81	82	83	84	85	86	87	88	89	90
E	D	C	E	C	E	E	A	E	B
91	92	93	94	95	96	97	98	99	100
A	A	E	C	D	D	A	D	E	D

SELECTIVE ATTENTION TEST
(Number Based Test)

In this type of test, a series of numbers are given. On the basis of the series of numbers, questions are asked.

1. How many odd numbers are there in the given number series?
2. How many even numbers are there in the given number series?
3. How many prime numbers are there in the given series?
4. Find the aggregate of numbers which are placed on even positions in the given series.
5. Find the aggregate of prime numbers in the given number series.
6. Find the aggregate of numbers which placed on odd position in the given series.

Example: In the following questions, a series of numbers is given. Find the aggregate of odd numbers.

7 5 3 2 7 9 3 7 6 8 4 2 3 5 8 2

A. 51   B. 52   C. 49   D. 50

Ans. C.

EXERCISE-1

Directions (Qs. 1-30): *Find the aggregate of even numbers in the following series.*

1. 2 2 3 4 5 6 3 2 3 4 4 5 6 7 8 3 8 8 3 9 8 7 6 5 4 3 2 1 2 2 8 4 3 2 5 6 7 8 8 9 3 2 1 1
A. 120   B. 115   C. 116   D. 114

2. 3 3 2 2 4 2 3 2 3 2 3 2 3 2 4 5 4 5 4 5 6 7 6 7 6 7 6 7 6 7 6 7 6 7 6 7 6 6 7 7 7
A. 102   B. 103   C. 104   D. 105

3. 1 2 3 4 5 6 1 2 3 4 5 6 1 2 3 4 5 6 1 2 3 4 5 6 1 2 3 4 5 6 1 2 3 4 5 6 1 2 3 4 5 6 1 2 3 4 5 6 1 1 2 2
A. 99   B. 100   C. 101   D. 102

4. 3 2 4 5 4 4 5 6 6 7 8 1 2 3 4 1 2 3 4 1 2 3 4 4 5 6 7 8 9 6 7 8 9 6 7 8 9 2 3 4 5
A. 102   B. 103   C. 104   D. 105

138

5. 1514131211121314 15 262728293031323334353
   6373812
   A. 55　　　　B. 56　　　　C. 57　　　　D. 58
6. 6061626364656667686970717273454466 78
   98231
   A. 120　　　　B. 122　　　　C. 123　　　　D. 124
7. 505152535455565758596162636466667689
   982
   A. 98　　　　B. 99　　　　C. 64　　　　D. 96
8. 1213141516171819201121222324253637383
   9404
   A. 60　　　　B. 61　　　　C. 62　　　　D. 63
9. 1198765432132345678923456789987654321 2
   12221
   A. 86　　　　B. 87　　　　C. 88　　　　D. 89
10. 342824681012141819202122234425363712
    A. 76　　　　B. 77　　　　C. 78　　　　D. 79
11. 2122232425262728313233343523637389 43
    2121
    A. 65　　　　B. 66　　　　C. 67　　　　D. 68
12. 30691215182124373048121620242829936404 14
    24344
    A. 95　　　　B. 94　　　　C. 96　　　　D. 97
13. 61 29 18 27 36 45 44 54 6 3 72 91 90 91 92 93 94 95 96 98
    98 98
    A. 83　　　　B. 84　　　　C. 85　　　　D. 86
14. 3031323327282980818283848586878889202324
    3839402
    A. 140　　　　B. 141　　　　C. 142　　　　D. 143
15. 2387195485329876543232322212892
    A. 83　　　　B. 64　　　　C. 65　　　　D. 66
16. 262524232221919181716151413122122232
    A. 72　　　　B. 73　　　　C. 74　　　　D. 75
17. 272829303141424344454647484950515253
    54
    A. 75　　　　B. 74　　　　C. 76　　　　D. 77
18. 2829304142666768697071727374757677 78
    79
    A. 80　　　　B. 81　　　　C. 82　　　　D. 83

19. 2 9 2 8 2 5 2 6 2 7 2 8 2 9 3 0 4 8 5 8 7 0 8 1 8 2 8 3 8 4 8 5 6 7 6 8 6 9

A. 126   B. 127   C. 128   D. 129

20. 3 0 3 1 5 0 5 1 2 2 2 3 8 5 4 5 5 5 6 5 7 5 8 5 9 6 0 6 1 2 8 7 8 9 8 8 8

A. 86   B. 87   C. 88   D. 89

21. 9 8 3 8 3 8 5 8 5 8 8 8 3 2 2 5 3 2 2 3 2 5 9 8 3 5 6 2 7 8 9 2 3 4 5 6 2 3 4 2 1

A. 111   B. 110   C. 112   D. 114

22. 7 8 9 2 3 4 5 3 2 5 6 1 2 3 4 5 6 7 8 9 8 8 9 2 3 4 5 6 7 8 9 9 8 8 3 1 2

A. 95   B. 98   C. 97   D. 96

23. 2 5 6 7 3 5 2 6 2 6 7 8 3 2 5 6 7 6 6 8 8 3 2 3 5 3 6 6 7 3 2 5 2 3 2 5 6 5 6 6 7 2

A. 108   B. 107   C. 106   D. 109

24. 6 7 8 3 3 2 4 6 3 2 5 6 3 8 9 8 7 6 5 4 3 2 1 8 7 8 7 6 6 3 2 1 2 2 3 4 5 6

A. 106   B. 104   C. 105   D. 102

25. 6 5 4 3 2 8 3 2 5 2 6 2 7 2 8 2 9 3 2 3 2 5 2 6 2 7 2 8 8 2 3 8 3 4 3 4 5 2

A. 94   B. 95   C. 96   D. 97

26. 9 8 7 6 5 3 2 1 1 2 3 4 5 6 7 8 7 8 7 8 6 5 3 2 3 2 8 6 8 6 7 8 5 2 5 2 3 2 4 2 6 1 7 2

A. 118   B. 111   C. 112   D. 113

27. 6 7 8 9 2 3 4 5 6 7 8 9 1 2 3 4 5 6 7 8 9 8 7 6 5 4 3 2 1 3 2 1 3 2 1 3 3 2 1 2 1 2 3 2 2

A. 87   B. 88   C. 89   D. 90

28. 1 2 3 4 5 6 7 8 1 2 3 4 5 6 7 8 1 2 3 4 5 6 7 8 1 2 3 4 5 6 7 8 1 2 3 4 5 6 7 8 8 7 6 5 3 2

A. 114   B. 115   C. 116   D. 117

29. 7 8 7 8 3 2 3 3 2 3 3 3 2 3 3 3 2 2 2 1 2 3 4 5 2 2 2 8 8 8 7 6 5 4 3 2 1

A. 80   B. 78   C. 76   D. 74

30. 1 2 4 5 1 2 4 5 1 2 4 5 1 2 4 5 1 2 4 5 1 2 4 5 4 5 4 5 4 6 6 7 8 3 2 1 2 3 2 1

A. 78   B. 75   C. 76   D. 77

ANSWERS

1	2	3	4	5	6	7	8	9	10
C	A	B	C	B	D	A	A	C	A

11	12	13	14	15	16	17	18	19	20
B	C	B	A	B	A	C	A	C	A

21	22	23	24	25	26	27	28	29	30
B	D	A	B	C	A	B	C	C	A

EXERCISE-2

Directions (Qs. 1-30): *Find the aggregate of numbers which placed on even postition in the following number series.*

1. 3 9 8 7 6 5 4 3 2 1 2 2 8 4 3 2 5 6 7 8 3 8 8 7 8 8 9 3 2 1 1
   A. 70   B. 65   C. 74   D. 68

2. 2 3 2 5 9 8 3 5 6 2 7 8 9 2 3 4 5 6 9 8 7 2 3 4 2 1
   A. 45   B. 71   C. 58   D. 55

3. 6 1 2 3 4 5 6 7 8 9 8 8 9 2 3 4 5 6 7 8 9 9 8 8 3 1 2 4 5 7 8 9
   A. 53   B. 91   C. 19   D. 68

4. 2 6 7 8 3 2 5 6 7 6 6 8 8 3 2 3 5 3 6 6 7 3 2 5 2 3 2 5 6 5 6 6 7 2
   A. 80   B. 85   C. 72   D. 95

5. 5 6 3 8 9 8 7 6 5 4 3 2 1 8 7 8 7 6 6 3 2 1 2 3 4 5 6 6 8 9 7 2 1
   A. 80   B. 78   C. 66   D. 85

6. 6 5 4 3 2 6 2 7 2 8 2 9 3 2 5 2 6 2 7 8 7 8 9 7 2 5 7 6 7 8 9
   A. 68   B. 86   C. 76   D. 55

7. 8 6 5 3 2 3 2 8 6 8 6 8 5 2 5 2 3 4 6 7 8 7 3 2 4 2 6 1 7 2
   A. 78   B. 112   C. 65   D. 70

8. 7 8 9 8 7 6 5 4 3 2 1 3 2 1 3 2 2 1 3 3 2 1 2 1 2 3 2 2 8 9 2 3 4 5 6 7 8
   A. 88   B. 77   C. 90   D. 69

9. 3 4 5 6 7 8 1 2 3 4 5 6 7 8 1 2 3 4 5 6 7 8 8 7 6 5 3 2 4
   A. 65   B. 122   C. 72   D. 95

10. 7 8 3 2 3 2 3 3 3 2 2 2 1 2 3 4 5 2 2 2 8 8 8 7 7 7 5 5 5 4
    A. 72   B. 60   C. 99   D. 79

11. 4 5 1 2 4 5 4 5 6 7 6 7 8 9 1 2 3 4 5 7 8 2 1 3 1 5 1 6 9
    A. 65   B. 77   C. 55   D. 69

12. 4 5 6 7 6 7 6 7 6 7 6 7 6 7 6 7 7 7 7 7 7 7 7 6 6 5 5 5 5
    A. 100   B. 105   C. 110   D. 95

13. 1 2 3 4 5 6 1 2 3 4 5 6 1 2 3 4 5 6 1 2 3 4 5 6 1 2 3 4 5 6 1 2 3 4 5 6
    A. 72   B. 82   C. 77   D. 65

14. 4 1 2 3 4 4 5 7 9 6 7 9 6 7 8 9 2 3 4 5 4 4 5 6 6 7 8 1 2 3 4 1 2 3
    A. 72   B. 66   C. 79   D. 85

15. 3 5 3 6 3 7 3 8 1 2 2 6 2 7 2 9 3 0 3 1 3 8 7 9 5 6 5 7 5 8 5 8 5 8 7 7
9 9 9

A. 99   B. 121   C. 100   D. 75

16. 6 9 7 0 7 1 7 2 7 3 4 5 4 4 6 6 7 8 6 0 6 1 6 2 6 3 6 4 6 5 6 6 6 7
6 8 9 8

A. 44   B. 65   C. 75   D. 82

17. 5 2 5 3 5 4 5 5 5 6 5 7 5 8 5 9 6 1 6 2 6 3 6 4 6 6 6 7 6 8 9
9 8 2

A. 76   B. 95   C. 86   D. 66

18. 11 21 22 23 24 25 36 37 38 39 40 41 1 2 3 4 5 1 6

A. 57   B. 61   C. 56   D. 95

19. 8 9 2 3 4 5 6 7 8 9 9 9 8 7 6 5 4 3 2 1 2 2 9 8 7 6 5 4 3 2 1

A. 80   B. 77   C. 85   D. 70

20. 8 2 4 6 8 1 0 1 2 1 4 1 8 1 9 2 0 2 1 2 2 2 2 3 4 4 4 5 5 5 6

A. 89   B. 38   C. 35   D. 40

21. 3 2 3 4 3 5 2 3 6 7 3 8 9 4 2 2 3 2 4 2 5 6 2 7 2 8 3 3 1 3 2
1 2 1

A. 60   B. 105   C. 65   D. 110

22. 4 8 1 2 1 6 2 0 4 2 8 2 9 3 3 6 7 6 8 5 4 2 1 3 3 4 5 6

A. 77   B. 59   C. 45   D. 53

23. 7 2 9 1 9 0 2 5 9 3 9 4 9 5 9 6 9 7 9 8 9 9 2 2 2 4 2 5 2 6

A. 68   B. 67   C. 57   D. 72

24. 8 2 8 3 8 4 8 5 8 6 8 7 8 8 8 9 9 1 9 2 9 5 7 4 7 5 7 8 1 2 3
3 4 5 1

A. 79   B. 69   C. 89   D. 99

25. 3 2 3 2 3 2 3 2 4 5 6 7 8 3 2 3 2 3 2 3 2 32 3 2

A. 44   B. 33   C. 35   D. 42

26. 2 4 2 3 2 2 2 1 1 9 1 8 1 7 16 1 5 1 4 1 3 1 2 2 1 2 2 2 3 2
4 2 6

A. 65   B. 70   C. 95   D. 94

27. 1 1 1 1 1 1 1 1 1 1 1 1 1 1 1 1 1 1 1 1 1 1 1 1 1 1 1 1 1 1 1 1 1 1 1

A. 99   B. 16   C. 15   D. 14

28. 4 5 4 5 4 5 4 5 4 5 4 5 4 5 1 2 3 4 7 8 1 2 3 4 7 8 9 6 2 6 3

A. 62   B. 70   C. 75   D. 60

29. 5 8 7 0 8 1 8 2 8 3 8 4 2 5 2 6 2 7 2 8 2 9 3 0 1 2

A. 45   B. 75   C. 55   D. 65

30. 3 0 3 1 5 3 3 4 3 8 3 9 7 9 8 7 6 5 4 3 1 2 3 4 5 6 7

A. 71   B. 109   C. 105   D. 61

ANSWERS

1	2	3	4	5	6	7	8	9	10
C	C	B	A	D	B	A	D	C	B
11	**12**	**13**	**14**	**15**	**16**	**17**	**18**	**19**	**20**
D	B	A	C	B	D	C	B	A	B
21	**22**	**23**	**24**	**25**	**26**	**27**	**28**	**29**	**30**
C	D	B	A	C	B	B	C	C	D

EXERCISE-3

Direction (Qs. 1-30): *Find the aggregate of odd numbers in the following series.*

1. 5 7 6 1 1 8 9 2 5 3 7 5 8 9 3
   - A 55
   - B 56
   - C 57
   - D 58
2. 8 7 6 5 3 2 1 4 5 6 5 9 6 1 8 7 6 3 2
   - A 30
   - B 44
   - C 70
   - D 46
3. 1 2 6 9 3 7 7 3 2 1 1 4 2 6
   - A 40
   - B 32
   - C 39
   - D 38
4. 3 7 5 5 1 8 2 4 6 9 1 5 9 7 6 2 5
   - A 70
   - B 72
   - C 66
   - D 78
5. 6 3 2 5 4 9 7 6 5 1 3 5 7 9 4 2 8 5
   - A 59
   - B 34
   - C 62
   - D 64
6. 1 9 5 6 4 2 7 3 2 5 4 9 1 7 1 2 3 5 7 9
   - A 55
   - B 69
   - C 108
   - D 72
7. 4 3 1 7 9 6 5 4 3 2 1 5 7 9 4 3 1 5 7 9
   - A 95
   - B 75
   - C 79
   - D 85
8. 1 3 5 7 4 6 2 8 5 7 6 4 9 2 1 8 1 4 9 6 2 8 5 4
   - A 70
   - B 53
   - C 59
   - D 65
9. 2 3 5 6 9 1 4 2 4 6 9 1 5 8 5 9 3 2 1 8
   - A 45
   - B 51
   - C 55
   - D 67
10. 7 6 5 1 2 8 9 4 6 2 5 7 9 8 4 1 1 2 3 7
    - A 55
    - B 45
    - C 35
    - D 105
11. 5 4 3 2 1 8 7 6 5 1 2 8 9 4 6 2 5 7 9 8 9 1 1 2 8 7 7 9 2 4 1 1 7 2 5
    - A 100
    - B 65
    - C 95
    - D 105
12. 2 3 5 6 9 7 4 2 4 6 9 1 5 8 1 7 2 5 7 9 2 4 1
    - A 79
    - B 89
    - C 59
    - D 69
13. 1 3 5 7 4 6 2 8 5 7 6 4 9 7 1 8 5 7 6 4 9 7 1 8 1 4 9 6 2 8 5 4
    - A 80
    - B 89
    - C 51
    - D 45
14. 4 8 1 7 9 6 5 4 3 2 1 5 7 9 4 3 1 5 7 9
    - A 74
    - B 82
    - C 80
    - D 72

15. 1 9 5 6 4 2 7 3 2 6 4 9 1 7 1 2 3 5 7 9
    A 77   B 67   C 87   D 107

16. 6 3 2 5 4 9 2 6 5 1 3 5 7 9 4 7 8 5
    A 59   B 89   C 69   D 79

17. 5 1 3 2 4 6 9 1 5 9 7 6 2 5
    A 55   B 48   C 45   D 40

18. 1 2 6 9 3 7 7 3 2 7 1 4 2 6 3 7 5
    A 93   B 53   C 43   D 103

19. 5 7 6 1 1 8 9 2 5 3 7 5 8 6 3 8 7 6 5 8 2 1 4 5 6 5 9 6 1 8 7 6 3 2
    A 89   B 80   C 71   D 99

20. 9 2 4 3 2 1 1 7 8 4 3 2 5 5 6 3 3 2 1 7 4 6 3 2 5
    A 67   B 66   C 65   D 56

21. 1 7 3 2 5 8 3 7 1 6 2 3 5 6 4 1 7 9 1 3 5 2 8 7 6 4
    A 48   B 78   C 68   D 108

22. 4 6 5 8 1 8 2 9 1 7 6 2 9 8 3 2 2 4 1 8 2 6 5 1 7 2 3 4 6 5 3
    A 90   B 80   C 60   D 70

23. 1 7 2 3 4 5 6 1 2 3 5 9 4 5 9 9 6 2 5 4 6 1 8 3 2 5
    A 71   B 78   C 68   D 44

24. 5 3 1 1 7 3 2 5 6 4 8 1 2 5 4 3 2 6 9 2 4 6 9 7 9 2 8 7 6
    A 78   B 88   C 68   D 108

25. 1 3 2 5 4 3 2 1 7 3 2 5 1 4 7 3 2 5 4 1 6 9
    A 79   B 54   C 68   D 64

26. 4 3 1 7 9 6 5 9 6 0 2 5 4 2 1 4 2 0 5
    A 55   B 49   C 45   D 69

27. 5 9 7 6 2 1 3 5 9 7 3 9 1 8 2 4 0 9 3 5 2 6 5 4 1 2 9 1 1 2 5 7
    A 78   B 66   C 67   D 105

28. 1 8 2 4 0 9 3 5 2 6 5 4 1 2 9 1 1 2 5 7 9 2 4 3 2 1 1 7 8 4 3 7 5
    A 65   B 89   C 83   D 79

29. 5 6 3 3 2 1 7 4 6 3 2 5 1 7 3 2 5 3 3 7 1 6 2 3 5 6 4 1 7 9 2 1
    A 78   B 70   C 83   D 95

30. 3 5 2 3 4 6 3 6 7 9 3 5 2
    A 38   B 30   C 16   D 25

ANSWERS

1	2	3	4	5	6	7	8	9	10
A	D	B	C	A	D	B	B	B	A

11	12	13	14	15	16	17	18	19	20
A	D	B	D	B	A	C	B	A	D

21	22	23	24	25	26	27	28	29	30
C	C	A	C	B	C	D	C	C	A

EXERCISE-4

Direction(Qs. 1-30): *How many even numbers are in the following series?*

1. 6 7 0 3 0 2 0 3 0 0 3 0 8 9 8 7 5
   A 5   B 4   C 7   D 9

2. 1 2 3 4 5 9 8 7 6 5 1 4 2 1
   A 9   B 10   C 8   D 6

3. 3 6 9 9 6 3 3 3 6 6 8 9 6 9 7 5 2 1
   A 8   B 3   C 9   D 7

4. 2 1 0 9 9 0 8 8 0 3 3 8 3 8 4 3 7 8
   A 9   B 4   C 7   D 5

5. 3 8 3 8 3 8 3 3 8 8 3 8 3 3 4 7 2 9
   A 10   B 6   C 11   D 8

6. 6 3 0 0 6 6 9 9 0 0 7 8 5 4 2 1
   A 9   B 7   C 10   D 6

7. 7 1 7 1 7 1 3 3 0 0 2 9 8 3 4 5 2
   A 4   B 5   C 7   D 6

8. 2 2 9 2 3 3 6 5 4 3 2 1 7 7
   A 7   B 9   C 6   D 8

9. 1 9 3 1 2 2 1 4 2 1 1 7 5 2 2 8 7 9
   A 4   B 7   C 3   D 6

10. 2 1 3 2 4 5 2 9 6 3 7 5 4 2 7 8 5
    A 5   B 7   C 10   D 8

11. 9 6 4 1 0 0 1 0 1 1 7 8 5 6 4 3 8
    A 9   B 7   C 6   D 8

12. 3 2 2 3 2 3 3 7 1 2 4 5 8 7
    A 9   B 5   C 10   D 6

13. 6 4 6 7 0 2 7 2 8 8 0 8 4 8 4 5 9 7 1
    A 11   B 10   C 12   D 9

14. 5 2 7 5 9 6 6 5 7 3 7 8 0 2 1
    A 3   B 5   C 8   D 4

15. 6 6 8 8 7 9 8 2 3 5 4 3 2 1
    A 8   B 4   C 7   D 5

16. 5 7 7 9 4 2 3 3 6 9 6 7 5 7
    A 10   B 12   C 4   D 9

17. 6 8 8 4 6 8 9 0 1 3 9 9 3 6
    A 7   B 8   C 9   D 10

18. 8 4 9 8 5 7 9 9 2 8 1 9 7 5 4
    A 10   B 6   C 2   D 5

19. 3 3 3 4 3 5 3 6 3 7 3 8 9
    A 5   B 4   C 3   D 7

20. 5 8 5 9 6 0 6 1 6 2 6 3 6 4 2 8
    A 15   B 10   C 16   D 11

21. 8 4 8 5 8 8 9 9 8 3 3 3 3 4 6 7 2
    A 11   B 10   C 15   D 9

22. 4 7 4 8 4 9 5 3 5 6 5 9 6 4
    A 7   B 9   C 10   D 8

23. 6 4 3 4 5 3 8 8 4 9 3 2 1 0 9 7 2
    A 4   B 5   C 3   D 8

24. 2 2 5 7 6 6 9 9 3 4 2 1 8 7 4 5
    A 8   B 12   C 6   D 9

25. 7 7 8 8 9 9 2 1 6 4 3 5 4 2 9
    A 9   B 8   C 10   D 7

26. 1 2 2 2 2 3 2 4 8 7 3 5 9 8 4
    A 6   B 7   C 9   D 12

27. 1 2 1 1 3 4 1 4 3 1 5 5 1 6
    A 6   B 4   C 9   D 10

28. 2 3 3 2 4 1 5 2 2 8 7 6 4 3 5
    A 8   B 11   C 7   D 12

29. 2 8 2 2 9 3 2 3 8 3 5 8 6 4 0
    A 15   B 7   C 9   D 10

30. 4 2 4 4 3 3 8 7 5 2 1 6 9 7 4
    A 7   B 5   C 10   D 8

ANSWERS

1	2	3	4	5	6	7	8	9	10
B	D	D	C	D	D	A	C	B	D

11	12	13	14	15	16	17	18	19	20
C	D	A	B	A	C	A	B	C	B

21	22	23	24	25	26	27	28	29	30
D	A	D	A	D	C	B	A	C	D

TABLE TEST OR COLUMN-ROW TEST

Table test is important test in aptitude test. This test is also known as column-row test. In this test, questions are based on given table and table is divided into some columns and some rows. Candidates are required to read the given table carefully to answer the questions.

EXERCISE-1

Directions (Qs. 1-10) : *The ten questions given below are based on the following table. Read the given table carefully and answer the questions that follow.*

Table

	Column 1	Column 2	Column 3	Column 4	Column 5
Row–1	E	D	A	B	D
Row–2	A	D	C	D	B
Row–3	D	C	A	E	B
Row–4	C	A	E	B	D
Row–5	A	C	D	B	E

1. What is the letter appearing between D and B in Row–1?
2. In Row–3, name the letter that is the third letter to the right of the first letter, which is to the left of C.
3. Name the letters in Column–3, which has appeared more than once.
4. In column–4, what is the first letter to the left of B, which has been placed against Row–5 at the bottom?
5. In Row–2, which letter has been repeated twice?
6. What is the letter below the third letter that has appeared above the last letter in Row–4?

7. In Column–5, which letter has not been repeated vertically?

8. Which letter has appeared twice in Column–1?

9. What is the letter that is located exactly above and on the upper left part of the second letter, which is located to the right of the last letter of Column–2?

10. What is the letter that is located exactly to the right hand side of the letter, which is located exactly to the left hand side of the last letter of Column–5?

ANSWERS

1	2	3	4	5	6	7	8	9	10
A	E	A	D	D	B	E	A	E	E

EXERCISE-2

Directions (Qs. 1-10) : *In the following table five columns, Column–I, Column–II, Column–III, Column–IV and Column V have been given. Further, five rows, Row–I, Row–II, Row–III, Row–IV and Row–V also have been given. Read the given table carefully and answer the questions that follow.*

Table

	Column I	Column II	Column III	Column IV	Column V
Row–I	B	D	E	D	A
Row–II	D	B	A	D	C
Row–III	E	B	D	C	A
Row–IV	B	D	C	A	E
Row–V	B	E	A	C	D

1. Which letter appears least along the diagonal of Row–I?

2. Which letter is second below the third letter above the last letter in Row–V?

3. Which letter is first above the third letter to the left of second letter above the second letter to the right of last letter of Column–II?

4. Starting from the lower most right corner, if we proceed to the upper right corner, then upper left corner and finally to the lower left corner, which letter would appear least?

5. If Row–III and Row–V are, interchanged, then which letter is second below the third letter to the left of the letter just above the letter 'A' in Cloumn–IV?

6. In Row–I, what is the letter between two D's?

7. Which letter is third to the right of first letter to the left of B in Row–III?

8. Which letter appears more than once in Column–III?

9. Which letter is second to the left of letter A of Column–IV and Row–IV?

10. If Column–III and Column–V are interchanged then which letter is second to the first letter below the first letter to the left of letter just above the letter 'A' in Row–IV?

ANSWERS

1	2	3	4	5	6	7	8	9	10
A	E	D	C	D	E	C	A	D	C

EXERCISE-3

Directions (Qs. 1-10) : *A table consisting of five rows and five columns is given below. Read the given table carefully and answer the questions that follow.*

Table

	Column I	Column II	Column III	Column IV	Column V
Row–I	A	B	C	D	E
Row–II	C	D	B	E	A
Row–III	B	E	A	D	B
Row–IV	B	E	D	A	C
Row–V	E	B	C	A	D

1. Which letter appears maximum times along the diagonal of Row–I?

2. If Row–I is interchanged with Row–III and that of Row–II with the Row–IV then which letter will be in Column–IV of the Row–III?

3. Which letter appears maximum times along the diagonal of Row–V up to Column–V?

4. Which letter has appeared more than once in the Column–III?

5. Which letter is to the left of letter A of Row–IV and Column–IV?

6. How many times the letter B has appeared in Column–I?

7. Which letter is just below the letter E of the Row–III and Column–II?

8. Which letter is just below the second letter from the bottom letter of the Column–V?

9. Starting from Row–I turn down at Column–V and proceed in Row–III. Which letter is second to the left of B which is just above the letter A?

10. Starting from Column–V of Row–I if one proceeds clockwise and after passing through the peripheral blocks finally reaches at the starting point then which letter will be exactly mid way between the two D's?

ANSWERS

1	2	3	4	5	6	7	8	9	10
A	D	E	C	D	B	E	C	C	No Middle letter

EXERCISE-4

Directions (Qs. 1-10) : *Answer the following questions based on the Table given below.*

Table

	Column 1	Column 2	Column 3	Column 4	Column 5	Column 6	Column 7
Row–1	C	A	B	D	E	D	B
Row–2	E	D	C	A	B	A	C
Row–3	C	B	D	B	D	E	A

	1	2	3	4	5	6	7
Row–4	D	E	A	A	A	C	B
Row–5	E	A	C	D	C	E	A
Row–6	A	B	C	E	E	C	D
Row–7	B	D	A	B	B	A	C

1. In Column–4, what is the letter between two A's?

2. In Row–7, which letter has shown the maximum number of appearances?

3. In Row–5, what is the letter that is fourth from the right of the letter that is the second letter to the left of D?

4. Which letter has shown the maximum number of appearances in the diagonal starting from the upper left corner and ending in the lower right corner?

5. Starting from the upper left corner go to the right corner then, start from upper right corner go to lower right corner. Again, go from lower right corner to lower left corner. Now, go from lower left corner to upper left corner. Which letters has shown the minimum number of appearances in this entire movement?

6. In Row–2, what is the letter appearing between two A's?

7. Starting from the lower left corner go to right corner. Now, from lower right corner go to upper right corner. Then, from upper right corner go to upper left corner. A last go from upper left corner to lower left corner what is the third letter that is to the left from the first letter. Which is to the right of the third D?

8. If Row–3 is re-written in the reverse order, then which letter will appear exactly above the letter D of Row–4?

9. The answer to this question is the letter, which has appeared more than twice in Column–6 or the letter that has shown the minimum number of appearances in Column–6.

10. Which letter has shown the maximum number of appearances in the diagonal starting from the letter B in the lower left corner and ending in the letter B in the upper right corner?

ANSWERS

1	2	3	4	5	6	7	8	9	10
B	B	E	C	E	B	D	A	D	B

EXERCISE-5

Directions (Qs. 1-10) : *Answer the following questions based on the Table given below.*

TABLE

	Column 1	Column 2	Column 3	Column 4	Column 5	Column 6	Column 7
Row–1	E	D	B	C	A	B	D
Row–2	B	A	C	E	D	C	A
Row–3	D	E	A	C	B	D	B
Row–4	A	C	B	D	E	A	A
Row–5	C	B	A	E	A	C	D
Row–6	E	C	D	A	B	C	E
Row–7	B	A	C	E	D	A	B

1. Which letter is in the middle of the two A's in the Column–3?

2. Starting from bottom left corner proceed to the bottom right corner then to top right corner and from top right corner to left corner and then to bottom left corner. Which letter is third to the left of first letter to right of fourth B?

3. Which letter appears maximum number of times along the diagonal from top left corner to bottom right corner?

4. Starting from the B of bottom left corner if one proceeds to D of the top right corner then which letter is appeared only once?

5. Which letter is in the middle of the two A's of Row–5?

6. If one proceeds from the top left corner to top right corner, then to the bottom right corner and from the bottom right corner to the bottom left corner and from bottom left corner to the top left corner, then which letter had been appeared minimum number of times?

7. Which letter is fourth to the right of second letter to the left of C of Row–3?

8. Which letter has appeared least number of times in Column–5?

9. If the letters of the Row–3 are written in the reverse order then which letter will be just above the letter B of Row–4?

10. Which letter has been repeated maximum number of times in the Row–4?

ANSWERS

1	2	3	4	5	6	7	8	9	10
B	C	A	A	E	C	D	E	B	A

SHAPE, SIZE AND COLOUR TEST

In this test, questions are asked related to shape, size and colour. Basic mental ability is measured by this test. In this type of question a figure is given in the left. Four definite rules are also given after the figure which determine the changes in the given figure. Then a blank space is left and a figure is given in last. Now one has to find out the specific rule from the previous given rules which can be filled in the blank, so that the last figure would be correct. In this context, few points are important; such as—

Level - 1 →	x
Level - 2 →	x
Level - 3 →	x

If there is cross (×) at Level-1, then you must change the shape. A cross (×) at Level-1 means, you have to change the size. If there is cross (×) at Level-3. Then you have to change the colour. You must keep in mind that changing shape means changing circle to rectangle and rectangle to circle, changing size means to increase or decrease size and changing colour means changing coloured to colourless and vice-versa. Understand this as:

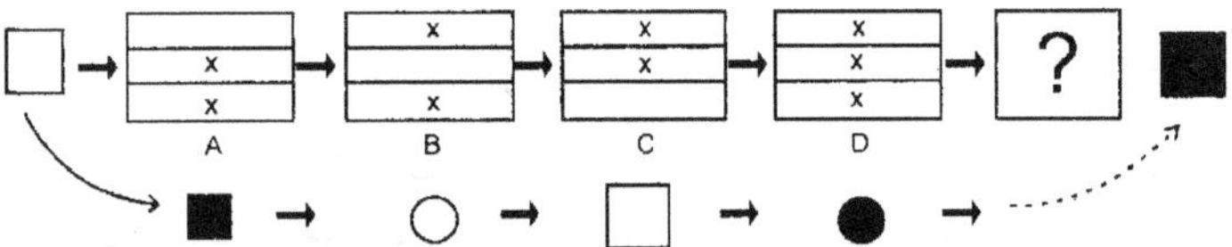

Here the figure on the left side, in option A, has been changed in size & colour and we get small black square. In option B, shape & colour have been changed and we get small white circle. Then, in option C, shape & size have been changed and we get big white square. Similarly, in option D, shape, size & colour have been changed and we get small, black circle. Now we have to see that to get the right-side figure correct what changes should be happen. The changes can be opted from the option A, B, C and D.

Small black circle convert to big black square. This means shape & size is changing here. The shape & size change is occurring in option C. Therefore, the answer should be C.

Hence, C has to be blackened in the answer sheet.

EXERCISE-1

Directions (Qs. 1-25) : *In each of the following questions the figure (on left side) changes to the right following a certain rule. The figure A, B, C and D are situated between the left and right figures showing the rule for change. Select the option to obtain the figure at the right side after effecting certain changes.*

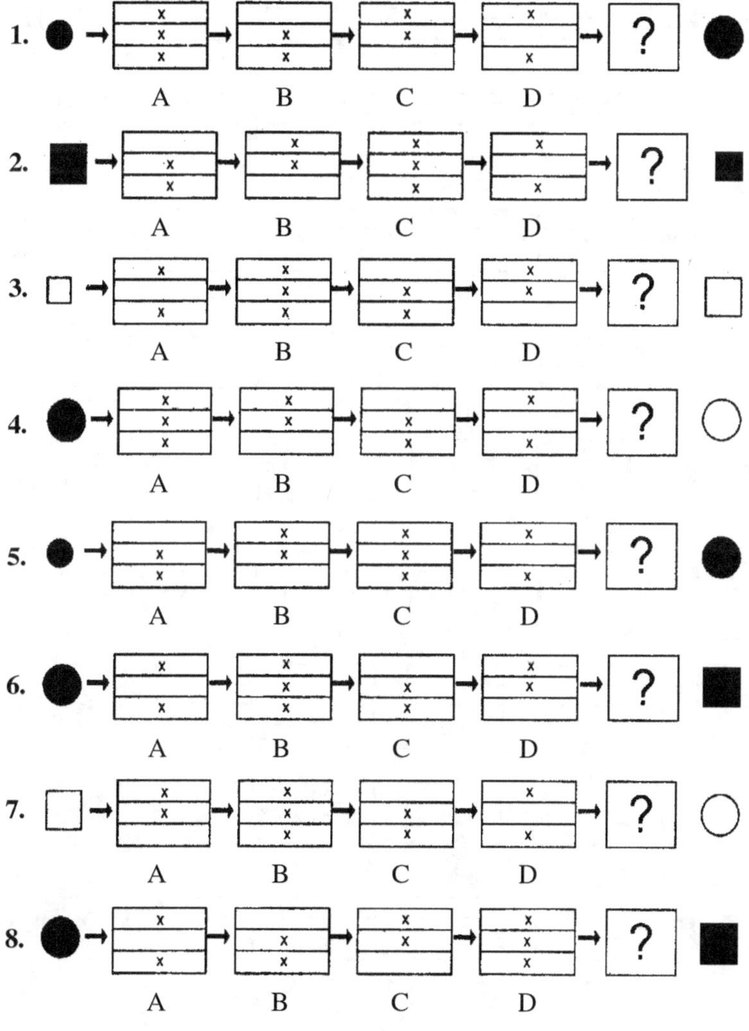

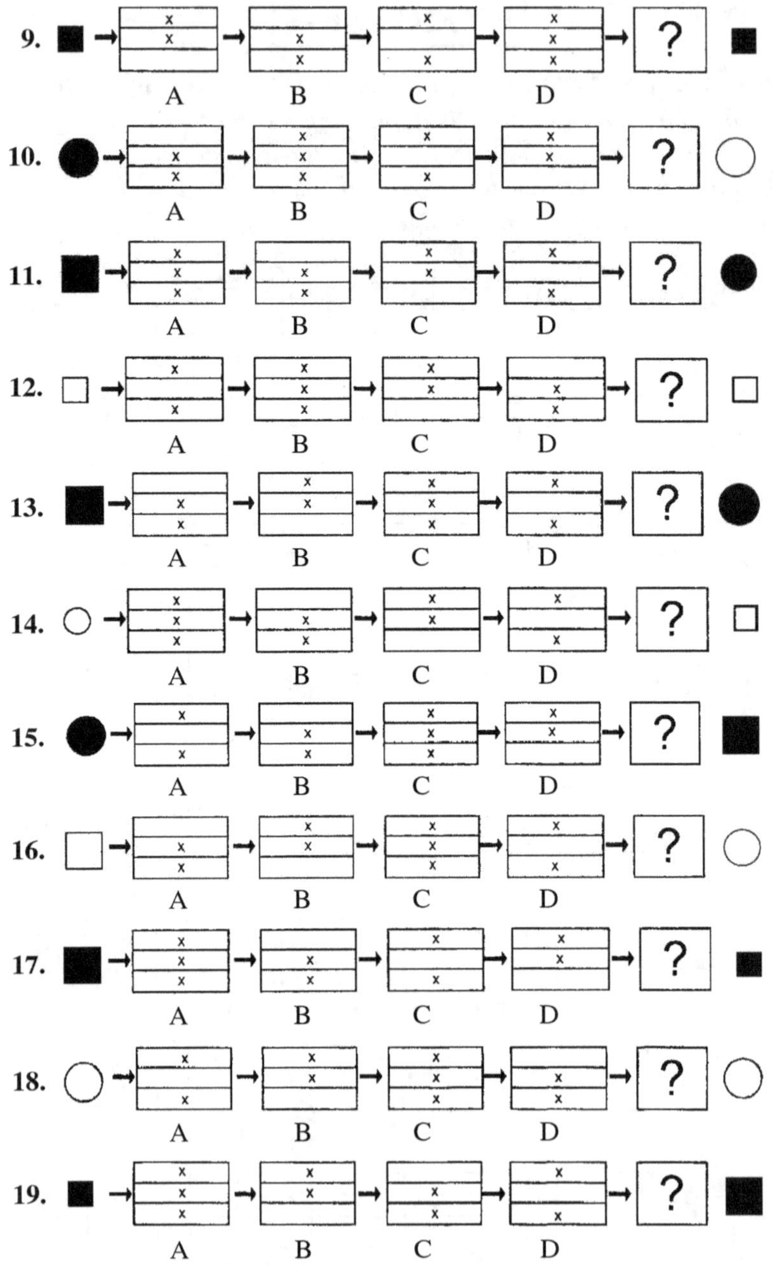

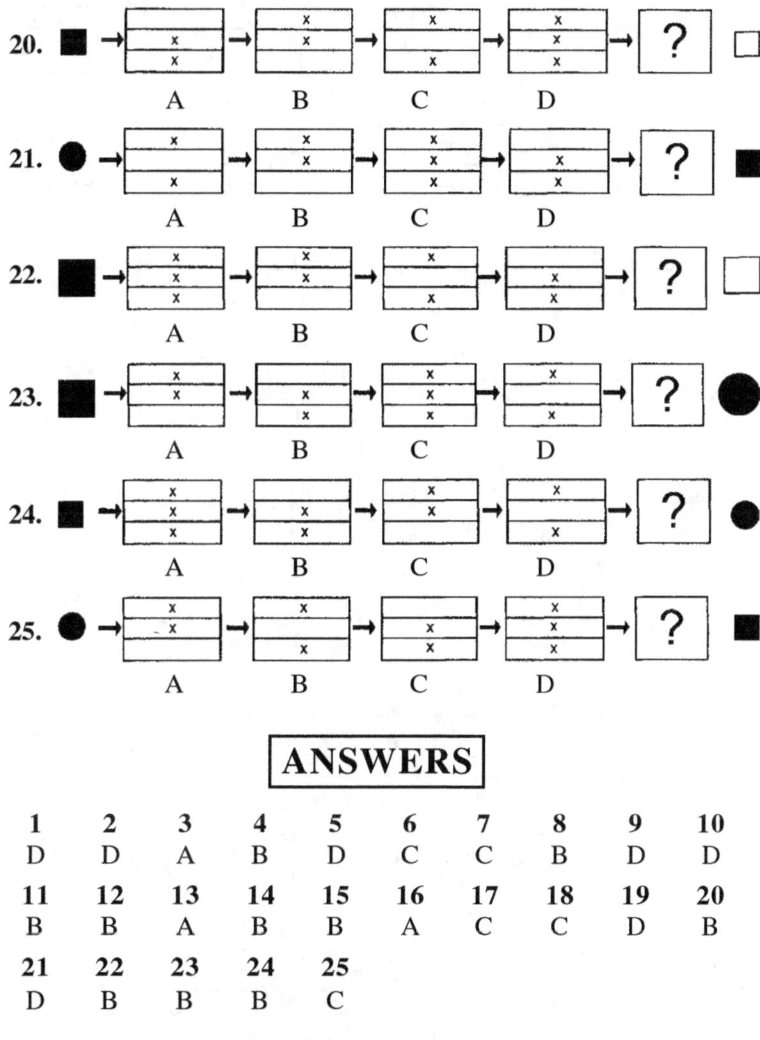

ANSWERS

1	2	3	4	5	6	7	8	9	10
D	D	A	B	D	C	C	B	D	D

11	12	13	14	15	16	17	18	19	20
B	B	A	B	B	A	C	C	D	B

21	22	23	24	25
D	B	B	B	C

EXERCISE-2

Directions (Qs. 1-25) : *In each of the following questions the figure (on left side) changes to the right following a certain rule. The figure A, B, C and D are situated between the left and right figures showing the rule for change. Select the option to obtain the figure at the right side after effecting certain changes.*

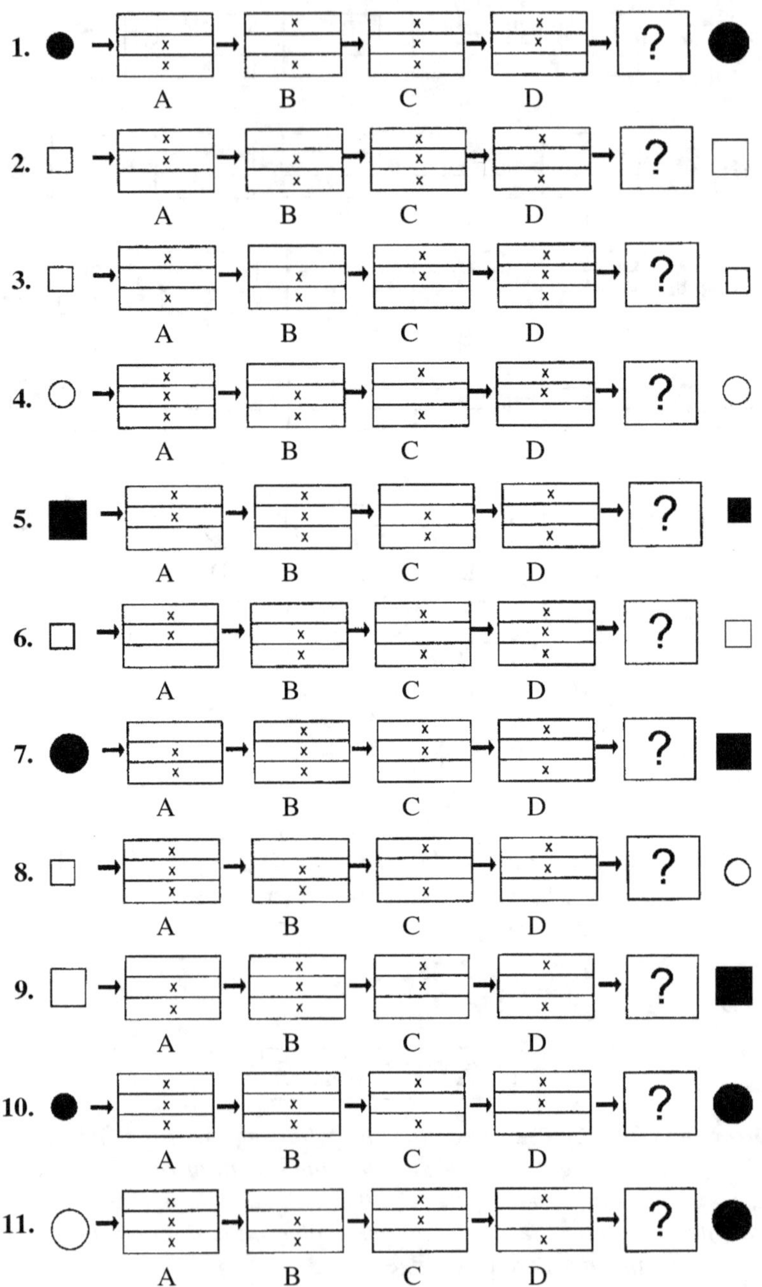

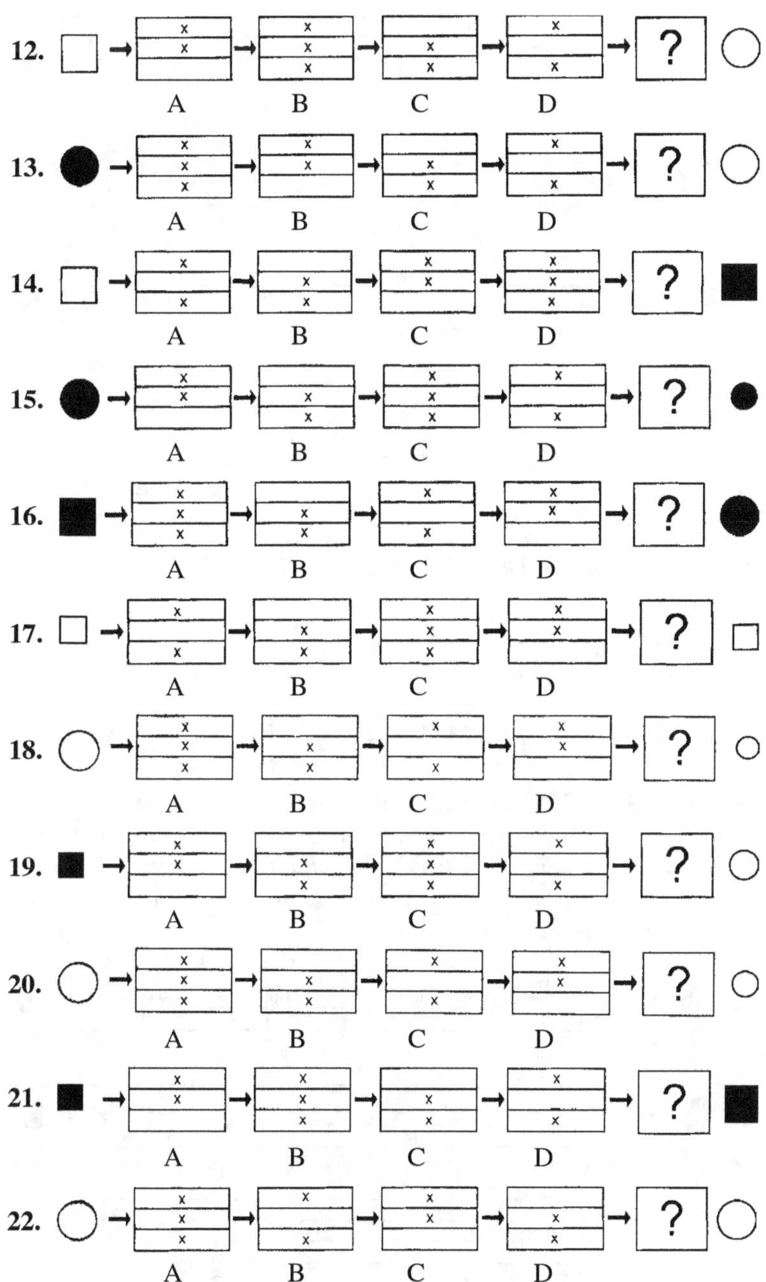

12.
A B C D
13.
A B C D
14.
A B C D
15.
A B C D
16.
A B C D
17.
A B C D
18.
A B C D
19.
A B C D
20.
A B C D
21.
A B C D
22.
A B C D

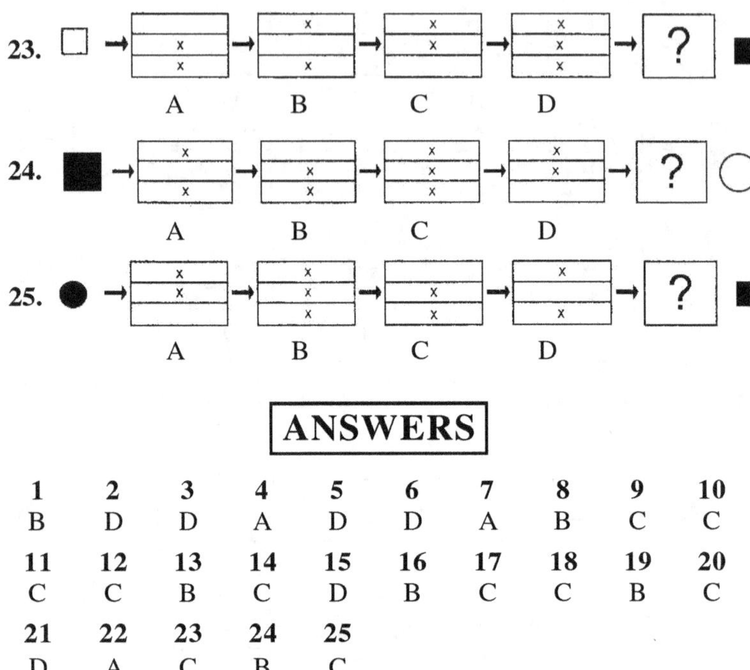

23. [options A, B, C, D] → ?

24. [options A, B, C, D] → ?

25. [options A, B, C, D] → ?

ANSWERS

1	2	3	4	5	6	7	8	9	10
B	D	D	A	D	D	A	B	C	C

11	12	13	14	15	16	17	18	19	20
C	C	B	C	D	B	C	C	B	C

21	22	23	24	25
D	A	C	B	C

EXERCISE-3

Directions (Qs. 1-25) : *In each of the following questions the figure (on left side) changes to the right following a certain rule. The figure A, B, C and D are situated between the left and right figures showing the rule for change. Select the option to obtain the figure at the right side after effecting certain changes.*

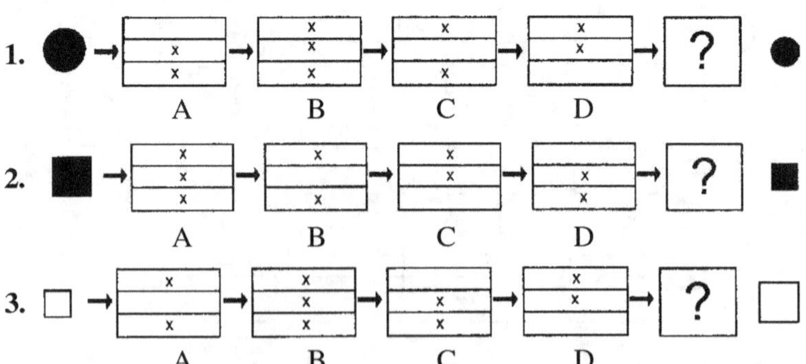

1. [options A, B, C, D] → ?

2. [options A, B, C, D] → ?

3. [options A, B, C, D] → ?

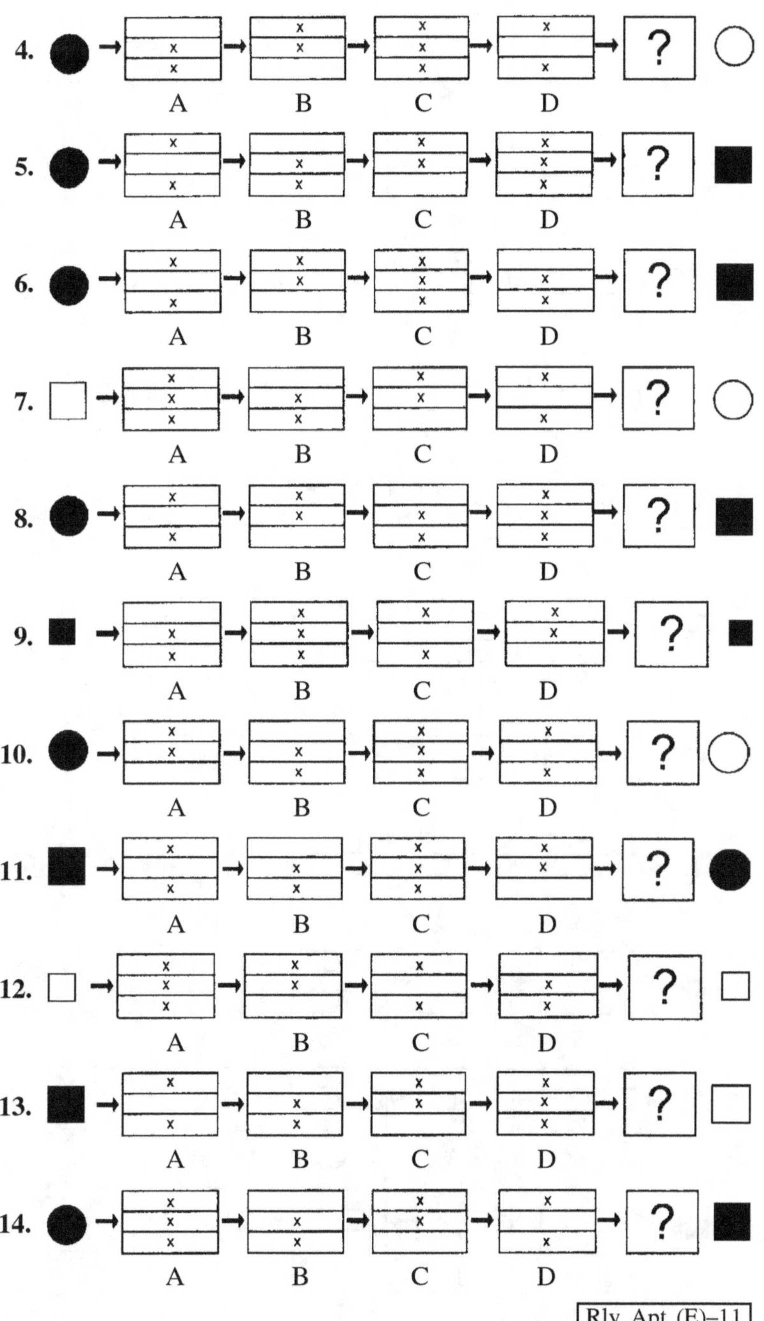

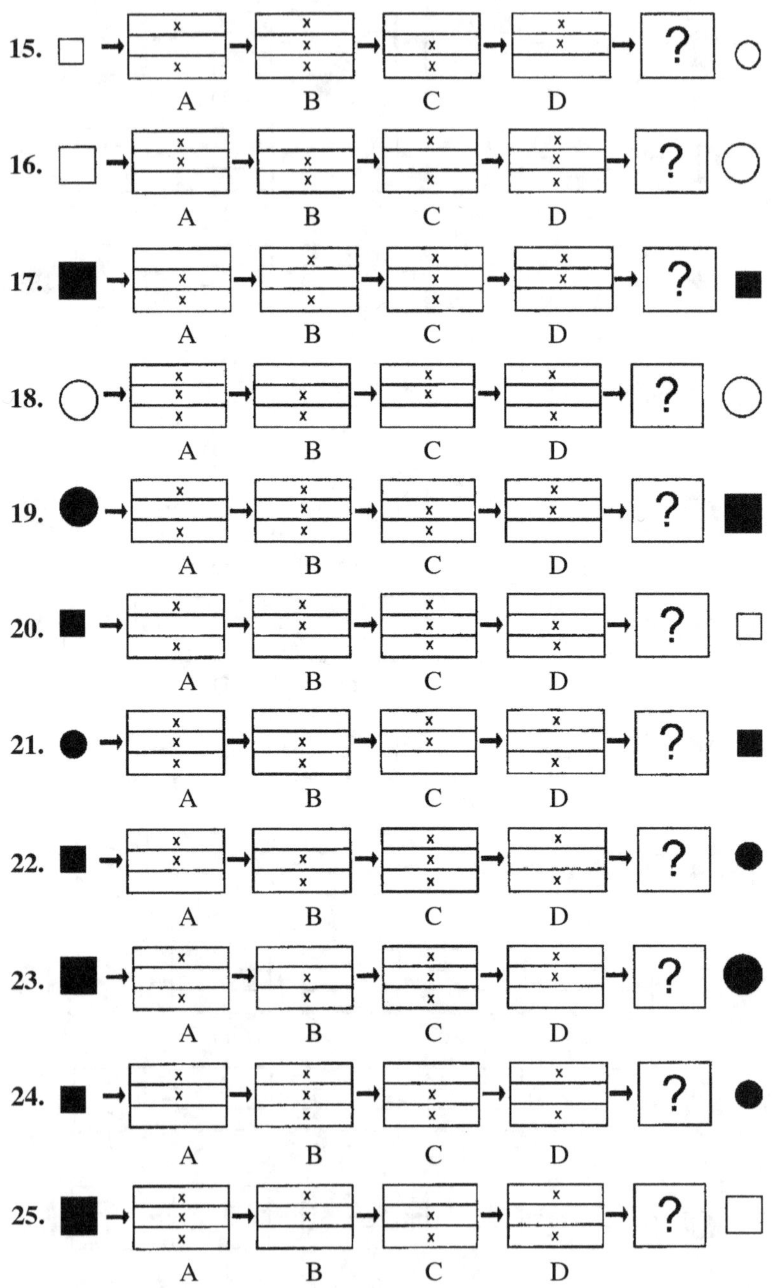

ANSWERS

1	2	3	4	5	6	7	8	9	10
C	B	A	B	B	D	B	C	B	A

11	12	13	14	15	16	17	18	19	20
B	A	C	B	C	B	B	D	C	B

21	22	23	24	25
B	B	B	C	B

EXERCISE-4

Directions (Qs. 1-25) : *In each of the following questions the figure (on left side) changes to the right following a certain rule. The figure A, B, C and D are situated between the left and right figures showing the rule for change. Select the option to obtain the figure at the right side after effecting certain changes.*

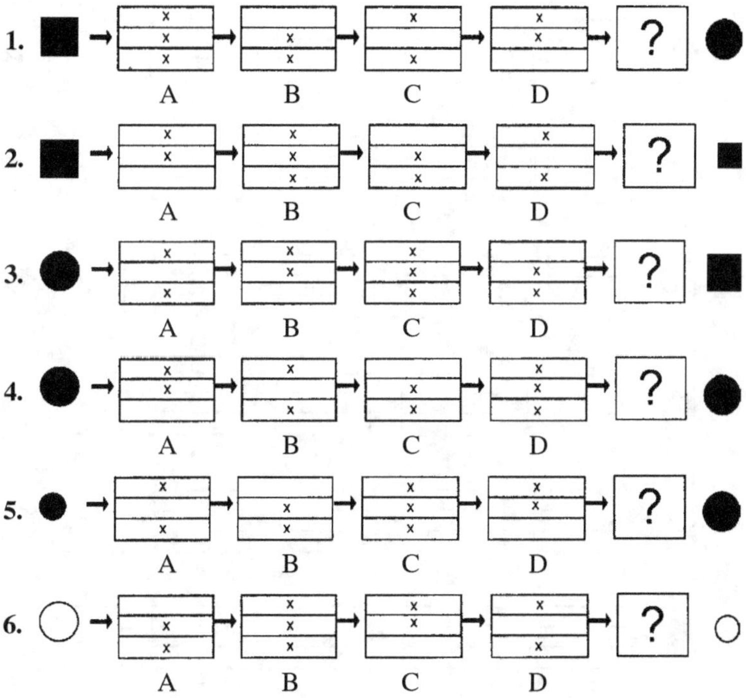

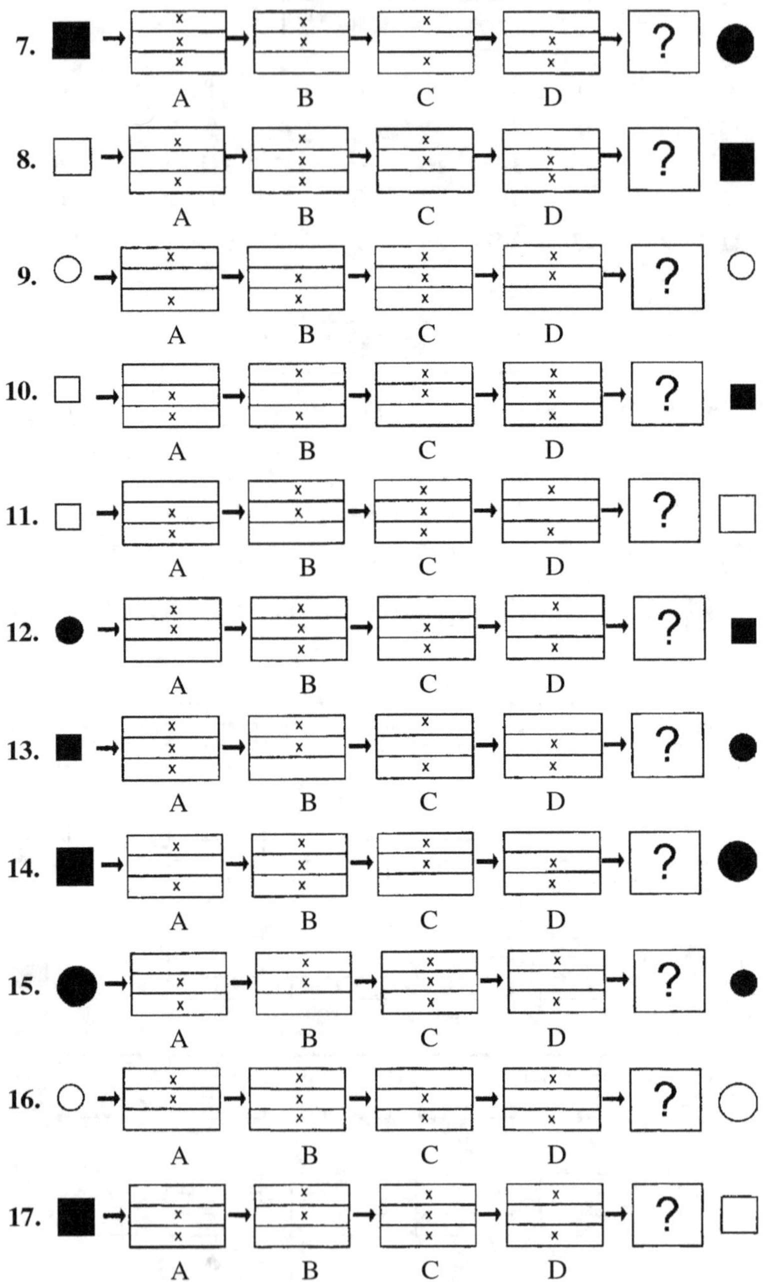

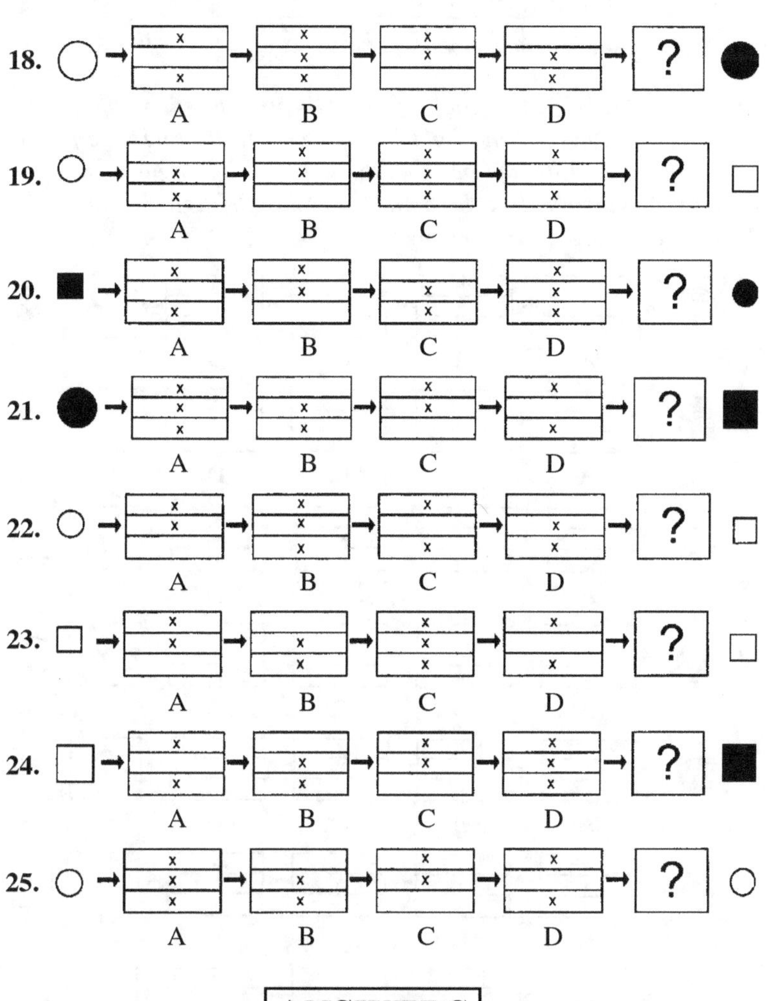

ANSWERS

1	2	3	4	5	6	7	8	9	10
B	D	D	D	A	D	D	C	C	C

11	12	13	14	15	16	17	18	19	20
D	C	D	D	D	D	B	C	A	C

21	22	23	24	25
B	D	C	C	A

EXERCISE-5

Directions (Qs. 1-25) : *In each of the following questions the figure (on left side) changes to the right following a certain rule. The figure A, B, C and D are situated between the left and right figures showing the rule for change. Select the option to obtain the figure at the right side after effecting certain changes.*

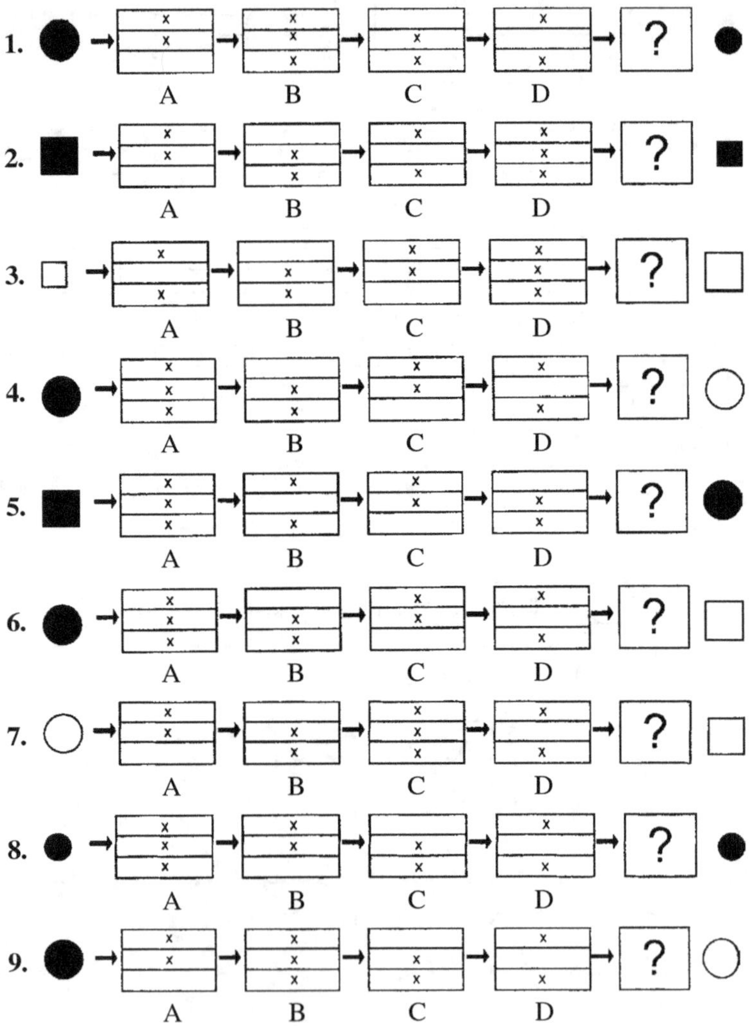

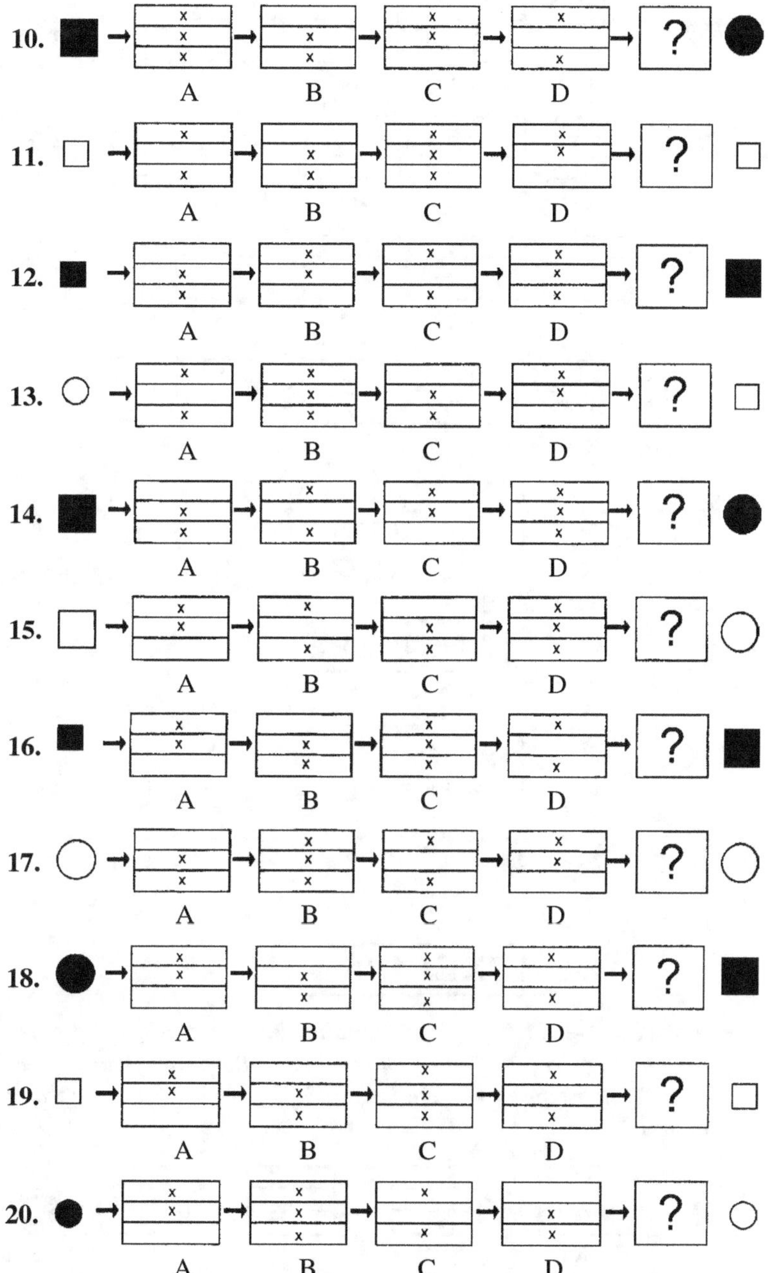

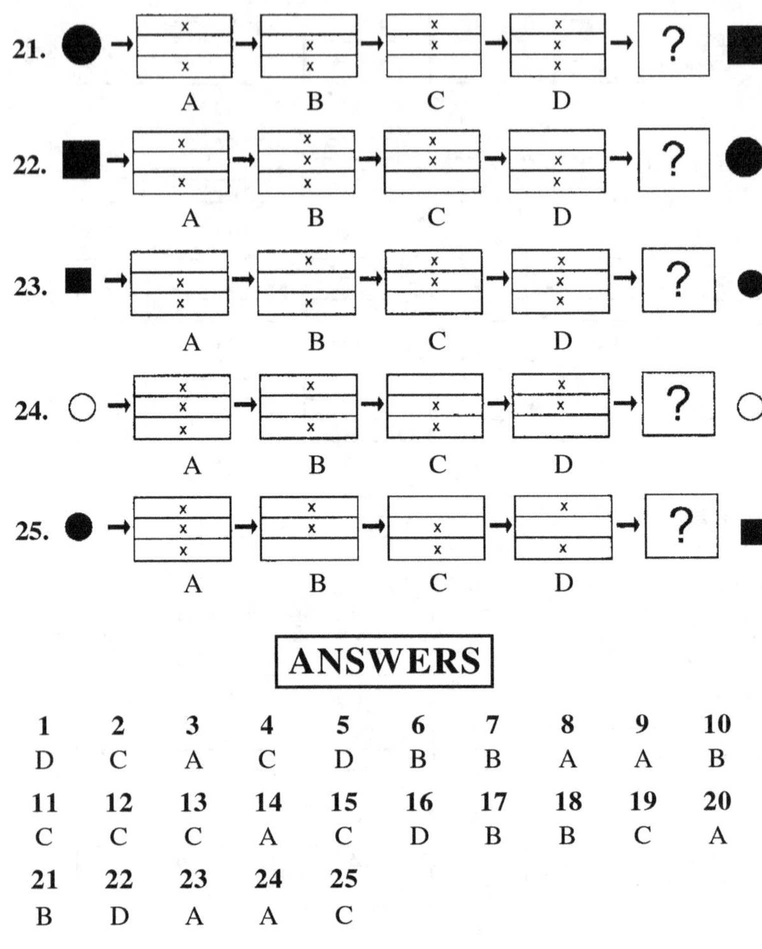

ANSWERS

1	2	3	4	5	6	7	8	9	10
D	C	A	C	D	B	B	A	A	B

11	12	13	14	15	16	17	18	19	20
C	C	C	A	C	D	B	B	C	A

21	22	23	24	25
B	D	A	A	C

EXERCISE-6

Directions (Qs. 1-25) : *In each of the following questions, two figure are given. One is 'Original figure while other is 'Resultant figure'. The question is: Which type of change is valid? Choose your answer from given options.*

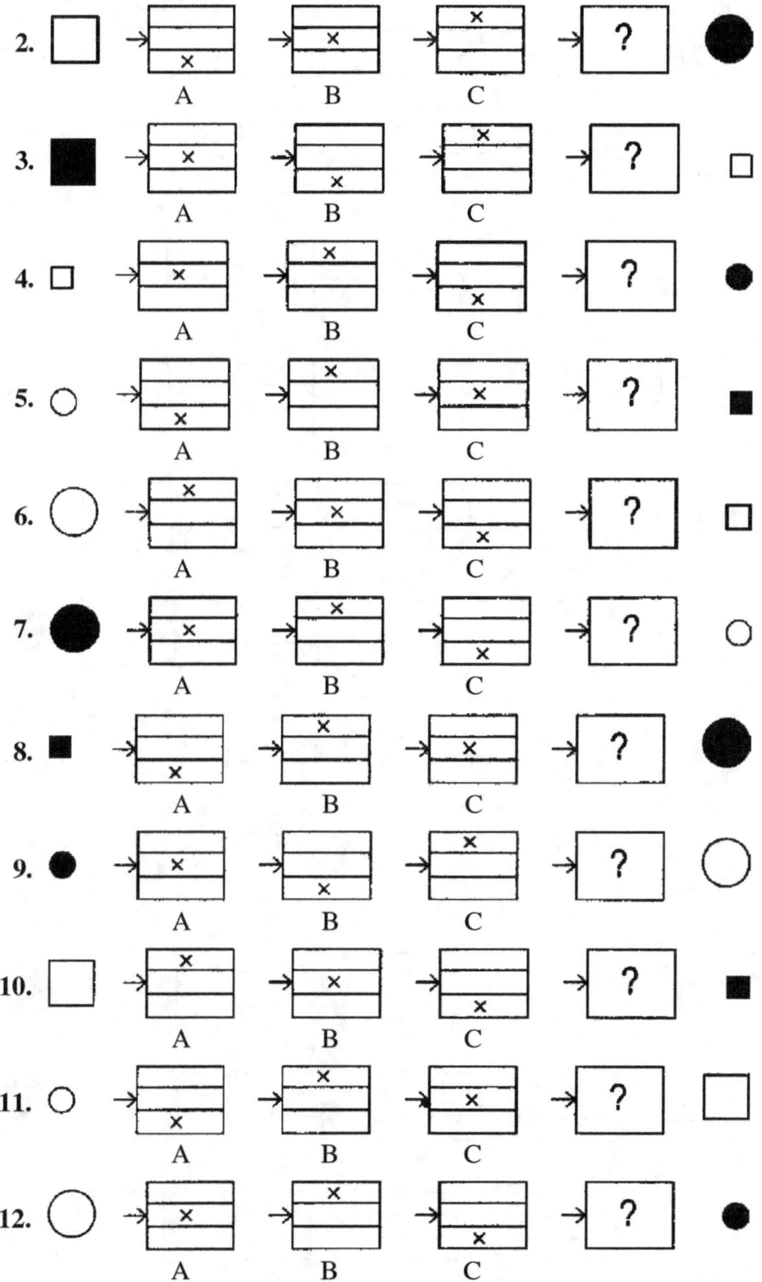

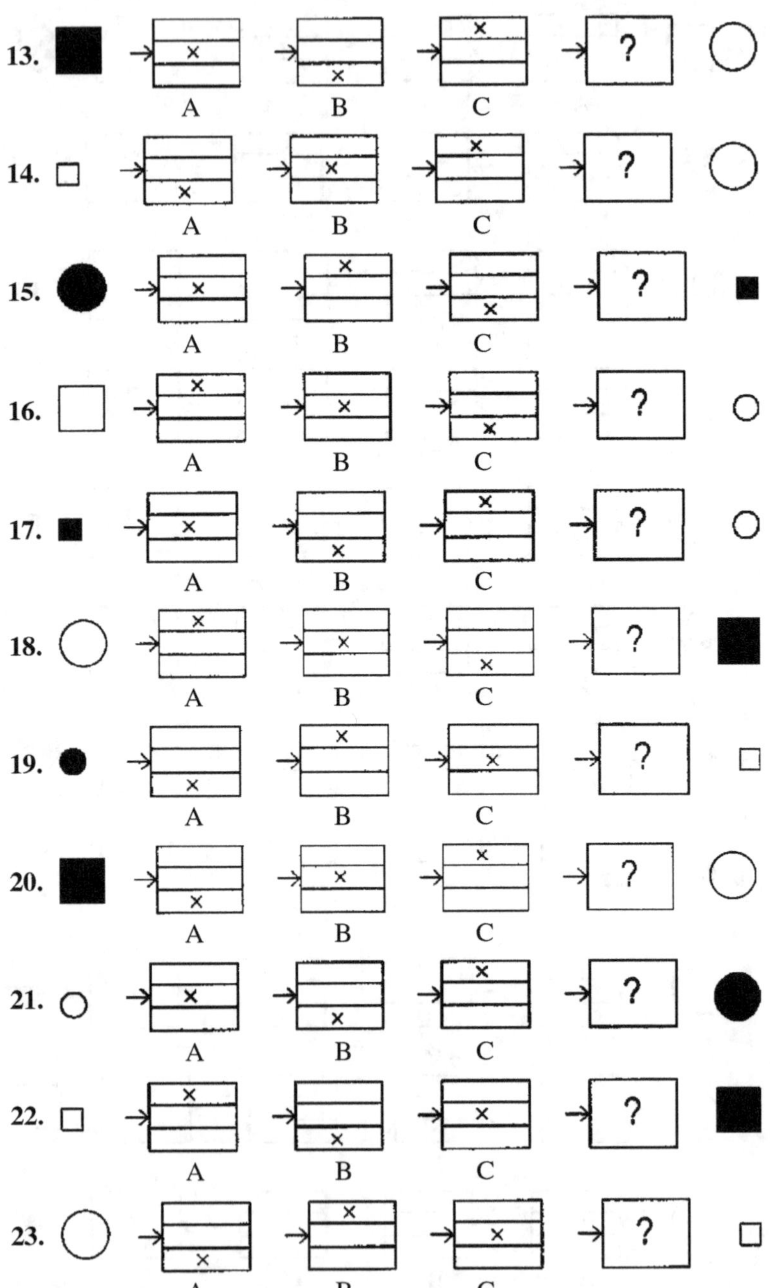

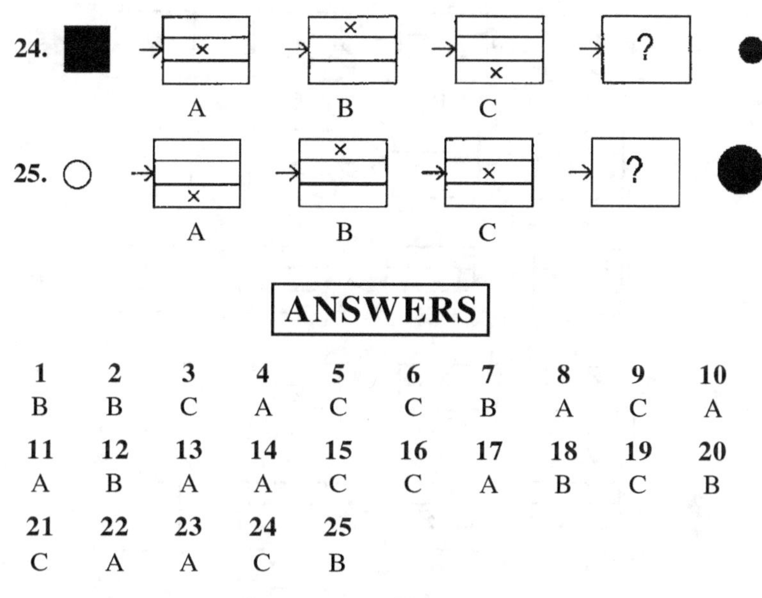

ANSWERS

1	2	3	4	5	6	7	8	9	10
B	B	C	A	C	C	B	A	C	A

11	12	13	14	15	16	17	18	19	20
A	B	A	A	C	C	A	B	C	B

21	22	23	24	25
C	A	A	C	B

EXERCISE-7

Directions (Qs. 1-25) : *In each of the following questions, two figure are given. One is 'Original figure while other is 'Resultant figure'. The question is: Which type of change is valid? Choose your answer from given options.*

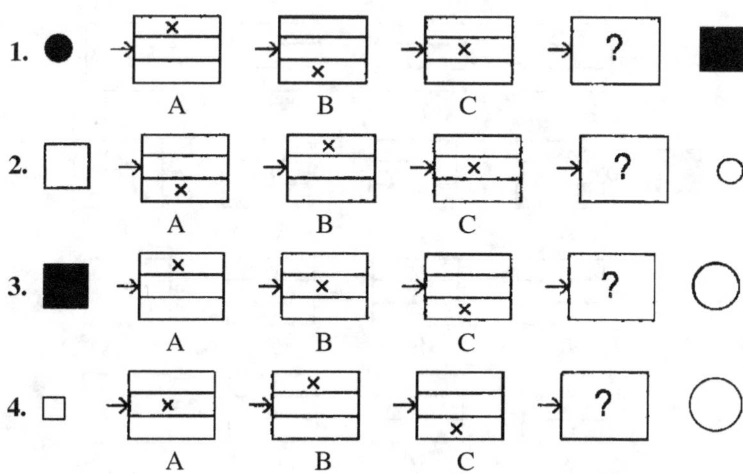

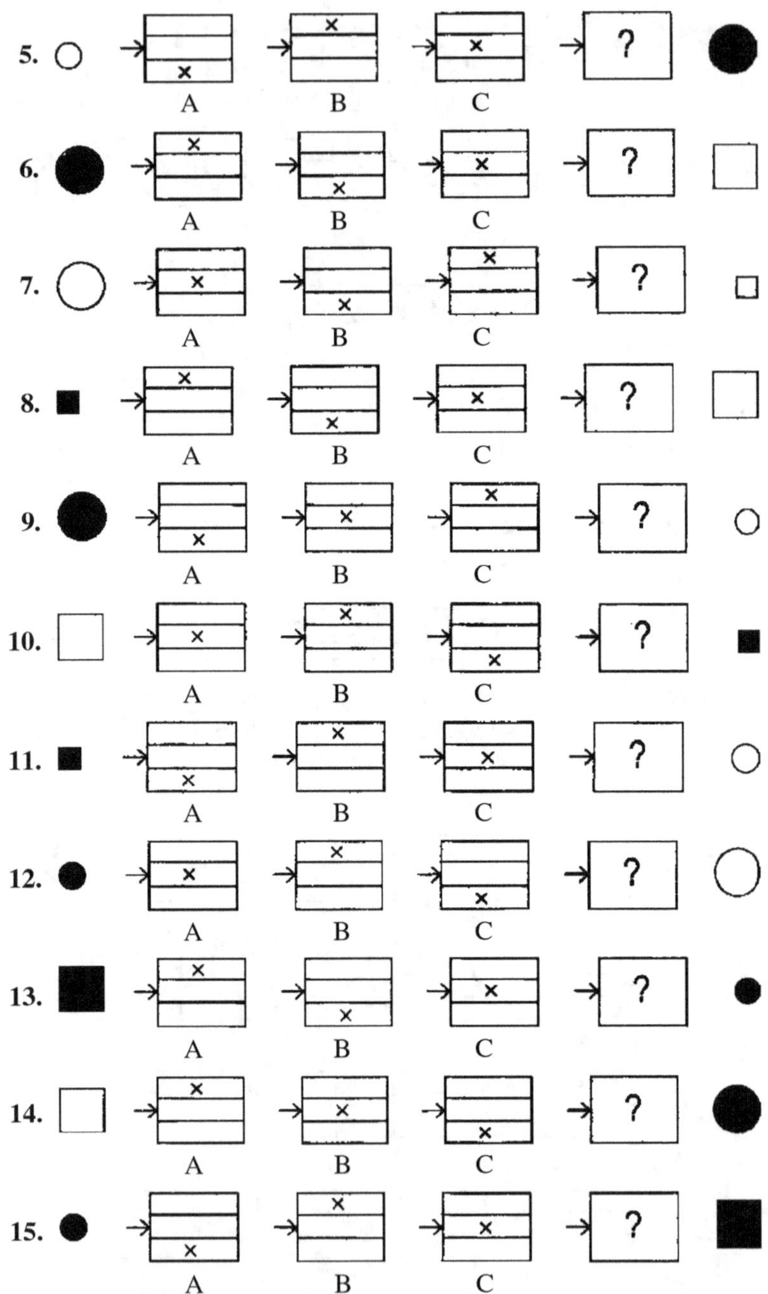
5.
A
B
C
?
6.
A
B
C
?
7.
A
B
C
?
8.
A
B
C
?
9.
A
B
C
?
10.
A
B
C
?
11.
A
B
C
?
12.
A
B
C
?
13.
A
B
C
?
14.
A
B
C
?
15.
A
B
C
?

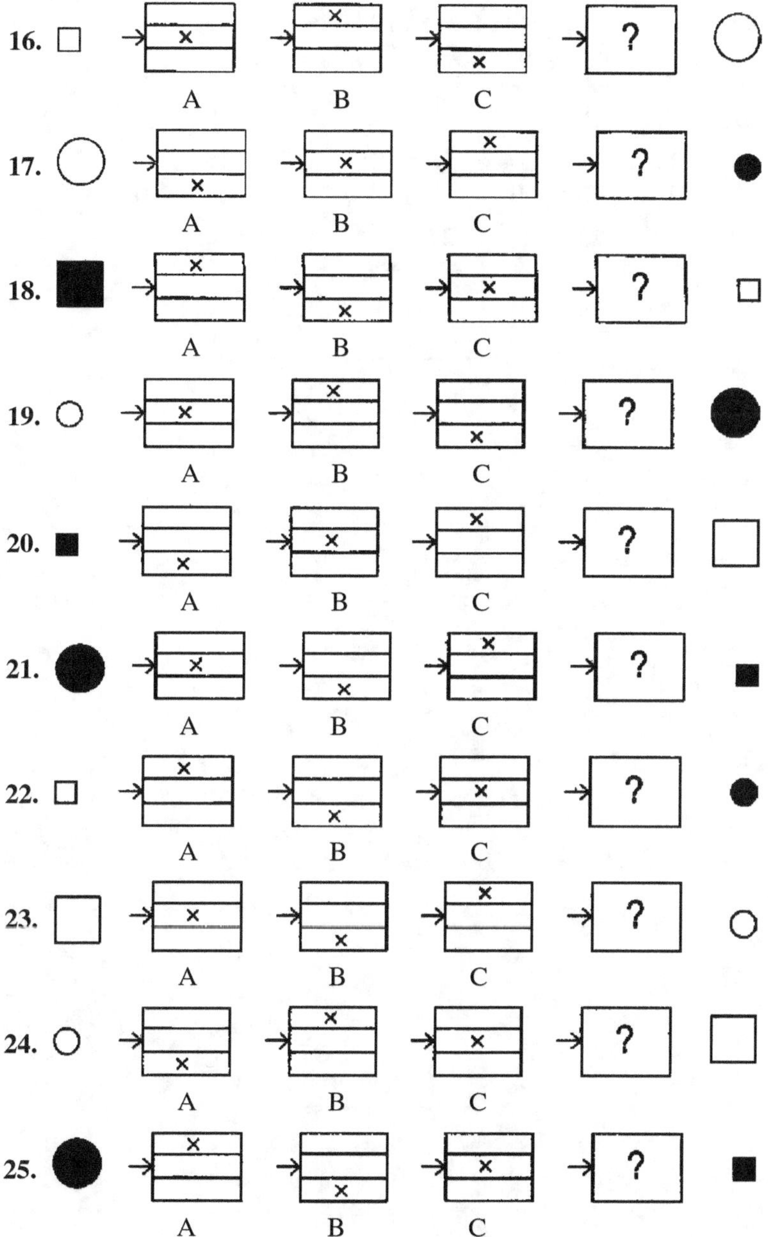

ANSWERS

1	2	3	4	5	6	7	8	9	10
B	A	B	C	B	C	B	A	C	B

11	12	13	14	15	16	17	18	19	20
C	B	B	B	A	C	C	A	B	C

21	22	23	24	25
B	C	B	A	B

PERSONALITY TEST
(Aptitude Test)

This type of test is used to judge the candidate's temperament, discretion and aptitude. In this type of test, a statement is given with four/three options as the answer. The candidates are required to select one of the given options according to their aptitude. Such questions are aimed at testing your reasoning power and mental ability in day-to-day life.

Example : When someone tells me to make a promise, then I
   A. do never make a promise
   B. think before finally making a promise
   C. make a promise immediately
   D. cannot say anything in this context

Answer (B) : From the foregoing discussion it is clear that psychological test is not so difficult as it is considered by majority of the candidates. However, without sufficient practice you cannot solve the questions quickly and accurately. Here, it must be noted that a minor mistake may lead to wrong answer because all the alternative choices are devised in such a manner that every option seems to be appropriate answer at a glance. But, the bare truth is that only one of the given alternative choices is correct in all respects and you have to select only that correct answer.

EXERCISE-1

Directions (Qs. 1-36) : *In the questions given below, four alternatives have been given below each one of them. You have to select the right alternative according to your aptitude and mark it in your answer sheet.*

1. If an argument starts with someone, then I invariably
   A. listen to the viewpoint of that person carefully and then, speak what is in my mind
   B. state my view at the very outset
   C. start saying whatever comes to my mind
   D. become confused and perplexed

2. If you were a woman and if it were within your control, then what would you like to become?
   A. Miss World   B. A player of international level
   C. Politician   D. Actress

3. I like to fight the intricate problems.
   A. Only sometimes   B. No
   C. Yes   D. Never

4. I read such books in leisure which deal with :
   A. moral values   B. sex
   C. violence   D. any theme

5. Whenever I join a new group, then
   A. I am not able to understand them
   B. I take some time to understand people
   C. I feel pretty soon that I have known all of them
   D. I take some time to identify and understand them

6. After having a meal to my heart's content, if someone requests me to eat a sweet, then I
   A. refuse politely
   B. eat some of the sweets
   C. do not care about the proposition
   D. scold the person who makes a request

7. When I accomplish a task in a foolish manner, then
   A. I feel proud
   B. I like the action very much
   C. I feel ashamed of it
   D. nothing happens

8. When someone knocks at my closed door, then first of all, I
   A. scold him from inside
   B. do not open the door
   C. open the door
   D. see through the lens installed in the door

9. Best ideas come to my mind
   A. when I work in a group
   B. when I work alone
   C. never
   D. do not know when they come

10. You inform your close friend
  A. all the important issues
  B. all the bad issues
  C. all the thoughts going on in your mind
  D. nothing at all

11. Normally, I am an extrovert and gregarious.
  A. Sometimes   B. No
  C. Yes   D. Never

12. Sometimes I feel disappointed.
  A. Yes   B. Cannot say
  C. No   D. Off and On

13. I inspired from the biographies of great personalities.
  A. Often   B. Sometimes
  C. Never   D. Regularly

14. When my bicycle goes out of order, then I
  A. show it to the bicycle mechanic
  B. try to repair it myself
  C. tell my friends to repair it
  D. buy a new bicycle

15. I search for the possibilities of the solution of every problem.
  A. Sometimes   B. Never
  C. Yes   D. No

16. I am punctual about
  A. eating   B. going to the cinema
  C. sleeping   D. time

17. If a person takes away my things without getting my permission,
then I feel pain.
  A. Yes   B. Sometimes
  C. No   D. Never

18. Whenever I talk to somebody, then I
  A. look at his face
  B. look into his eyes
  C. look at the things around him
  D. look at his feet

19. Whenever someone interrupts my speech, then I
  A. do not pay attention to him
  B. start speaking at a faster pace than before

Rly Apt (E)–12

    C. stop my speech and let him speech
    D. nothing is certain

20. You have adorned a new shirt. Your companion passes a remark that your shirt is misfit for your personal. So, you will
    A. start scolding him in the presence of all others
    B. change the shirt immediately
    C. not change the shirt but singe from the heart of your hearts
    D. laugh away the remark, starting that it is your style

21. I always take care of ..... in my life.
    A. sleeping   B. time
    C. taking meal   D. making enjoyments

22. When you go to buy cloth for yourself, then what is the most important issue/factor looked after by you?
    A. The cloth must be suitable for you
    B. The cloth that is stated to be good by the shopkeeper
    C. The costliest cloth
    D. The design of the cloth should be different from those of all others

23. If I were to acquire a lot of money, then I will
    A. distribute it among neighbours
    B. spend it and have whale of a time
    C. save most of it for the future
    D. cannot say anything about it

24. If I were a bat, them I would
    A. fly during the day
    B. fly during the night
    C. fly during the day as well as the night
    D. increase the number of ultrasonic waves

25. During the period of difficulty, I invariably take the help of another person.
    A. Never   B. Yes
    C. No   D. Sometimes

26. I like to meet new people.
    A. Always   B. Sometimes
    C. Never   D. Cann't say

27. I will to spend my idle time by
    A. chatting aimlessly with friends
    B. reading a book containing interesting facts

C. reading comics
D. None of these

28. If you are a woman, then, while talking to others
A. you fly into a rage when the talk related to age is commenced
B. you tell your age by reducing a few years from the actual age
C. refrain from going any set of information related to age
D. you inform about your correct age, if asked about the same

29. I love to live alone.
A. Sometimes   B. Yes
C. No   D. Never

30. Excessive consumption of ghee and oil is
A. tasty for the health
B. beneficial to the health
C. injurious to the health
D. cannot state anything in this context

31. The secret of my success is
A. studying newspaper   B. awakening in night
C. hard labour   D. gossiping

32. When my little child cries loudly, then I
A. give him food
B. thrash him with vigour
C. make him sleep
D. give him feed of milk

33. I like to use new procedures of work.
A. Never   B. Yes
C. Sometimes   D. No

34. During winter days, I
A. get up at a fixed time
B. get up only in the morning
C. get up late
D. get up at an uncertain time

35. I like to be convinced by facts.
A. Sometimes   B. No
C. Yes   D. Never

36. Find the odd man out of the following
A. Cow   B. Dog
C. Buffalo   D. Goat

ANSWERS

1	2	3	4	5	6	7	8	9	10
A	B	C	A	B	A	C	D	B	A

11	12	13	14	15	16	17	18	19	20
C	C	A	A	C	D	A	B	C	D

21	22	23	24	25	26	27	28	29	30
B	A	C	B	D	A	B	D	A	C

31	32	33	34	35	36
C	D	B	A	C	B

EXERCISE-2

Directions (Qs. 1-36) : *In the questions given below, three alternatives have been given below each one of them. You have to select the right alternative according to your aptitude and mark it in your answer sheet.*

1. Which one of the following is different?
   A. AIDS   B. Cancer
   C. Typhoid

2. I found a purse full of money in college premise. I
   A. donated the amount among poors
   B. gave it to the principal
   C. none of these

3. I am punctual regarding
   A. going to bed   B. time
   C. meals

4. I was travelling on a boat which capsized. Firstly, I
   A. rescued others   B. saved myself
   C. closed by eyes

5. When someone asks you for help in odd situations then
   A. you give him/her all possible help
   B. you promise him/her help
   C. you do not help him/her

6. In case my wrist watch is out of order, I
   A. would try to repair it myself

B. would give it to watch maker

C. would buy a new watch

7. Often I change my opinion in the last moment.
   A. Yes   B. No
   C. Sometimes

8. Generally, I am extrovert and well behaved.
   A. Yes   B. No
   C. Sometimes

9. I like to use new technique of work.
   A. Yes   B. No
   C. Some times

10. When someone considers you wrong then
    A. you do not react
    B. you consider him/her wrong
    C. you try to ward off the misunderstanding on proper occasion.

11. "Best" is related to "worst" in the same way as "slow" is related to
    A. Slowest   B. Very fast
    C. Fast

12. If you are a female and you are talking with a male
    A. You hide your age
    B. You are afraid
    C. You talk without hesitation

13. I do like rules and regulations.
    A. Yes   B. No
    C. Sometimes

14. Excellent ideas come to my mind
    A. while working alone
    B. while working in group
    C. I do not know

15. Whenever my little baby cries loudly, then I
    A. beat him/her   B. feed milk to him/her
    C. make him/her sleep

16. When I see a mad person, I
    A. approach towards him/her

B. maintain distance from him/her

C. throw stone at him/her

17. While driving my car I offer lift who ask for the lift

A. always   B. sometimes

C. never

18. When someone tries to convince you then

A. You get convinced

B. You do not get convinced

C. You hear him/her passionately

19. I never gossip with my colleagues.

A. Yes   B. No

C. Can not say

20. I speak to others about my expectation and dreams.

A. rarely   B. often

C. some times

21. The antonym of antonym of 'Proper' is

A. Wrong   B. Improper

C. Right

22. When I do any foolish work then

A. I feel ashamed

B. I feel proud of my self

C. Nothing happens

23. If I were correspondent of any newspaper then I will write on the following subject

A. Cinema and theatre   B. Political events

C. Neither, A nor B

24. If I were not human being then

A. I wish to be a bird   B. I wish to be a horse

C. Can not say

25. Suppose, you have worn a new shirt your friend passed a comment that it is not looking good on you. You

A. will change the shirt immediately

B. will take it lightly as it is your style

C. will not change the shirt but feel offended

26. I am keen to know current social issues.
A. Yes
B. No
C. Can not say

27. I am slow in expressing my views.
A. Yes
B. No
C. Can not say

28. Before doing any work I ask myself 'Is it appropriate'?
A. Yes
B. No
C. Sometimes

29. If I see the GOD, I will ask for
A. huge wealth
B. honesty
C. love

30. People call you selfish:
A. Always
B. Sometimes
C. Never

31. While talking to friends I do not like to express my very personal matters.
A. Yes
B. No
C. Sometimes

32. Charioteer means
A. selfish
B. companion
C. driver of chariot

33. Consultation with others helps me to take any decision.
A. Yes
B. No
C. I get confused

34. Which of the following words is different from others ?
A. probable
B. perhaps
C. may be

35. After failure
A. One repents
B. One tries again to succeed
C. Nothing special is happened

36. I want to be convinced by arguments
A. Yes
B. No
C. Sometimes

ANSWERS

1	2	3	4	5	6	7	8	9	10
C	B	B	B	A	B	B	A	A	C

11	12	13	14	15	16	17	18	19	20
C	C	A	A	B	B	B	A	A	A

21	22	23	24	25	26	27	28	29	30
C	A	B	A	B	A	B	A	C	C

31	32	33	34	35	36
C	C	A	A	B	A

EXERCISE-3

Directions (Qs. 1–36) : *In the questions given below, four alternatives have been given below each one of the them. You have to select the right alternative according to your aptitude and mark it in your answer sheet.*

1. I fully remember people's names.
   - A. Yes
   - B. No
   - C. Can not say
   - D. None of these

2. I do remember God
   - A. in distress
   - B. in happier time
   - C. always
   - D. off and on

3. If I were the correspondent of a newspaper, then I will write on the following subject
   - A. Health
   - B. Cinema and theatre
   - C. Political events
   - D. None of these three

4. P, who is the brother of M, is the father of L. And further, the father of M is the father of S. So, ... is the uncle of L.
   - A. S
   - B. P
   - C. M
   - D. None of these

5. If the hands of a watch meet exactly 65 minutes later (according to the working watch), then this watch is
   - A. not working properly
   - B. slow
   - C. fast
   - D. giving the right time

6. The house of my hate-worthy neighbour is on fire. I
  A. am very happy to learn about this
  B. am going to put out the fire
  C. am not going to put out the fire
  D. am still thinking

7. I get help when I discuss things/issues with others.
  A. Sometimes   B. No
  C. Yes   D. I get into a fix

8. I play lead role in social works.
  A. Yes   B. No
  C. Can not say   D. None of these

9. If ''better'' is related to 'worst,' then ''very slow'' is related to
  A. extremely slow   B. fast
  C. very fast   D. medium fast

10. Upon seeing a lunatic, I
  A. start making hue and cry
  B. throw stones on him
  C. go near him
  D. keep myself away from him

11. I like pre-defined rules and regulations.
  A. Sometimes   B. No
  C. Yes   D. According to the occasion

12. I myself open the door of the car to enable my wife to sit inside the car.
  A. If I am happy   B. Sometimes
  C. Never   D. Always

13. Quite often, I change my mind at the last moment.
  A. No   B. Yes
  C. Sometimes   D. According to my benefit

14. Before startings my scooter, first of all, I
  A. check its brakes
  B. check the quantity of petrol in the fuel tank
  C. check air in the tyres
  D. check the headlight

15. When I decide somethings, then I
  A. get into a fix
  B. think about the decision
  C. feel myself to be contented and satisfied
  D. change my decision afterwards

16. When I am alone at my home, then, quite often, I
  A. sing a song   B. sleep
  C. watch television   D. read literature

17. I like to explore various possibilities/opportunities, even though
it may lead to delay in the piece of work.
  A. Sometimes   B. Yes
  C. No   D. Never

18. A is the father of B but B is not the son of A. Then what is B?
  A. Sister   B. Wife
  C. Brother   D. Daughter

19. Before doing any piece of work, I ask myself, ''Is it correct?''
  A. Sometimes   B. Yes
  C. No   D. Never

20. In the interview the quality which is sought mostly is:
  A. handsomeness   B. clothing
  C. personality   D. hair style

21. While talking to my friends, I do not like to express my personal
feelings.
  A. Sometimes
  B. Yes
  C. No
  D. It depends of the gravity of feelings

22. When I go by the car, I always give lift to hitchhikers.
  A. Only to ladies   B. Always
  C. Never   D. Sometimes

23. If put under pressure, I give emphasis on giving myself more time
so that I may be able to think more clearly.
  A. I get into a fix   B. Yes
  C. No   D. Sometimes

24. I believe in taking risks to suceed.
  A. Yes   B. No
  C. Can not say   D. None of these

25. While doing work, invariably, I
  A. remain in a dilly-dally situation—"to do or not to do"
  B. feel difficulty during the beginning
  C. find the end to be tedious
  D. start doing it immediately

26. I like to carry out the agricultural work according to the scientific method.
  A. For sometime
  B. Always
  C. Sometimes
  D. Never

27. If I find two persons fighting each other, on my way, I
  A. try to help them arrive at a truce/settlement of the dispute
  B. start fighting on behalf of the weaker person
  C. let them fight and move on
  D. watch the show

28. If I meet God sometime, then I would ask from Him.
  A. Gold and Silver
  B. Unlimited property/assets
  C. Honesty
  D. Love

29. If I were not a man, then I
  A. would like to be a cow
  B. would become a horse in a big stable
  C. would like to be a bird
  D. can not say anything in this context

30. Whenever someone demands anything from me, I
  A. return him empty-handed
  B. abuse him
  C. give something
  D. do not talk to him

31. It is necessary for progress
  A. to deceive others
  B. to resort to unlawful means
  C. to be sincere towards one's own duty
  D. No need of special attention

32. Whenever I take a decision, then I
  A. do not change it
  B. change it
  C. never change it
  D. do not know

33. Any dispute can be solved by
  A. quarrelling
  B. dialogue
  C. court
  D. Can't say

34. While driving during night there must be
    A. helmet   B. light source
    C. smooth road   D. controlled speed

35. I like to
    A. wander   B. study
    C. watch television   D. indulge in gossips

36. When I go to appear in an interview, then I wear a clean
    A. shirt   B. pantaloon
    C. dress   D. under wear

ANSWERS

1	2	3	4	5	6	7	8	9	10
A	C	C	C	D	B	C	A	B	D

11	12	13	14	15	16	17	18	19	20
C	D	A	B	C	D	C	D	B	C

21	22	23	24	25	26	27	28	29	30
A	D	B	A	B	B	A	D	C	C

31	32	33	34	35	36
C	C	B	B	B	C

INFORMATION ORDERING TEST

GUIDELINES

1. This is the test of ability to do as per given instructions.
2. Questions in the test include two tables 1 and 2 which you should use to solve it.
3. All quesitons have a test figure included.
4. Every quesiton has a series of process boxes from A to D.
5. All process boxes are divided into three parts-level 1, 2, and 3.
6. Each part in a process box will either have a 'X' or lack it.
7. The value of the part which will have a 'X' needs to be added or subtracted.
8. The value of the part which lacks a 'X' needs to be ignored.

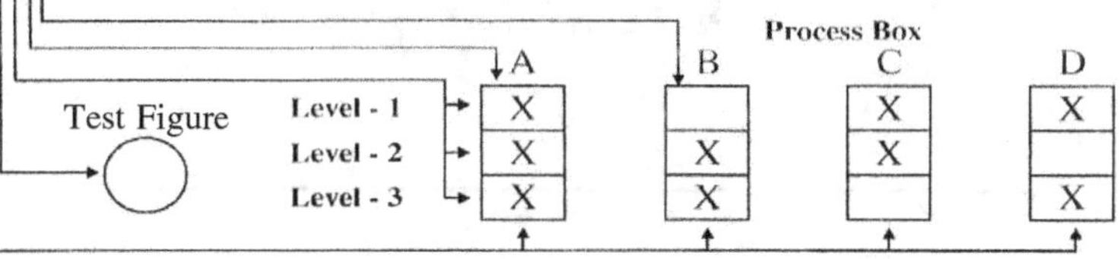

Table -1

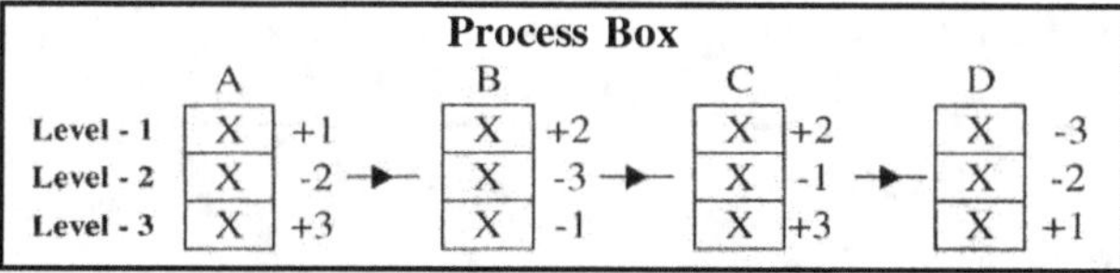

	Process Box							
	A		**B**		**C**		**D**	
Level - 1	X	+1	X	+2	X	+2	X	-3
Level - 2	X	-2	X	-3	X	-1	X	-2
Level - 3	X	+3	X	-1	X	+3	X	+1

Table -2

Figures and their corresponding values

□	☐	■	■	○	○	●	●	△	△	▲	▲
1	2	3	4	5	6	7	8	9	10	11	12

Solve the test using following orders:

1. Firstly, find the value of test figure from figure table 2
2. Either add or subtract the value of X from A-D levels of each process box in the value of test-figure.
3. Find the corresponding figure from the figure table 2 which is related to the value of number obtained at the last level of process box D.
4. Select the answer from options corresponding to the obtained figure.

EXAMPLE

Question Figure

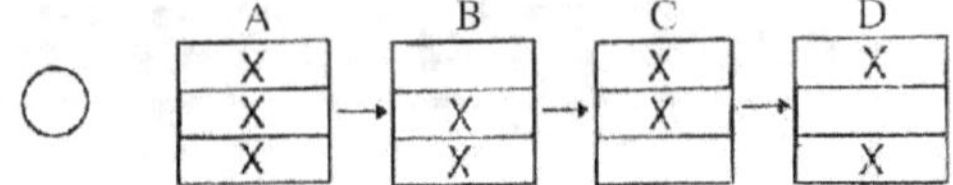

Answer Figure

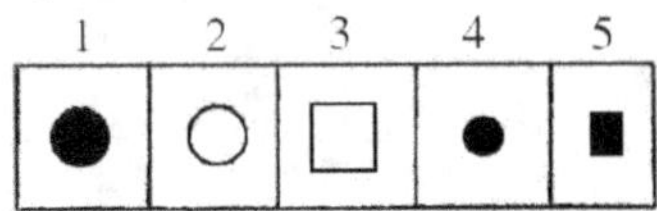

Sol.

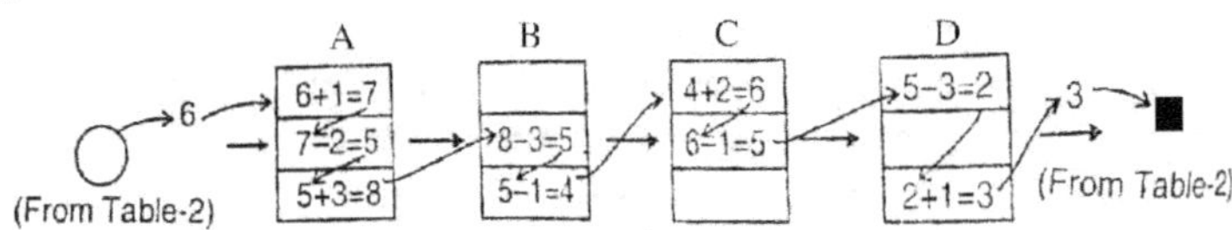

EXERCISE

Table-1

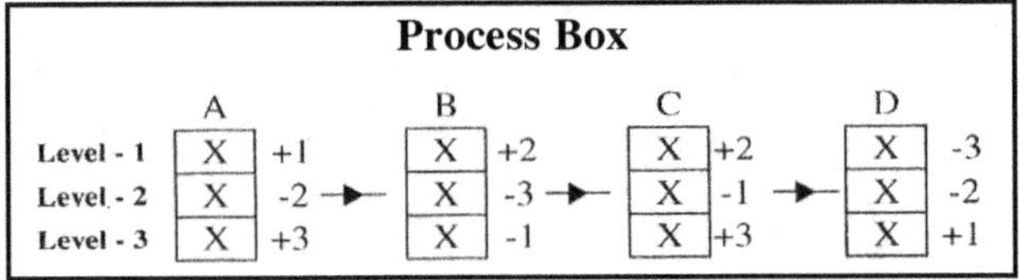

	A		B		C		D	
Level - 1	X	+1	X	+2	X	+2	X	-3
Level - 2	X	-2	X	-3	X	-1	X	-2
Level - 3	X	+3	X	-1	X	+3	X	+1

Table-2

Figures and their corresponding values

□	☐	■	■	○	◯	●	●	△	△	▲	▲
1	2	3	4	5	6	7	8	9	10	11	12

1. Test Figure   **Process Box**

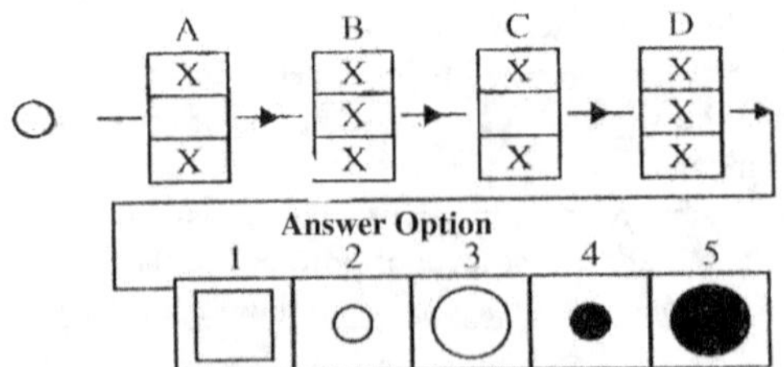

2. Test Figure   Process Box

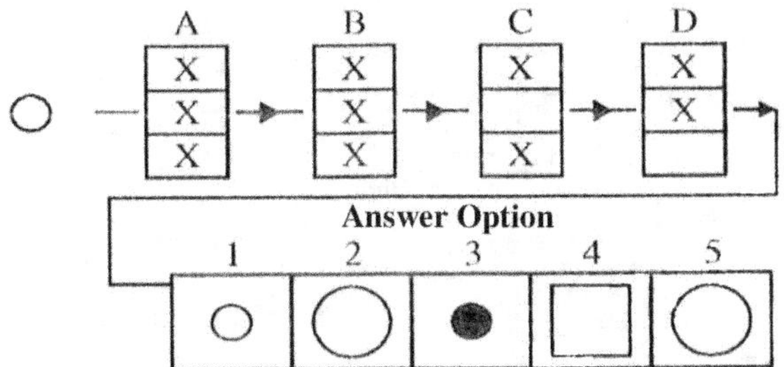

3. Test Figure   Process Box

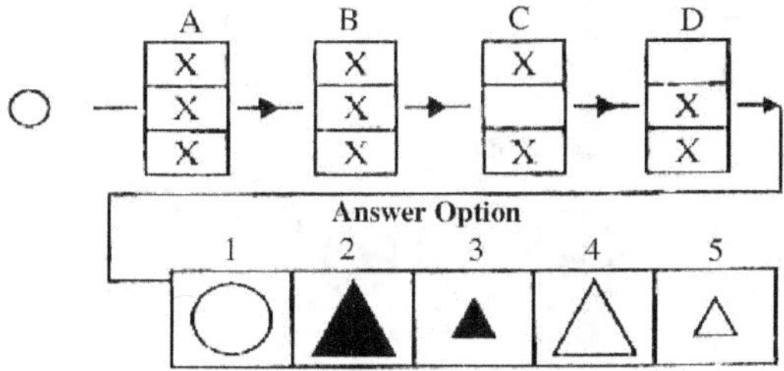

4. Test Figure   Process Box

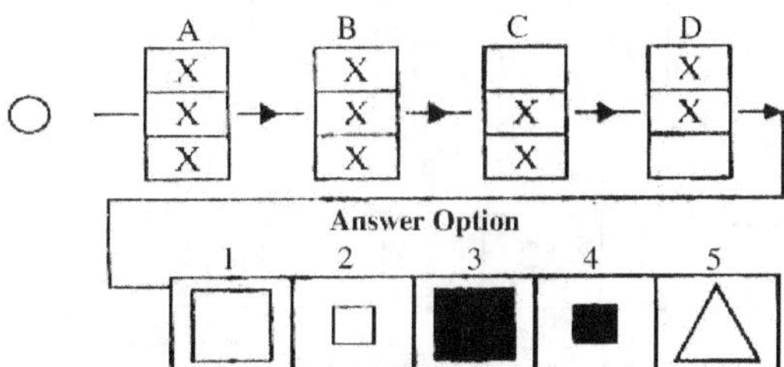

5. Test Figure   Process Box

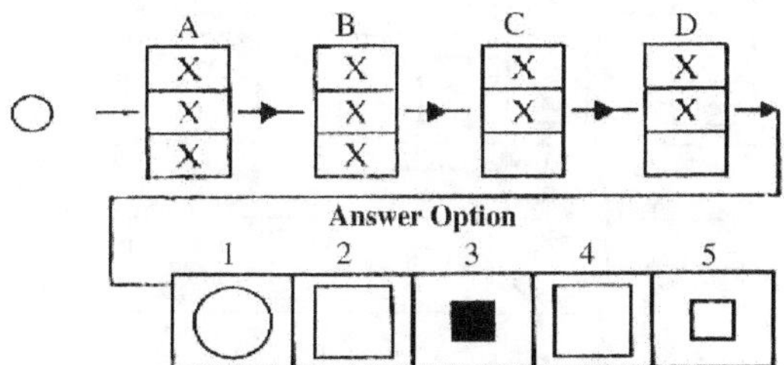

6. Test Figure   Process Box

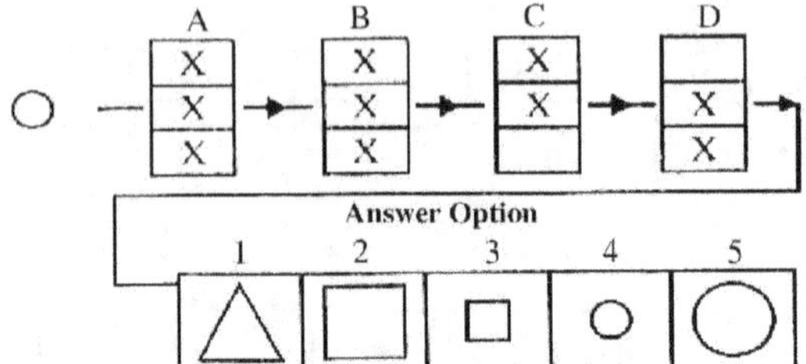

7. Test Figure   Process Box

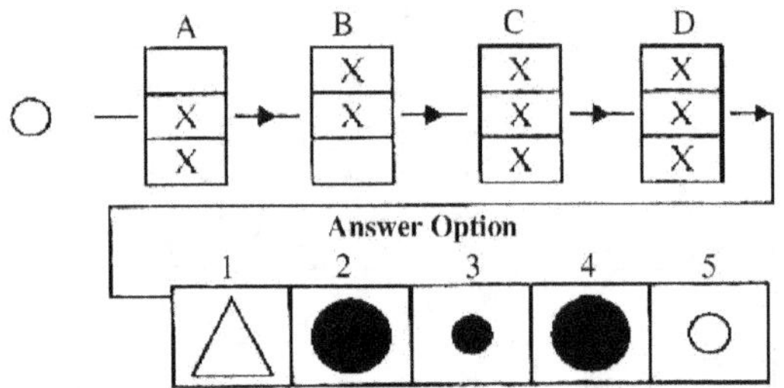

8. Test Figure   Process Box

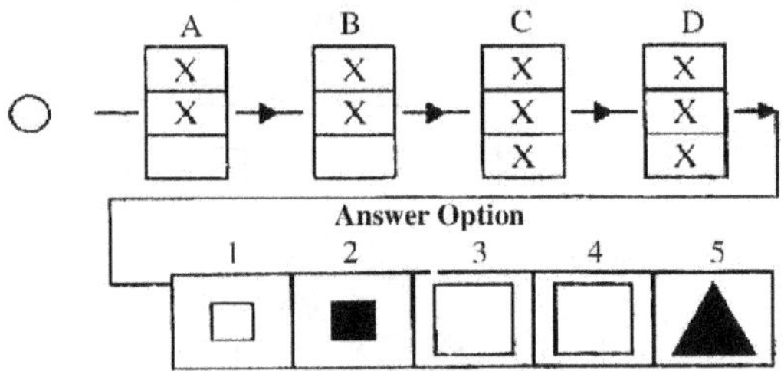

9. Test Figure   Process Box

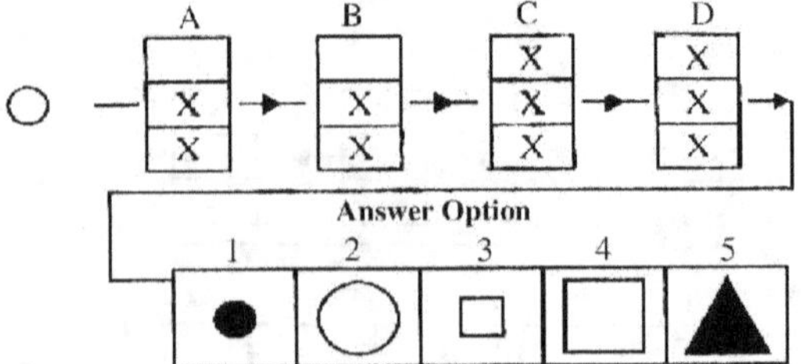

10. Test Figure   Process Box

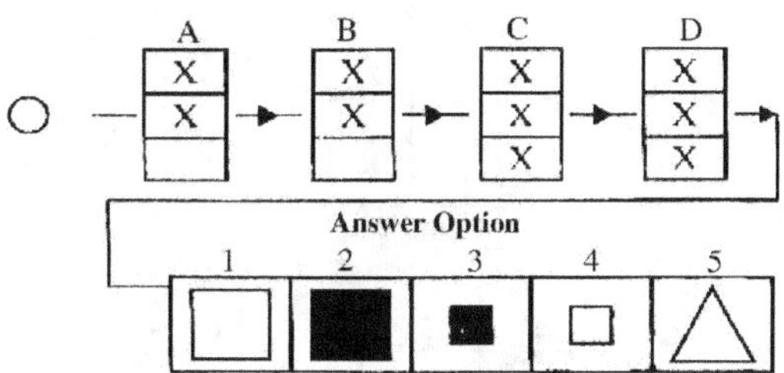

11. Test Figure   Process Box

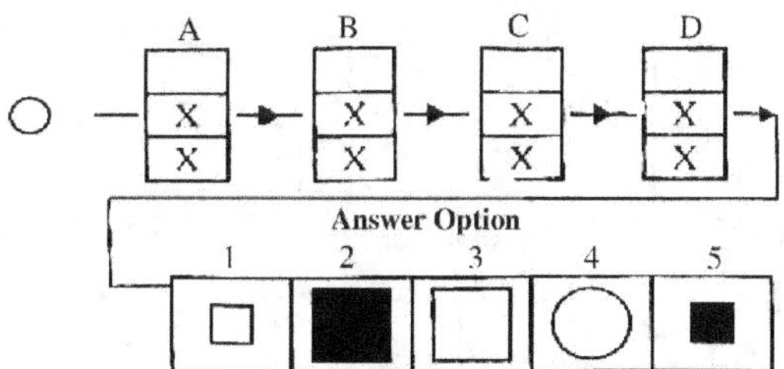

12. Test Figure   Process Box

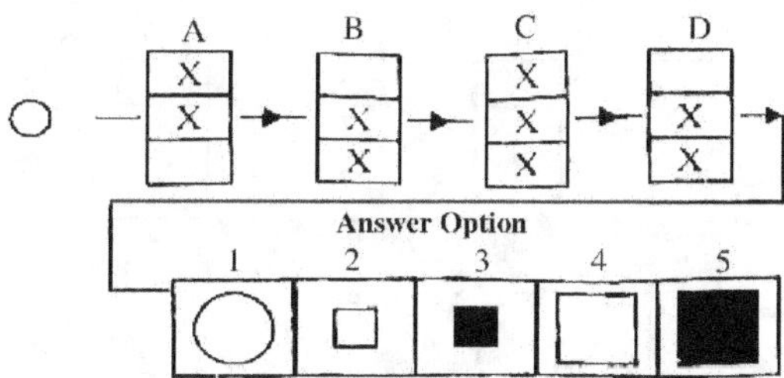

13. Test Figure   Process Box

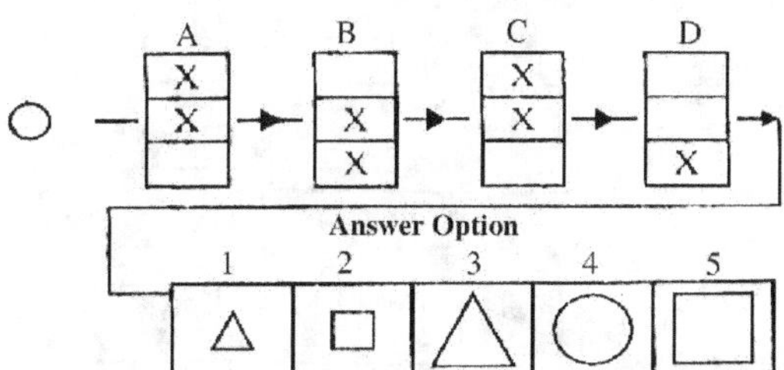

14. Test Figure   **Process Box**

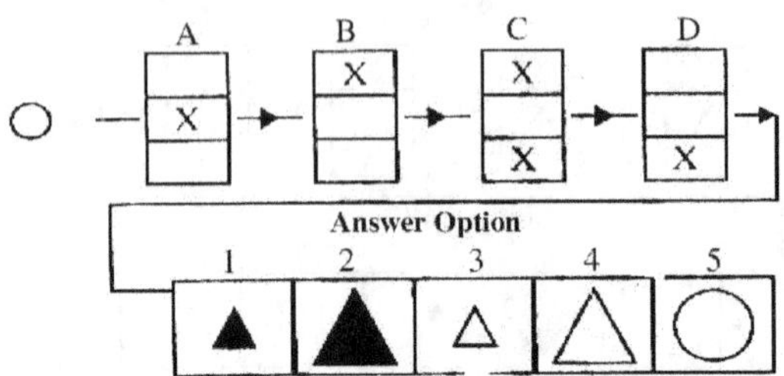

15. Test Figure   **Process Box**

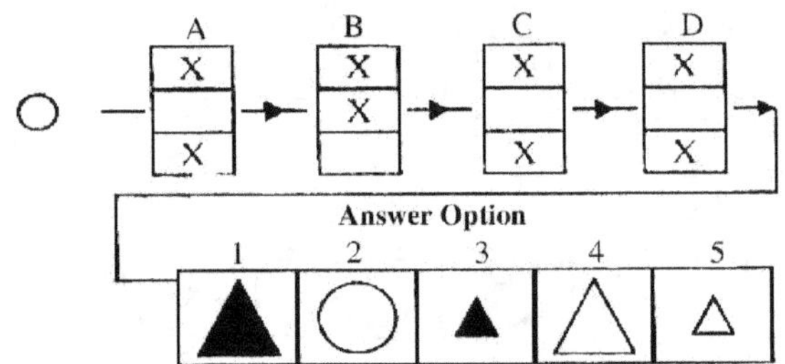

16. Test Figure   **Process Box**

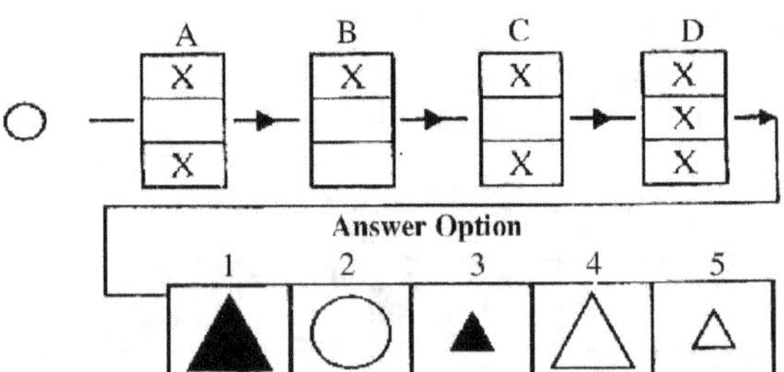

17. Test Figure   **Process Box**

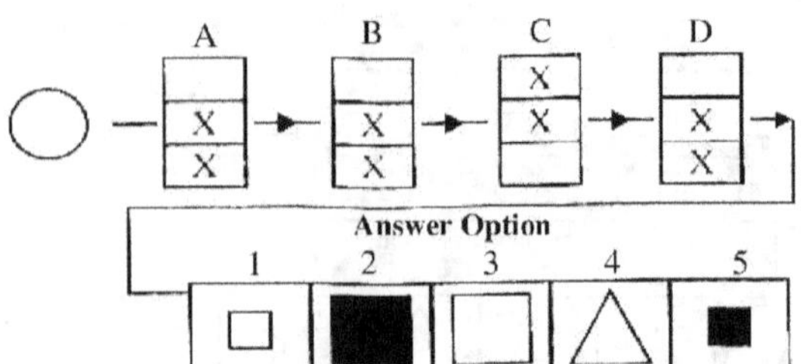

18. Test Figure   **Process Box**

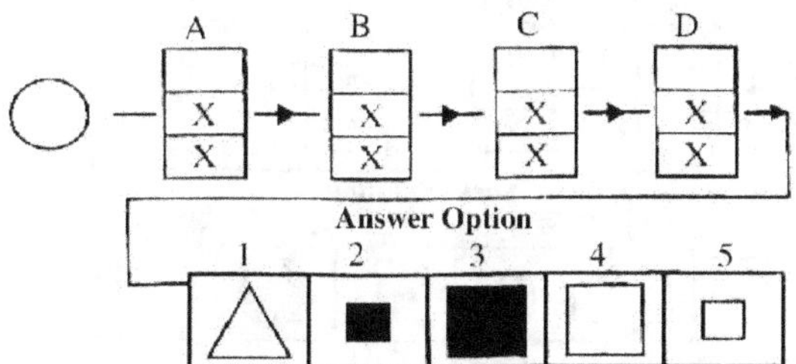

19. Test Figure   **Process Box**

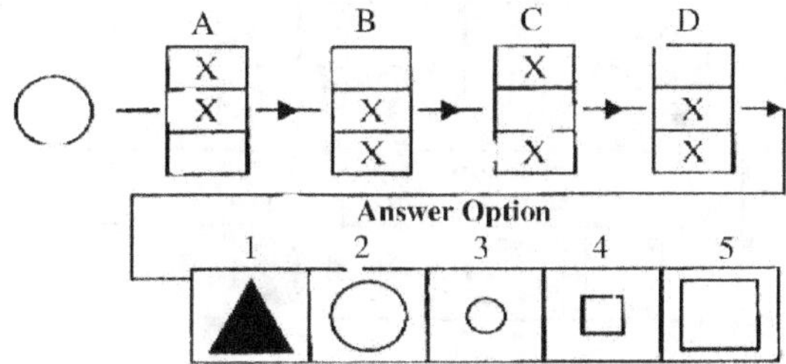

20. Test Figure   **Process Box**

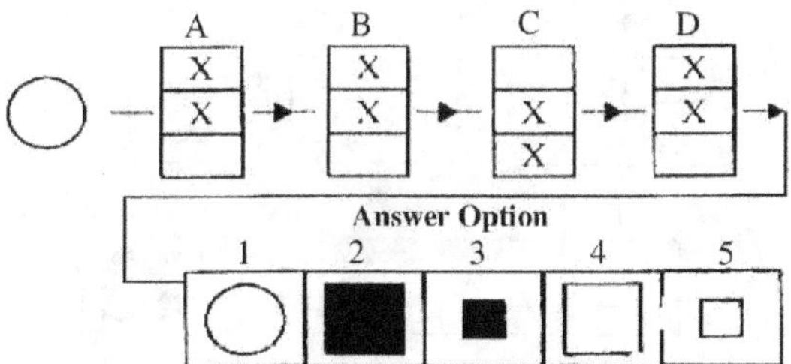

21. Test Figure   **Process Box**

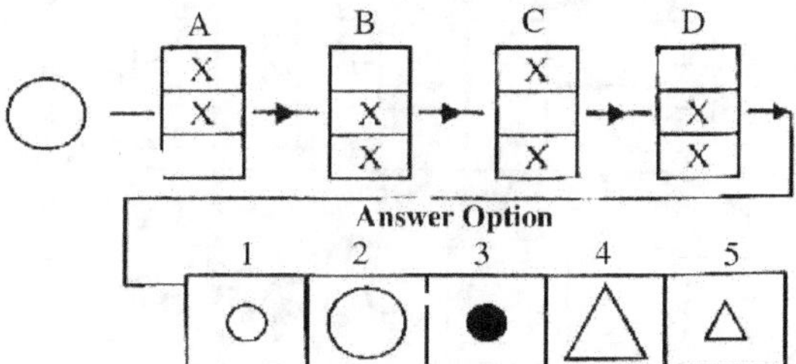

22. Test Figure   Process Box

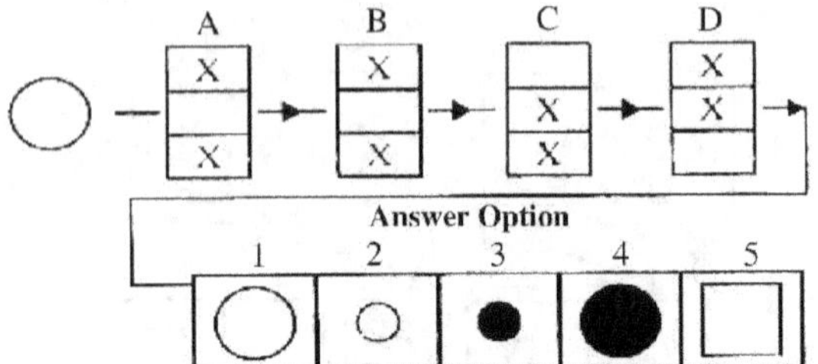

23. Test Figure   Process Box

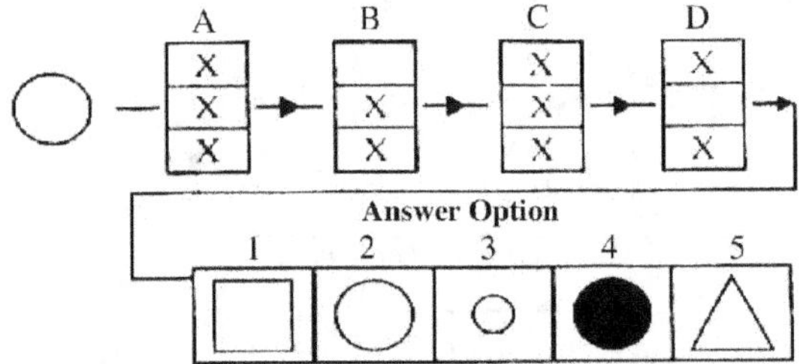

24. Test Figure   Process Box

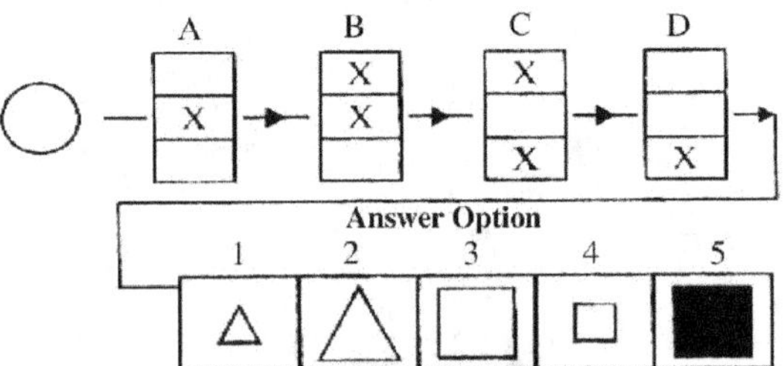

25. Test Figure   Process Box

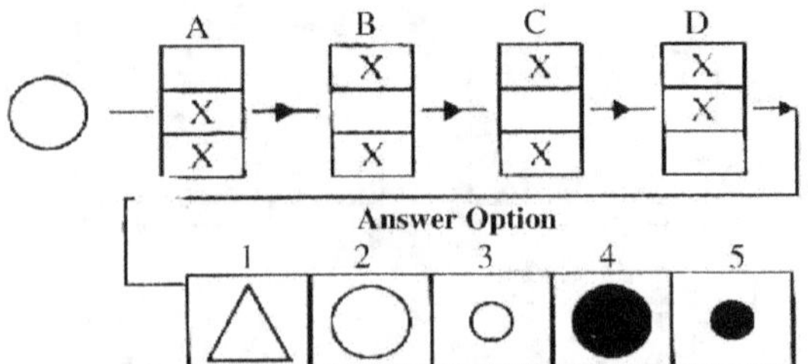

26. Test Figure   Process Box

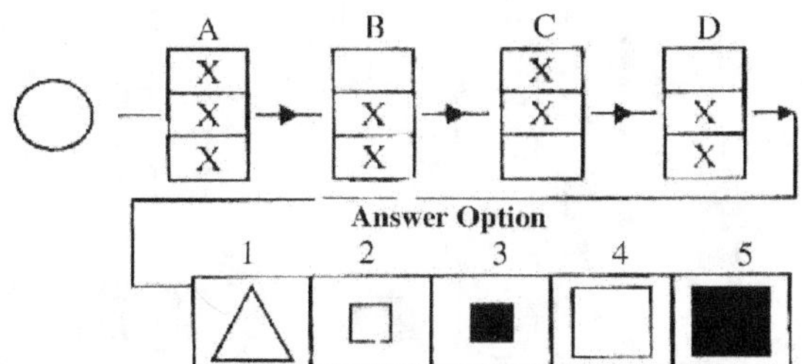

27. Test Figure   Process Box

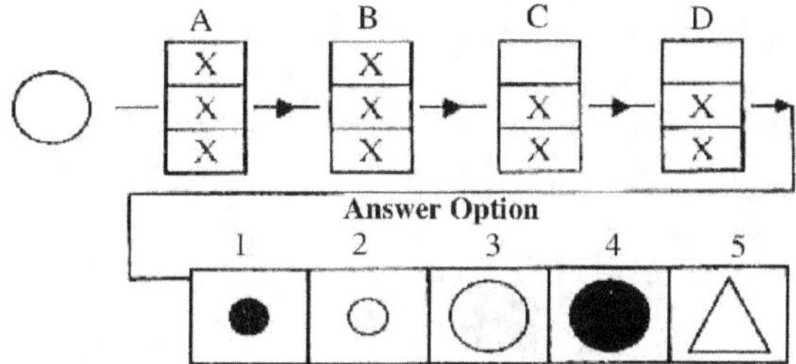

28. Test Figure   Process Box

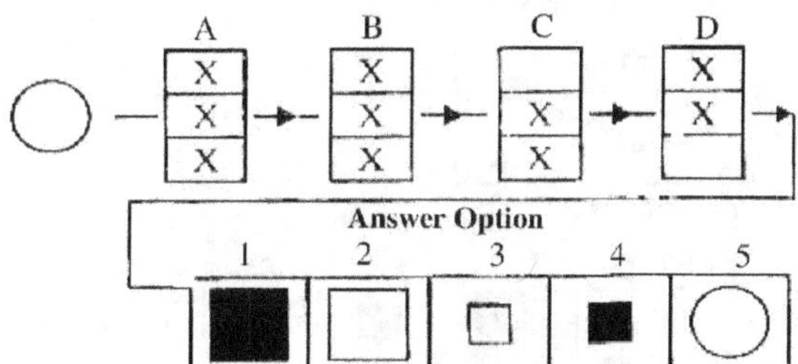

29. Test Figure   Process Box

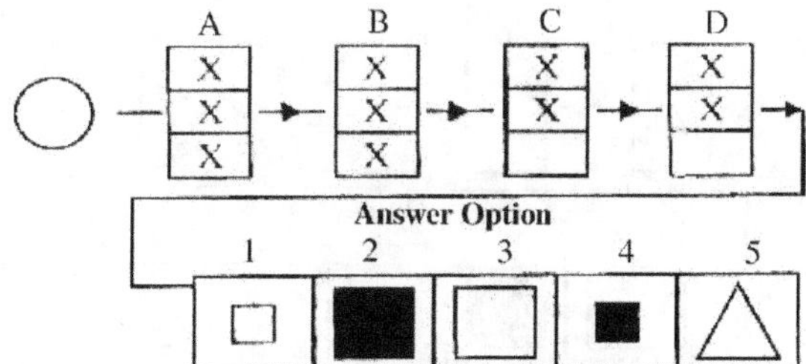

30. Test Figure   Process Box

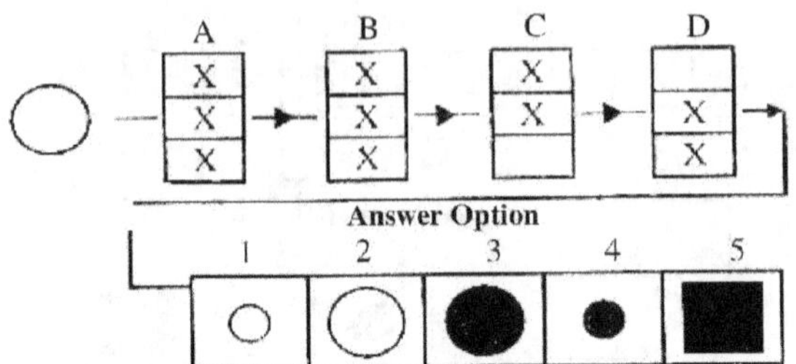

31. Test Figure   Process Box

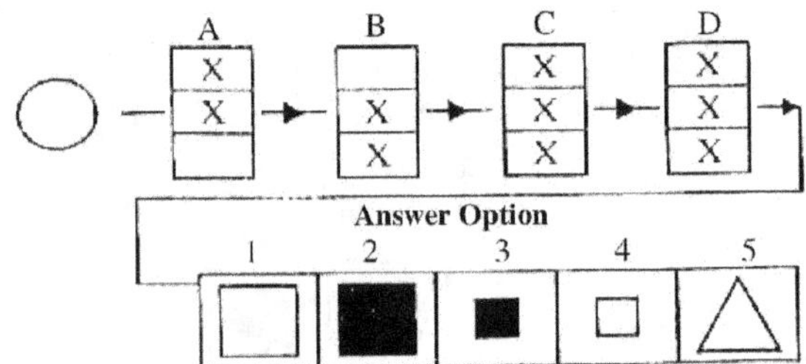

32. Test Figure   Process Box

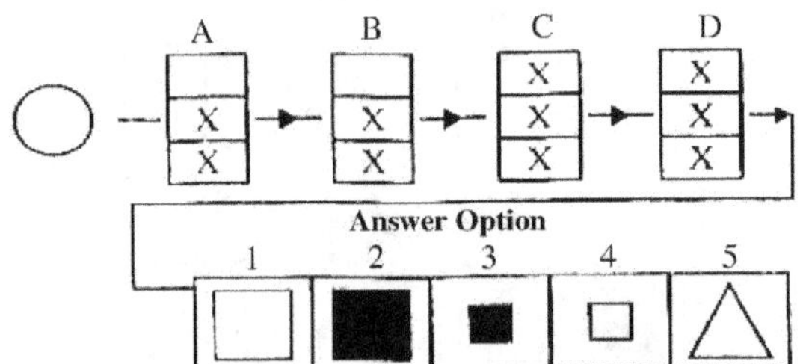

33. Test Figure   Process Box

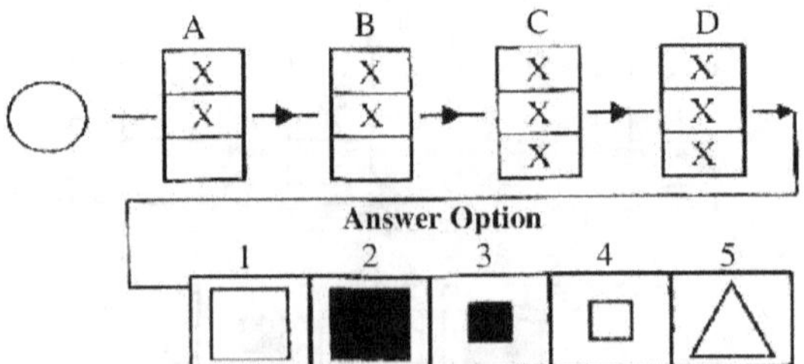

34. Test Figure   **Process Box**

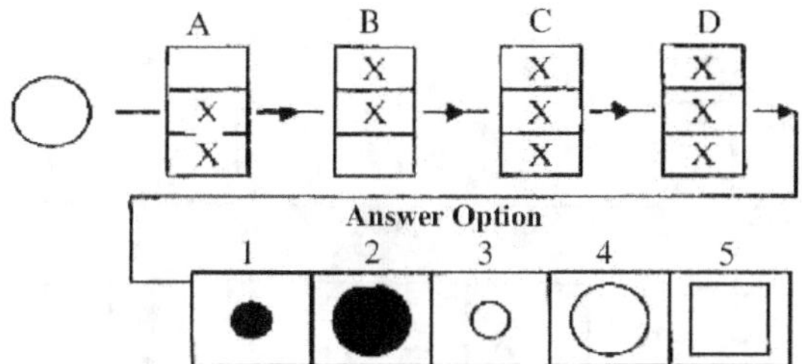

35. Test Figure   **Process Box**

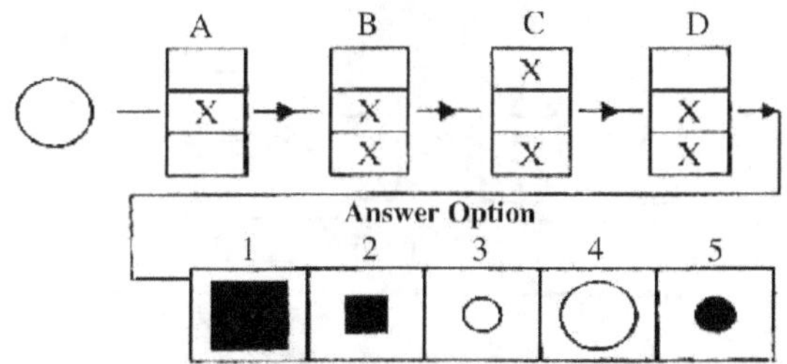

36. Test Figure   **Process Box**

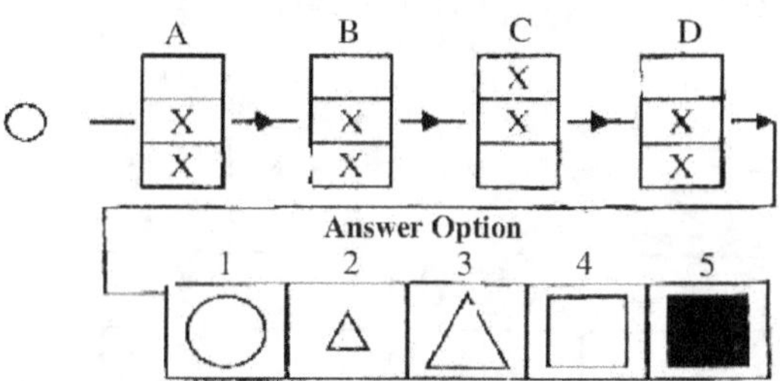

37. Test Figure   **Process Box**

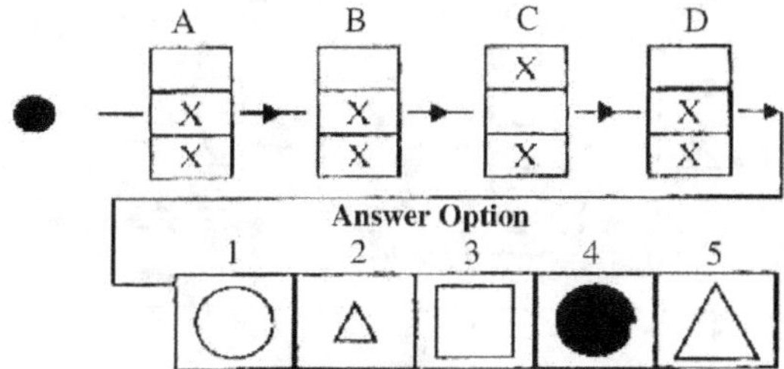

38. Test Figure   Process Box

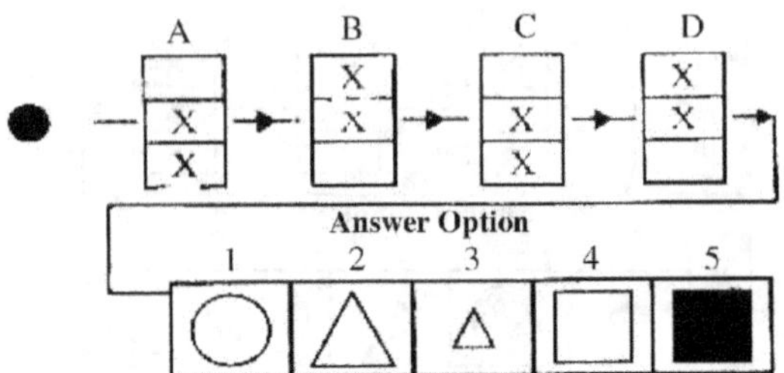

39. Test Figure   Process Box

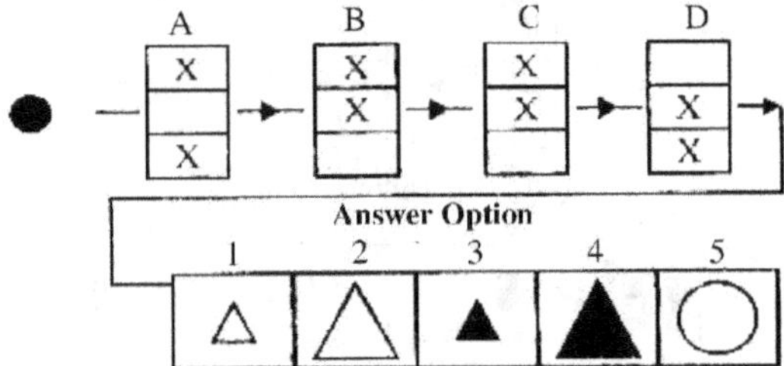

40. Test Figure   Process Box

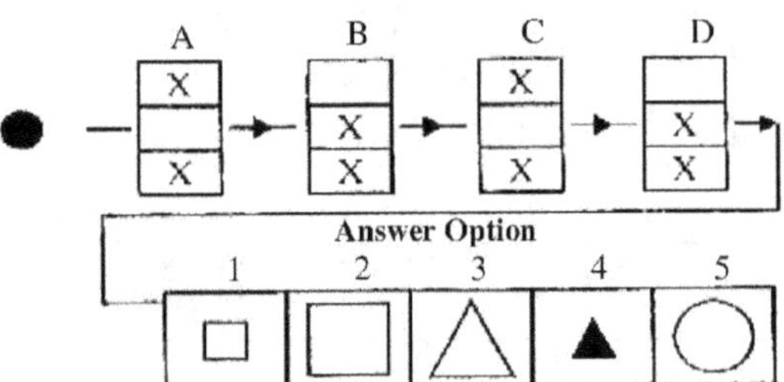

41. Test Figure   Process Box

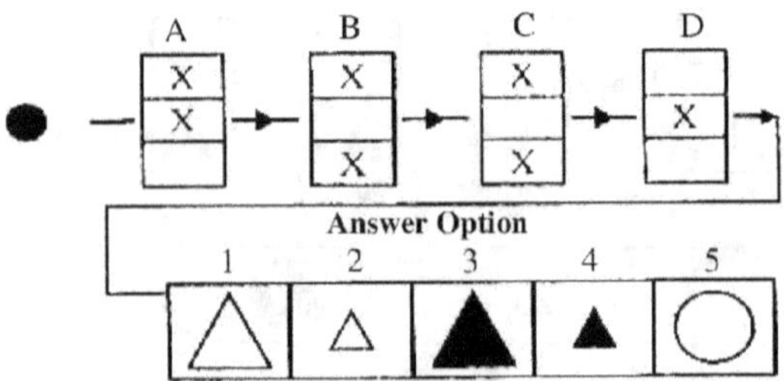

42. Test Figure   **Process Box**

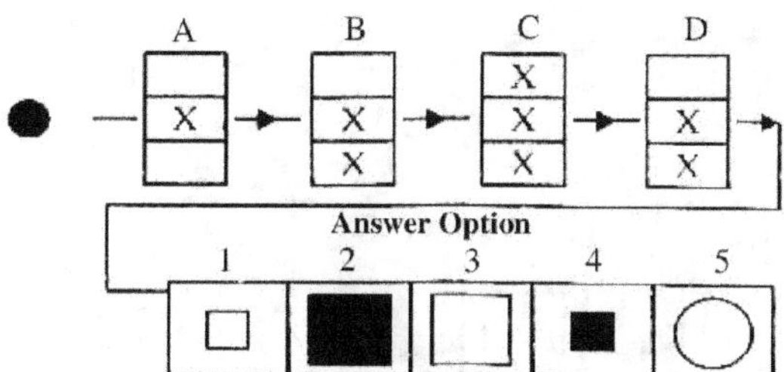

43. Test Figure   **Process Box**

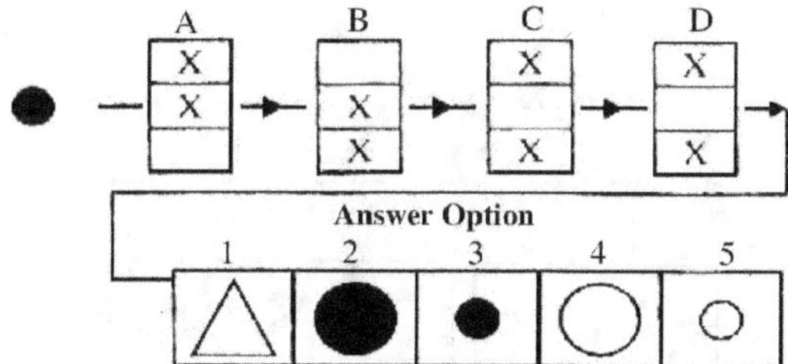

44. Test Figure   **Process Box**

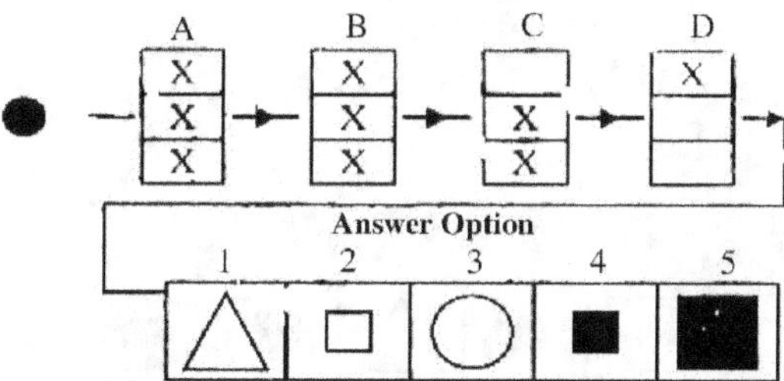

45. Test Figure   **Process Box**

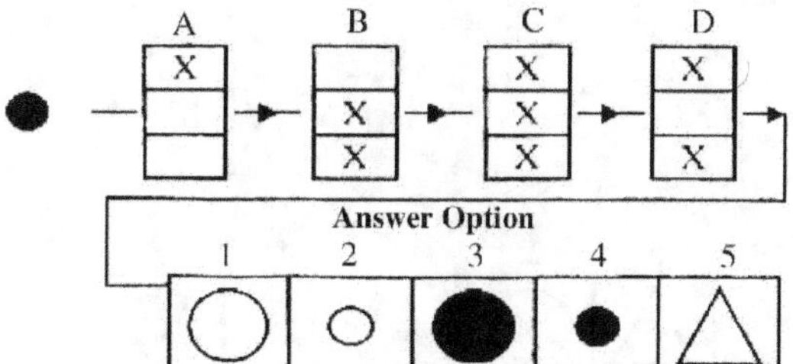

46. Test Figure   Process Box

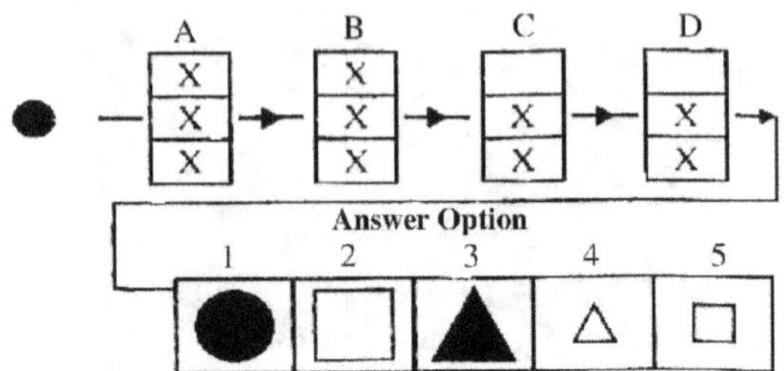

47. Test Figure   Process Box

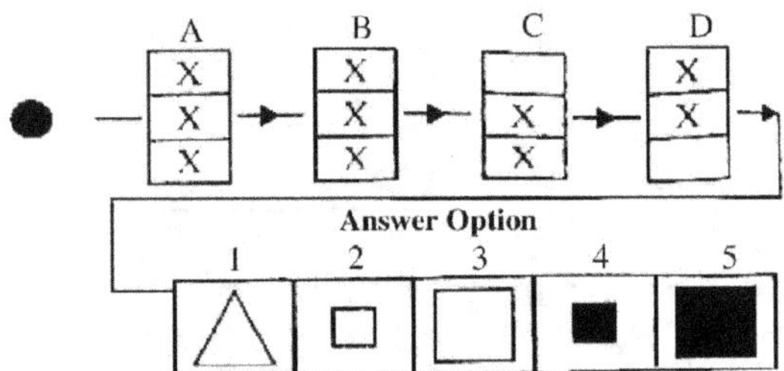

48. Test Figure   Process Box

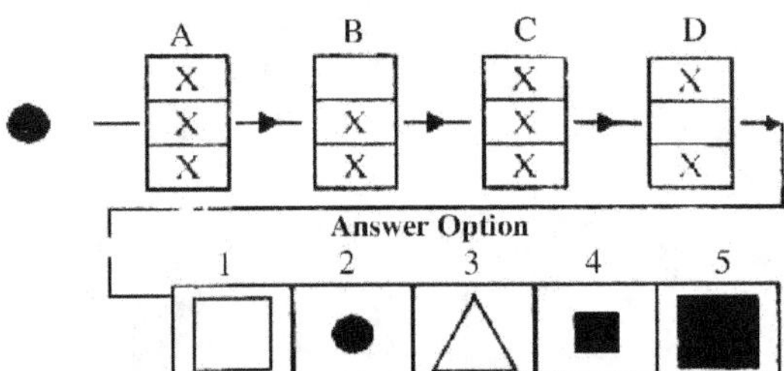

49. Test Figure   Process Box

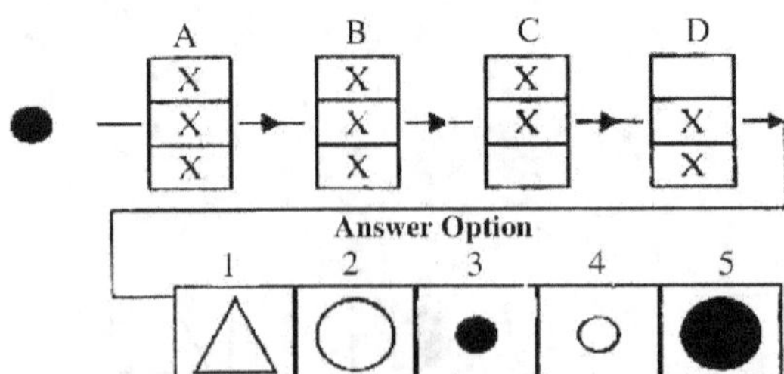

50. Test Figure   Process Box

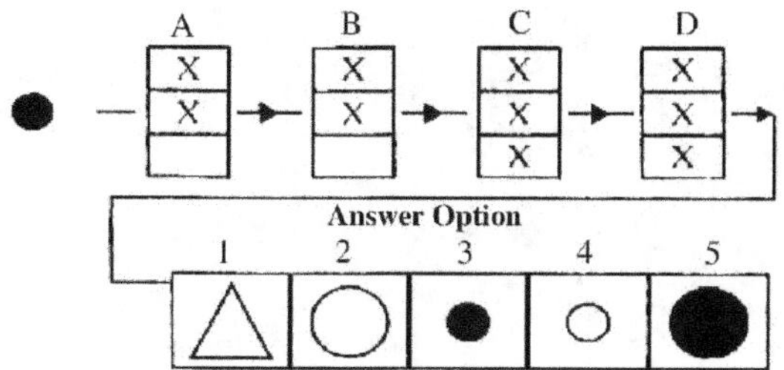

ANSWERS

1	2	3	4	5	6	7	8	9	10
(4)	(1)	(5)	(1)	(5)	(4)	(5)	(2)	(4)	(3)

11	12	13	14	15	16	17	18	19	20
(5)	(3)	(5)	(1)	(3)	(1)	(5)	(3)	(3)	(5)

21	22	23	24	25	26	27	28	29	30
(1)	(4)	(2)	(1)	(4)	(4)	(1)	(4)	(3)	(2)

31	32	33	34	35	36	37	38	39	40
(4)	(3)	(2)	(4)	(1)	(4)	(4)	(5)	(2)	(4)

41	42	43	44	45	46	47	48	49	50
(1)	(2)	(5)	(3)	(1)	(1)	(5)	(2)	(3)	(4)

TEST PAPERS
(SOLVED)

Directions (Qs. 1-72): *In the following questions, similar type of four questions are given on the left side and these figures have been reproduced on the right side which are named as A, B, C, D and E. You have to find the exact reproduction of the question figures from the given five answer figures A, B, C, D and E.*

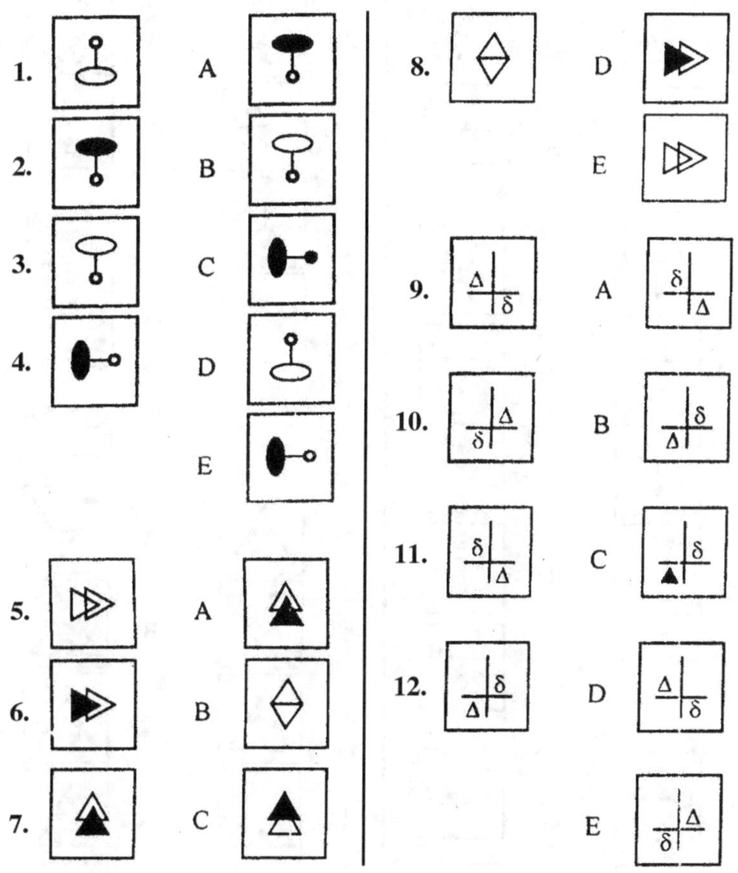

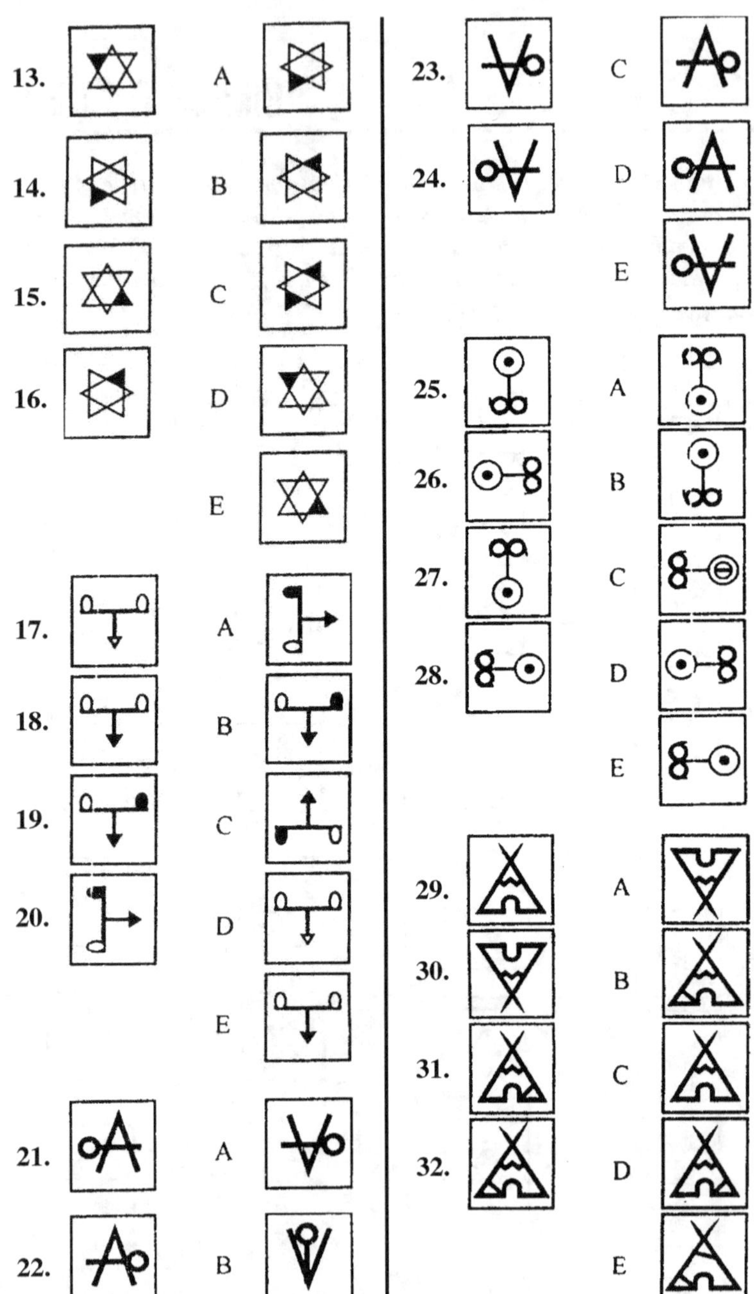

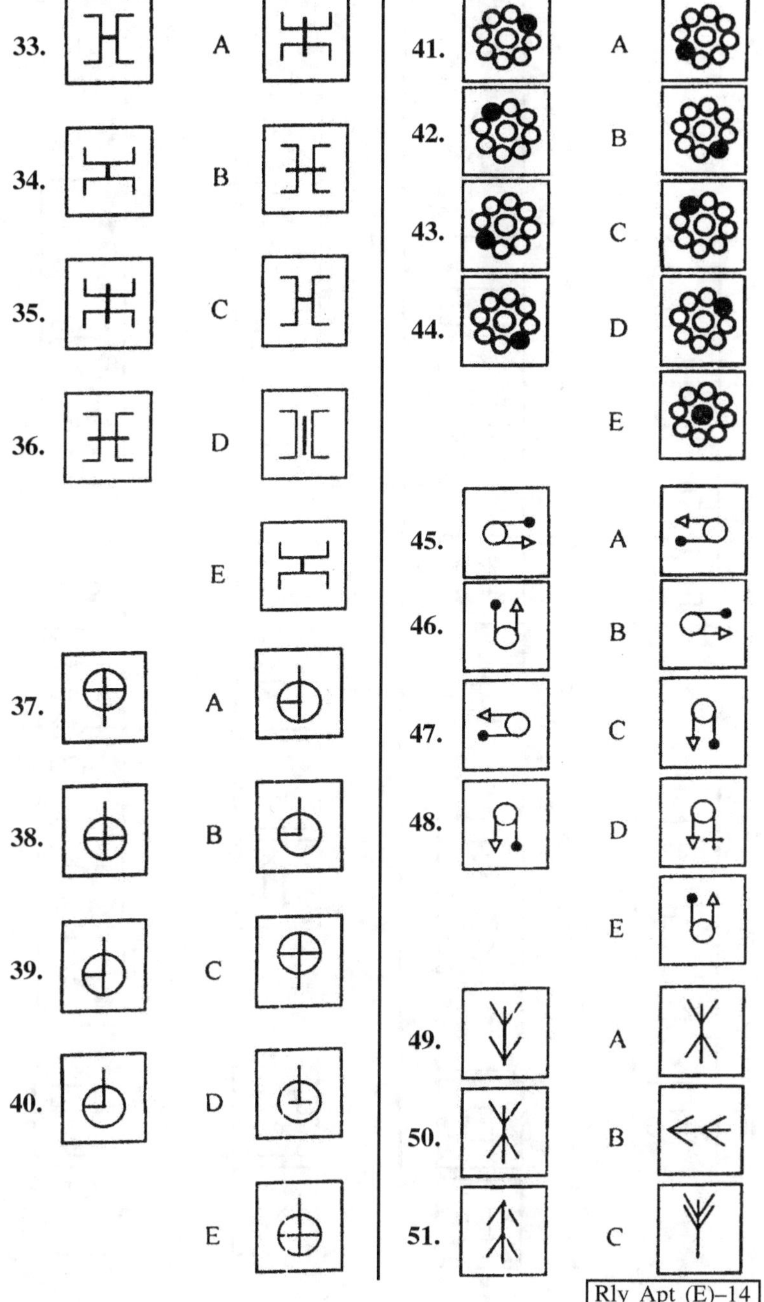

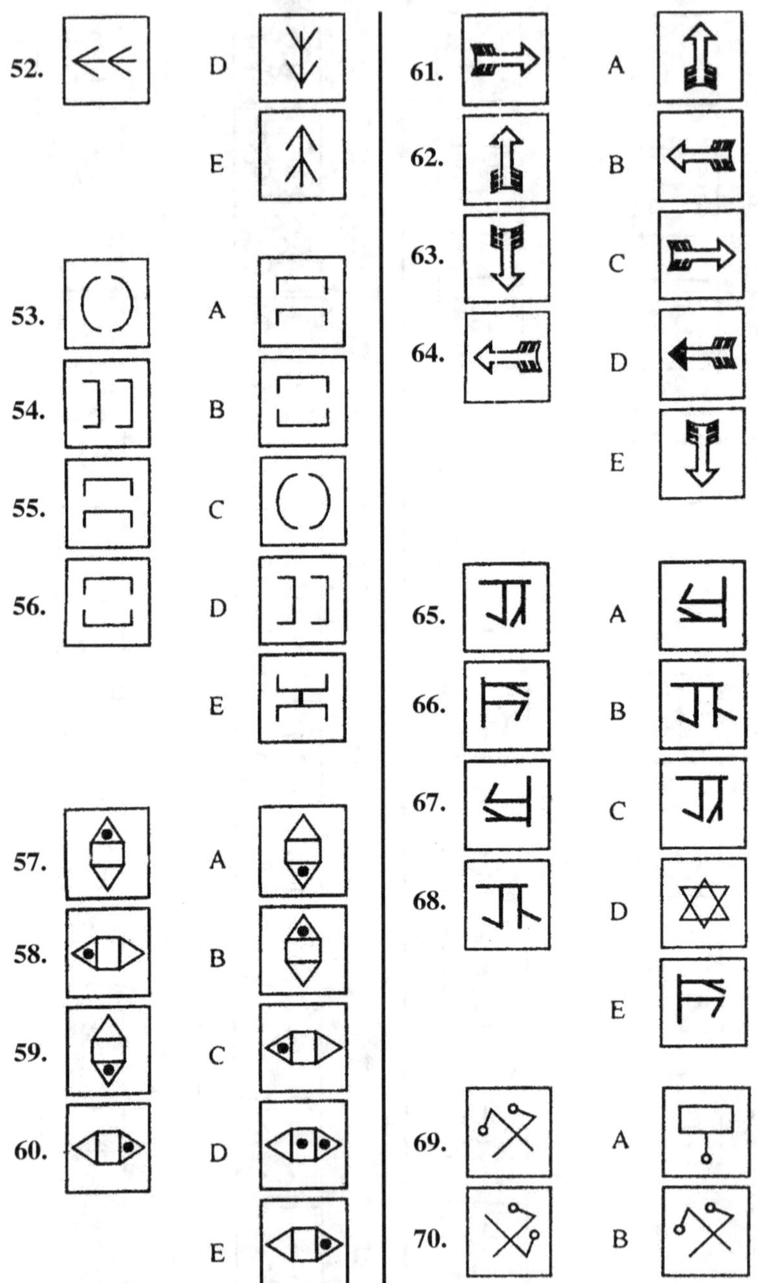

71.  C  **72.** 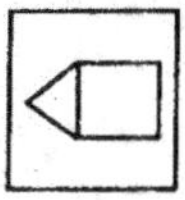 D

E

ANSWERS

1	2	3	4	5	6	7	8	9	10
D	A	B	E	E	D	A	B	D	E

11	12	13	14	15	16	17	18	19	20
A	B	D	A	E	B	D	E	B	A

21	22	23	24	25	26	27	28	29	30
D	C	A	E	B	D	A	E	C	A

31	32	33	34	35	36	37	38	39	40
D	B	C	E	A	B	C	E	A	B

41	42	43	44	45	46	47	48	49	50
D	C	A	B	B	E	A	C	D	A

51	52	53	54	55	56	57	58	59	60
E	B	C	D	A	B	B	C	A	E

61	62	63	64	65	66	67	68	69	70
C	A	E	B	C	E	A	B	B	D

71	72
A	C

FIGURE AND NUMBER COMPARISON TEST

Directions (Qs. 1-21): *Carefully observe the pictures and the correponding numbers on the memory page and mark the correct number on the question-page against the corresponding pictures.*

Memory Page

	12		94		88
	24		23		79
	28		5		64
	27		34		83
	99		51		32

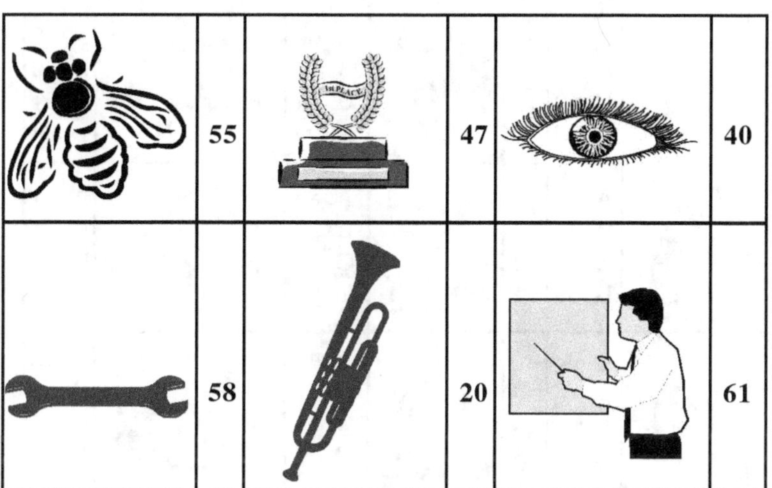

(bee)	55	(trophy)	47	(eye)	40
(wrench)	58	(trumpet)	20	(teacher)	61

Questions Page

No.		Options	No.		Options	No.		Options	No.		Options
1	(teacher)	A. 61 B. 41 C. 30 D. 37	5	(eye)	A. 87 B. 49 C. 40 D. 56	9	(dolphin)	A. 99 B. 70 C. 95 D. 51			
2	(helicopter)	A. 40 B. 11 C. 32 D. 60	6	(trumpet)	A. 24 B. 71 C. 55 D. 20	10	(ferry)	A. 34 B. 48 C. 90 D. 16			
3	(printer)	A. 80 B. 41 C. 83 D. 18	7	(bee)	A. 07 B. 95 C. 55 D. 89	11	(people)	A. 98 B. 40 C. 25 D. 28			
4	(snake)	A. 39 B. 21 C. 99 D. 22	8	(scroll)	A. 79 B. 54 C. 33 D. 23	12	(figure)	A. 55 B. 59 C. 64 D. 39			

13		A. 58 B. 72 C. 09 D. 29	**16**		A. 66 B. 41 C. 24 D. 99	**19**		A. 98 B. 40 C. 51 D. 88
14		A. 5 B. 45 C. 90 D. 39	**17**		A. 87 B. 32 C. 47 D. 94	**20**		A. 41 B. 71 C. 94 D. 30
15		A. 88 B. 60 C. 90 D. 27	**18**		A. 47 B. 33 C. 80 D. 23	**21**		A. 12 B. 58 C. 91 D. 98

ANSWERS

1	2	3	4	5	6	7	8	9	10
A	C	C	C	A	A	D	C	D	C

11	12	13	14	15	16	17	18	19	20
A	C	C	D	D	A	D	C	D	C

21
A

Directions (Qs. 1-50): *There are 50 questions based on bricks' mutual contact below. These questions are divided in 10 sections. In each section, a different arrangement of bricks is done to form a cube or some other figure. Some of the bricks have been marked A, B, C, D, and E. You have to count the number of bricks which are in contact with the particular brick.*

SECTION-1

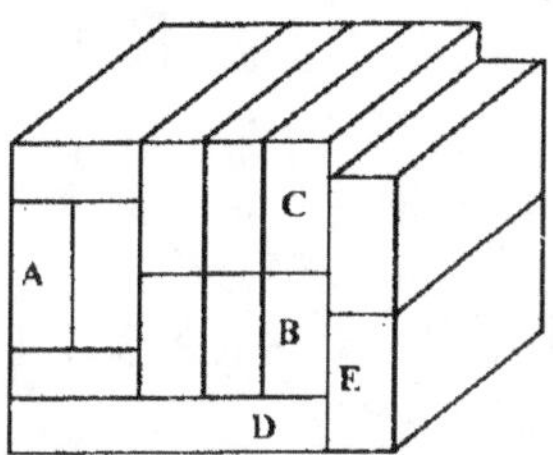

Question: How many bricks are touched by bricks :
1. A. (?)   2. B. (?)   3. C. (?)
4. D. (?)   5. E. (?)

SECTION-2

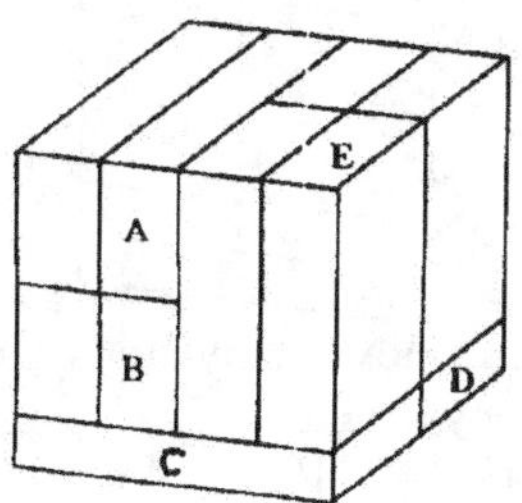

Question: How many bricks are touched by bricks :
6. A. (?)   7. B. (?)   8. C. (?)
9. D. (?)   10. E. (?)

SECTION-3

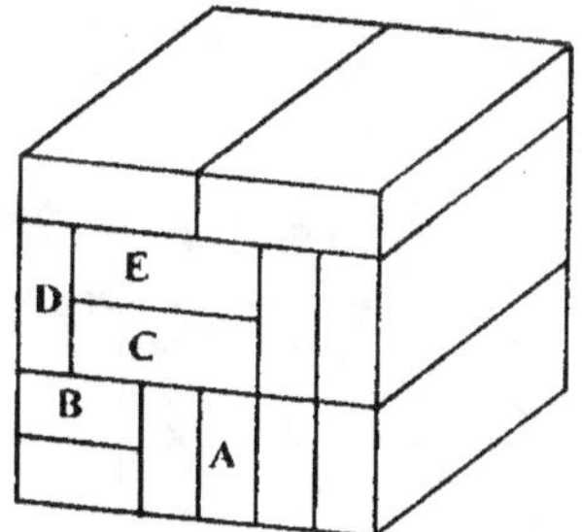

Question: How many bricks are touched by bricks :
11. A. (?)   12. B. (?)   13. C. (?)
14. D. (?)   15. E. (?)

SECTION-4

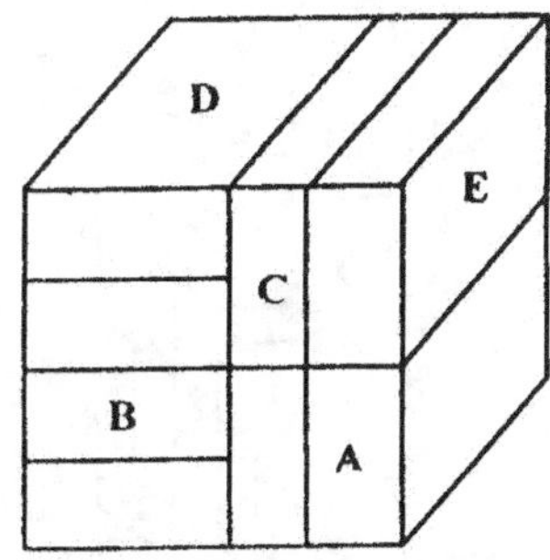

Question: How many bricks are touched by bricks :
16. A. (?)   17. B. (?)   18. C. (?)
19. D. (?)   20. E. (?)

SECTION-5

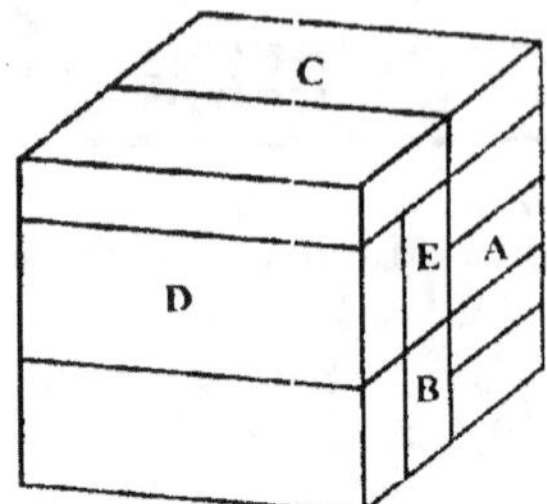

Question: How many bricks are touched by bricks :
21. A. (?) 22. B. (?) 23. C. (?)
24. D. (?) 25. E. (?)

SECTION-6

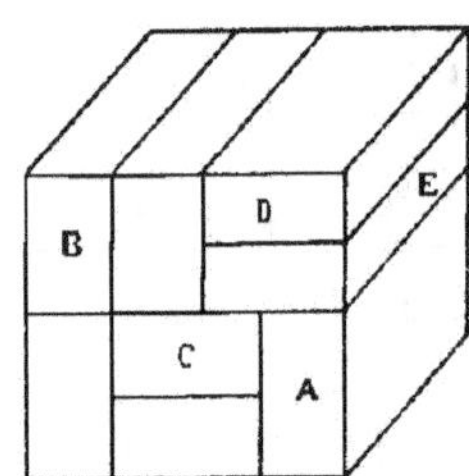

Question: How many bricks are touched by bricks :
26. A. (?) 27. B. (?) 28. C. (?)
29. D. (?) 30. E. (?)

SECTION-7

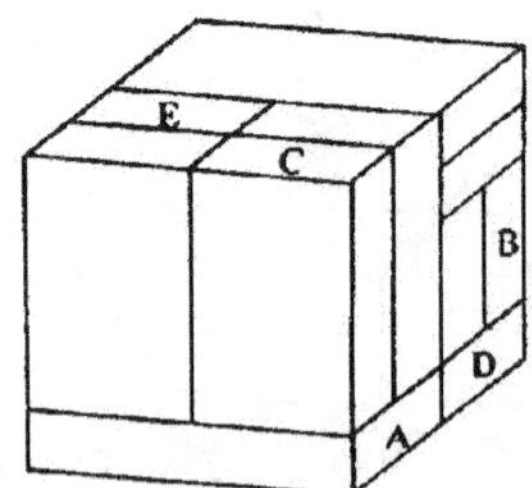

Question: How many bricks are touched by bricks :
31. A. (?) 32. B. (?) 33. C. (?)
34. D. (?) 35. E. (?)

SECTION-8

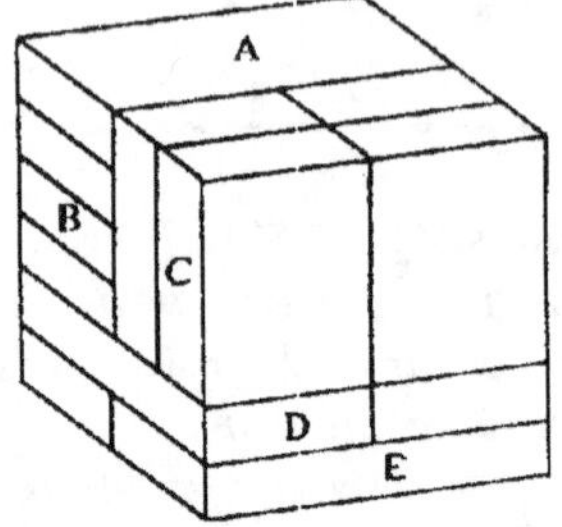

Question: How many bricks are touched by bricks :
36. A. (?) 37. B. (?) 38. C. (?)
39. D. (?) 40. E. (?)

SECTION-9

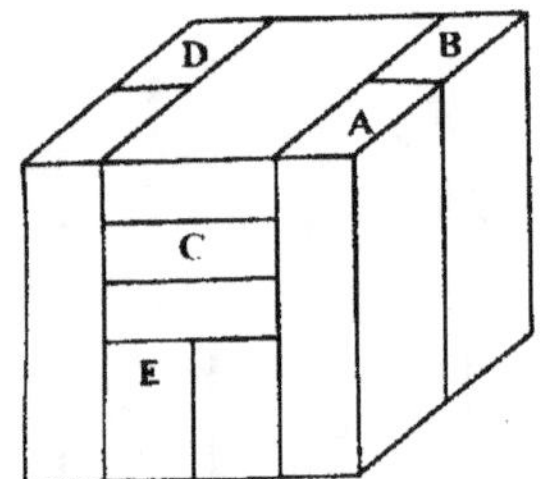

Question: How many bricks are touched by bricks :
41. A. (?) 42. B. (?) 43. C. (?)
44. D. (?) 45. E. (?)

SECTION-10

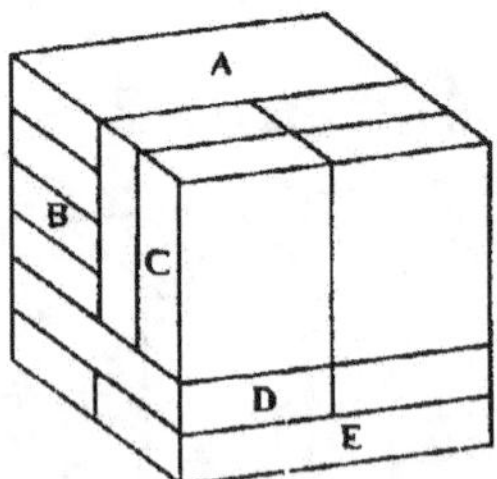

Question: How many bricks are touched by bricks :
46. A. (?) 47. B. (?) 48. C. (?)
49. D. (?) 50. E. (?)

ANSWERS

1	2	3	4	5	6	7	8	9	10
(3)	(5)	(3)	(5)	(3)	(4)	(5)	(5)	(5)	(3)

11	12	13	14	15	16	17	18	19	20
(3)	(4)	(6)	(4)	(5)	(2)	(3)	(4)	(2)	(2)

21	22	23	24	25	26	27	28	29	30
(3)	(4)	(2)	(3)	(5)	(3)	(2)	(5)	(2)	(4)

31	32	33	34	35	36	37	38	39	40
(5)	(3)	(3)	(3)	(6)	(3)	(2)	(3)	(6)	(3)

41	42	43	44	45	46	47	48	49	50
(5)	(5)	(6)	(5)	(4)	(3)	(4)	(3)	(6)	(3)

Directions (Qs. 1-75): *In the following questions there are four large numbers under the column A, B, C and D. Select the option having digit '6'. Indicate your answer 'E' if digit '6' does not appear in any option or it appears in more than one options.*

1. A. 191988768 B. 7654321 C. 544789231 D. 231453247
2. A. 30313263 B. 3031323 C. 353378 D. 3940417567
3. A. 43444523 B. 400047489 C. 49505152 D. 5354558
4. A. 1298324 B. 9187344554 C. 543621 D. 1234517
5. A. 18358350 B. 228351923 C. 40675321 D. 1234578
6. A. 19876543 B. 92323631 C. 1562312 D. 8345671
7. A. 1987543 B. 3213212 C. 712321 D. 3343577
8. A. 37335346 B. 363323130 C. 63031323 D. 3334635
9. A. 009383987 B. 198543 C. 8854321 D. 99123451
10. A. 456410152 B. 303546041 C. 455051 D. 789232
11. A. 24681012 B. 1411820 C. 2224264545 D. 2527283
12. A. 233031323 B. 134353637 C. 3738639 D. 494142463
13. A. 112445584 B. 0764849 C. 90650721 D. 2312336
14. A. 4344454 B. 4478449 C. 5051525 D. 53545556
15. A. 559849849 B. 39849845 C. 274984984 D. 32149855
16. A. 987543 B. 875432 C. 78910162 D. 336213151
17. A. 247486 B. 49505152 C. 4535455 D. 5575859
18. A. 4748987 B. 8546987 C. 987892 D. 928754
19. A. 11999987 B. 889754 C. 321632133 D. 4545789
20. A. 495056152 B. 5356455 C. 55758767 D. 59612349
21. A. 5234588 B. 7891061112 C. 136141517 D. 1819202
22. A. 02324252 B. 023246252 C. 232425 D. 62322589
23. A. 229988877 B. 54321 C. 5213234 D. 55321623
24. A. 44354555 B. 5575185 C. 98991765 D. 12345455457
25. A. 215649819 B. 19819819 C. 39996998 D. 19654980

26. A. 1919323　　B. 1981997　　C. 1989998　　D. 1998889

27. A. 7702103104　B. 105101007　C. 108109110　D. 7711211314

28. A. 15165251　　B. 17714　　C. 3167183　　D. 1819202

29. A. 1234555　　B. 455454321　C. 2134511　　D. 78910675

30. A. 82232642　　B. 25242627　C. 282682930　D. 3132545

31. A. 3577372　　B. 383140　　C. 41424312　　D. 344543215

32. A. 178678　　B. 2342387864　C. 23645832　　D. 783454

33. A. 134547　　B. 589102　　C. 578234　　D. 1346578

34. A. 1234567　　B. 7654321　　C. 234578　　D. 2346489

35. A. 123498　　B. 987543　　C. 121234　　D. 56789

36. A. 9867543　　B. 321453　　C. 6782345　　D. 2368974

37. A. 3343212　　B. 2122443　　C. 345321　　D. 123456

38. A. 997543　　B. 321537　　C. 478923　　D. 278911

39. A. 888699　　B. 2345632　　C. 4434567　　D. 578911

40. A. 8922968　　B. 2335321　　C. 9234555　　D. 5463212

41. A. 545234523　B. 2323632　　C. 2345573　　D. 789611

42. A. 78993213　　B. 2345232　　C. 5453263　　D. 42345630

43. A. 79234506　　B. 37869234　　C. 47890232　　D. 7892622

44. A. 23654071　　B. 2436409　　C. 283213　　D. 246222

45. A. 43141516　　B. 227181920　C. 202612223　D. 2324625252

46. A. 4122232425　B. 2522728　　C. 272936031　D. 12336345

47. A. 01323556　　B. 94353631　　C. 9637381　　D. 38394601

48. A. 10770415　　B. 94883959　　C. 95979896　　D. 9910162034

49. A. 77014105　　B. 19161084　　C. 160111　　D. 77211411

50. A. 13475016　　B. 101101　　C. 10101103　　D. 1011601103

51. A. 44923456　　B. 789231　　C. 789231　　D. 732123

52. A. 987659　　B. 554578961　C. 11312345　　D. 24535889

53. A. 272829565　B. 373839　　C. 404146243　D. 444547

54. A. 48495213465　B. 5051525　　C. 52537754　　D. 555444758

55. A. 12234532543　B. 83845　　C. 999783　　D. 97070715

56. A. 22987054　　B. 19819976　　C. 5677812　　D. 923454554

57. A. 1986705　　B. 5564321　　C. 9768078　　D. 33455576

58. A. 198998　　B. 5432121　　C. 2345447　　D. 4569788

59. A. 8564532123 B. 89362333   C. 00587896   D. 03457896

60. A. 54321188   B. 23457786   C. 878999   D. 987543216

61. A. 121326134   B. 454545   C. 321321633   D. 6344555

62. A. 789231   B. 78923211   C. 2687814141   D. 543654421

63. A. 1989768954   B. 19876534345 C. 0254356   D. 002345732

64. A. 319681999   B. 39898699   C. 63989998   D. 8756321

65. A. 0102986999   B. 23453   C. 654321   D. 3213216333

66. A. 0098969   B. 98654321   C. 32326333   D. 4532156

67. A. 6123325   B. 57890896   C. 231362331   D. 5543216

68. A. 1987453548   B. 32122334   C. 57894367   D. 234578

69. A. 5599398   B. 8886777   C. 6543216   D. 234523

70. A. 7986717223   B. 747567222   C. 67787980   D. 818286381

71. A. 858878   B. 8886990   C. 91929394   D. 9599798

72. A. 6273747   B. 7267374   C. 75777   D. 7892361

73. A. 23456123   B. 62345123   C. 344389231   D. 23145622

74. A. 1987500   B. 65432114   C. 005432811   D. 154321179

75. A. 198757   B. 00789231   C. 6954321   D. 99213213321

ANSWERS

1	2	3	4	5	6	7	8	9	10
E	E	E	C	C	E	E	E	E	E

11	12	13	14	15	16	17	18	19	20
E	E	E	D	E	E	A	B	C	E

21	22	23	24	25	26	27	28	29	30
E	E	D	C	E	E	E	E	D	E

31	32	33	34	35	36	37	38	39	40
E	E	D	E	D	E	D	E	E	E

41	42	43	44	45	46	47	48	49	50
E	E	E	E	E	E	E	E	E	E

51	52	53	54	55	56	57	58	59	60
A	E	E	A	E	E	E	D	E	E

61	62	63	64	65	66	67	68	69	70
E	E	E	E	E	E	E	C	E	E

71	72	73	74	75
B	E	E	B	C

MEMORY TEST

Directions (Qs. 1-12): *Carefully observe the memory page and find out the exact position of the pictures/figures given on the question page.*

SET-1

MEMORY PAGE

QUESTION PAGE

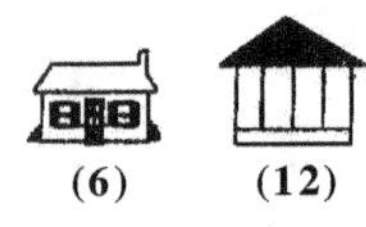

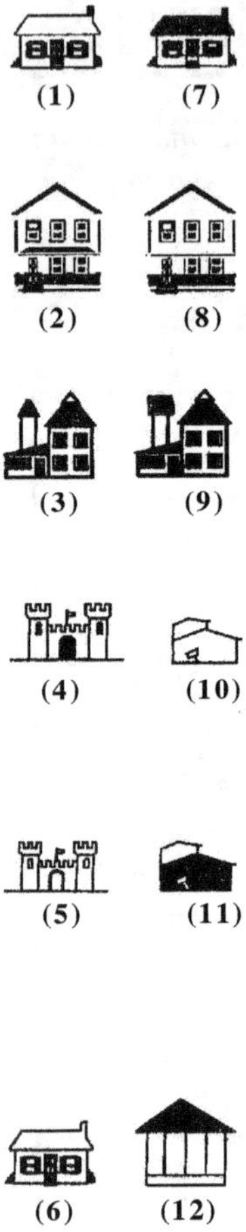

(1) **(7)** **(2)** **(8)** **(3)** **(9)** **(4)** **(10)** **(5)** **(11)** **(6)** **(12)**

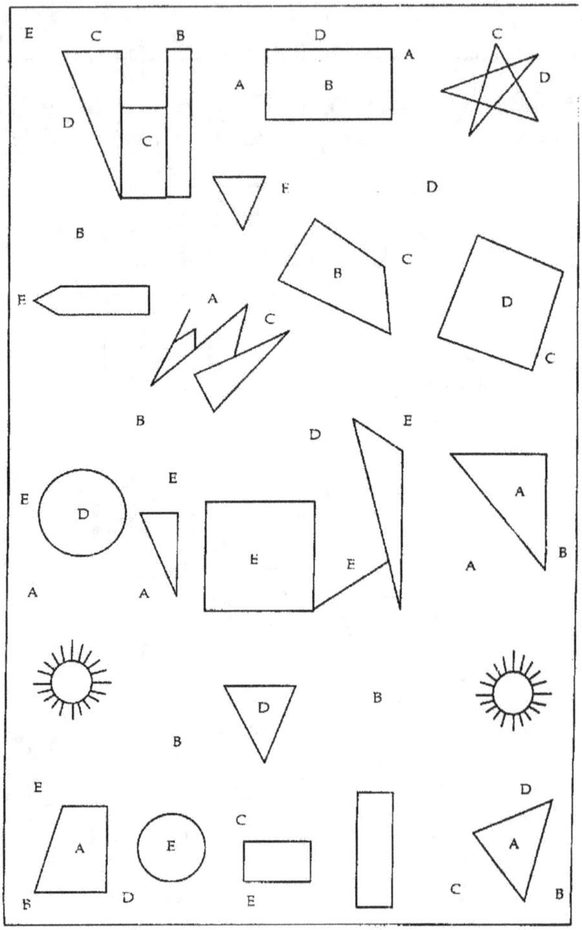

ANSWERS

1	2	3	4	5	6	7	8	9	10
B	D	C	E	B	A	D	D	A	A

11	12
C	B

Directions (Qs. 1-12): *Carefully observe the memory page and find out the exact position of the pictures/figures given on the question page.*

SET-2

MEMORY PAGE

QUESTION PAGE

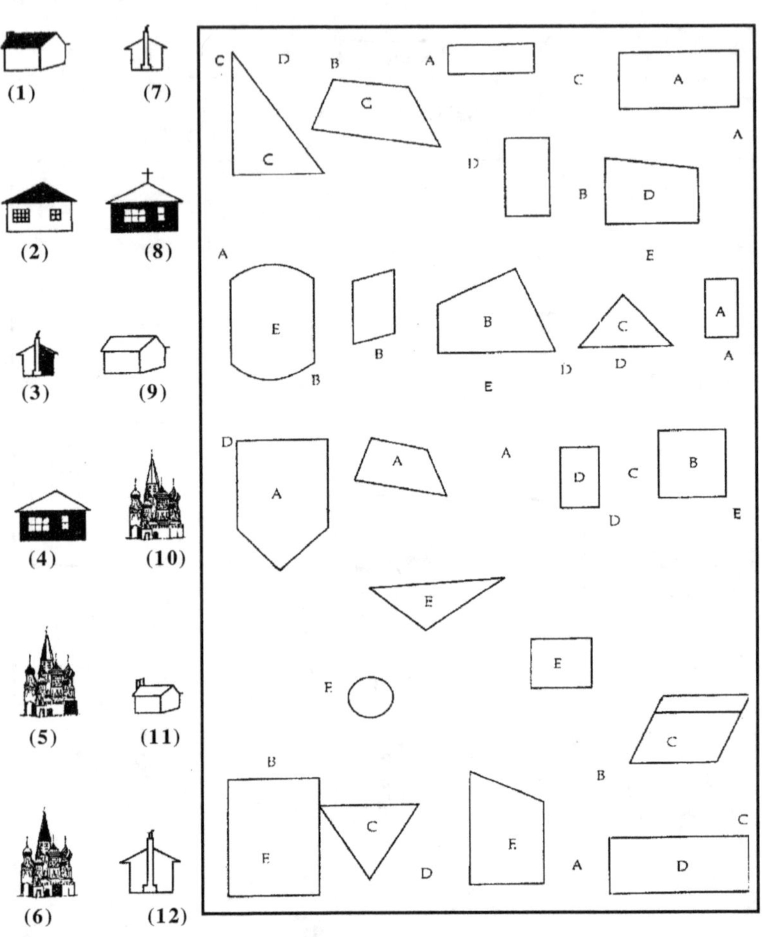

ANSWERS

1	2	3	4	5	6	7	8	9	10
C	E	C	B	A	E	D	B	A	A

11	12
C	E

Directions (Qs. 1-96): *In the following questions a number of multiple digits is given on left side and another number is given on the right side of (=) sign. If the numbers on the left and the right side of (=) sign are identical in all respect then you answer should be 'Yes' otherwise 'No'.*

1.	89835013	=	89835013	Yes	No
2.	14143898	=	14143898	Yes	No
3.	512946262	=	512946262	Yes	No
4.	892387	=	892387	Yes	No
5.	846367	=	846367	Yes	No
6.	44029696	=	44029696	Yes	No
7.	6644861	=	6644861	Yes	No
8.	39269101	=	39269101	Yes	No
9.	6265975	=	6265975	Yes	No
10.	5476753	=	5467573	Yes	No
11.	28805177	=	28805177	Yes	No
12.	8524319	=	8524319	Yes	No
13.	796576	=	796576	Yes	No
14.	9602241	=	9602241	Yes	No
15.	858509	=	858509	Yes	No
16.	5204278	=	5204278	Yes	No
17.	67073011	=	67073011	Yes	No
18.	3066082	=	3006628	Yes	No
19.	68479224	=	68479224	Yes	No
20.	6548103	=	6548103	Yes	No
21.	5594254	=	5594254	Yes	No
22.	592503202	=	925530202	Yes	No
23.	87505121	=	87505121	Yes	No
24.	88741166	=	88741166	Yes	No

Rly Apt (E)–15

25.	5290275	=	5290275	Yes	No
26.	5216556	=	5216556	Yes	No
27.	0429257	=	0429257	Yes	No
28.	905828	=	905828	Yes	No
29.	5637499	=	563949	Yes	No
30.	2804988	=	2804988	Yes	No
31.	8768245	=	8768245	Yes	No
32.	6252655	=	6252655	Yes	No
33.	77786511	=	77786511	Yes	No
34.	28220959	=	2822059	Yes	No
35.	5323202	=	5323202	Yes	No
36.	5179574	=	5179574	Yes	No
37.	16553150	=	16553150	Yes	No
38.	1619753434	=	1619753434	Yes	No
39.	9716359	=	9716359	Yes	No
40.	698832	=	698823	Yes	No
41.	407808	=	407808	Yes	No
42.	810484	=	810484	Yes	No
43.	25101212	=	25101212	Yes	No
44.	4337520	=	4337520	Yes	No
45.	579182	=	579182	Yes	No
46.	43253434	=	43253434	Yes	No
47.	236786	=	237668	Yes	No
48.	6350605605	=	6350605605	Yes	No
49.	168025443	=	168052443	Yes	No
50.	52994721	=	52994721	Yes	No
51.	74522551	=	74522551	Yes	No
52.	6810922	=	6810922	Yes	No
53.	040330991	=	040330991	Yes	No
54.	56933591	=	369353991	Yes	No
55.	124438121	=	124438121	Yes	No
56.	60574272	=	60574272	Yes	No

57.	96388277	=	96388277	Yes	No
58.	703632551	=	703632551	Yes	No
59.	674785428	=	67478528	Yes	No
60.	68201	=	68201	Yes	No
61.	4084366421	=	4084364121	Yes	No
62.	310736231	=	31706321	Yes	No
63.	6523321	=	6523321	Yes	No
64.	330288121	=	330288121	Yes	No
65.	47252888	=	47528288	Yes	No
66.	1719354242	=	1719354242	Yes	No
67.	26451424	=	26451424	Yes	No
68.	904196124	=	9049161124	Yes	No
69.	1282788941	=	12827878914	Yes	No
70.	1225886155	=	1225886155	Yes	No
71.	6728282823	=	6728282824	Yes	No
72.	881017994	=	880197994	Yes	No
73.	82733214	=	82733214	Yes	No
74.	7438045	=	7438045	Yes	No
75.	443025002	=	440302502	Yes	No
76.	945004001	=	945004004	Yes	No
77.	560652541	=	560652542	Yes	No
78.	805089669	=	805099696	Yes	No
79.	875595717	=	758595771	Yes	No
80.	7540145	=	7540145	Yes	No
81.	60747542	=	607475421	Yes	No
82.	81404771	=	81404771	Yes	No
83.	4039522	=	4039523	Yes	No
84.	5606524522	=	5606521522	Yes	No
85.	601080404	=	601080404	Yes	No
86.	404431322	=	4044133322	Yes	No
87.	434885661	=	4348856661	Yes	No
88.	837633321	=	8376333321	Yes	No

89.	64101854	=	64101845	Yes	No
90.	4221284828	=	4221284828	Yes	No
91.	8261041424	=	861041424	Yes	No
92.	3206305	=	32063025	Yes	No
93.	783301464	=	783301464	Yes	No
94.	30626300	=	30626300	Yes	No
95.	527143131	=	5271143131	Yes	No
96.	761805214	=	7618052214	Yes	No

ANSWERS

1	2	3	4	5	6	7	8	9	10
Yes	Yes	Yes	Yes	Yes	Yes	Yes	Yes	Yes	No

11	12	13	14	15	16	17	18	19	20
Yes	Yes	Yes	Yes	Yes	Yes	Yes	No	Yes	Yes

21	22	23	24	25	26	27	28	29	30
Yes	No	Yes	Yes	Yes	Yes	Yes	Yes	No	Yes

31	32	33	34	35	36	37	38	39	40
Yes	Yes	Yes	No	Yes	Yes	Yes	Yes	Yes	No

41	42	43	44	45	46	47	48	49	50
Yes	Yes	Yes	Yes	Yes	Yes	No	Yes	No	Yes

51	52	53	54	55	56	57	58	59	60
Yes	Yes	Yes	No	Yes	Yes	Yes	Yes	No	Yes

61	62	63	64	65	66	67	68	69	70
No	No	Yes	Yes	No	Yes	Yes	No	No	Yes

71	72	73	74	75	76	77	78	79	80
No	No	Yes	Yes	No	No	No	No	No	Yes

81	82	83	84	85	86	87	88	89	90
No	Yes	No	No	Yes	No	No	No	No	Yes

91	92	93	94	95	96
No	No	Yes	No	No	No

Directions (Qs. 1-72): *In the following questions, similar type of four questions are given on the left side and these figures have been reproduced on the right side which are named as A, B, C, D and E. You have to find the exact reproduction of the question figures from the given five answer figure A, B, C, D and E.*

1.   (A)

2.   (B)

3.   (C)

4.   (D)

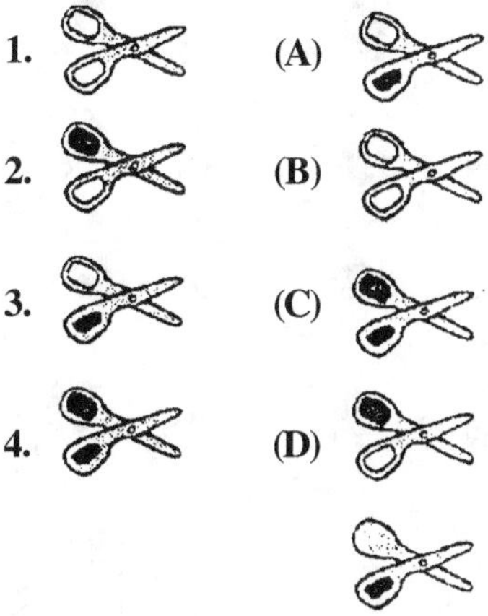

5.   (A)

6.   (B)

7.   (C)

8.   (D)

          (E)

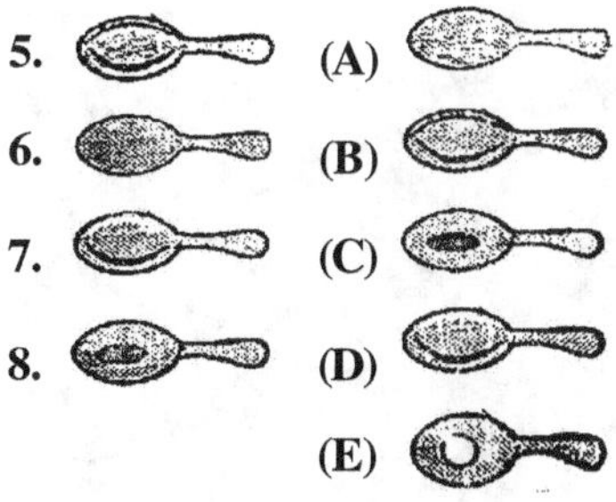

9.   (A)

10.   (B)

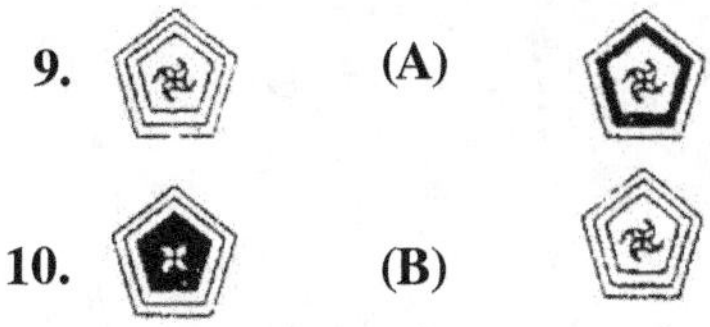

11.   (C)

12.   (D)

          (E)

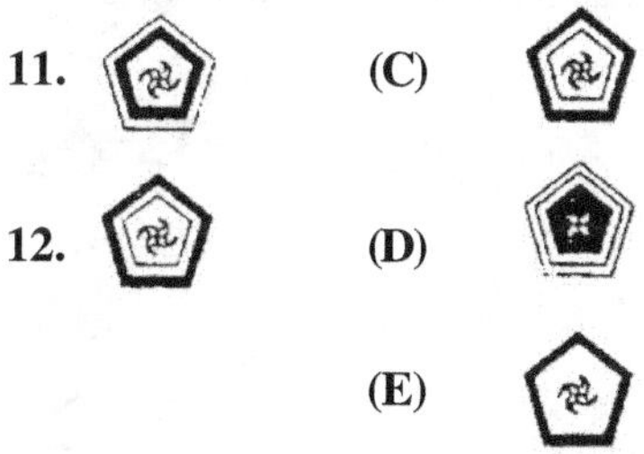

13.   (A)

14.   (B)

15.   (C)

16.   (D)

          (E)

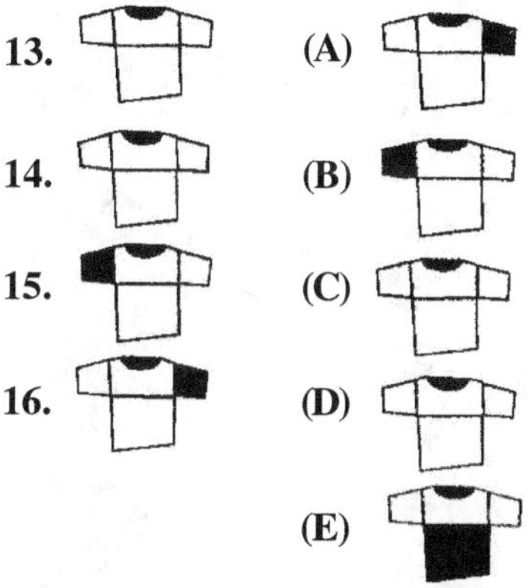

17.   (A)

18.   (B)

19.   (C)

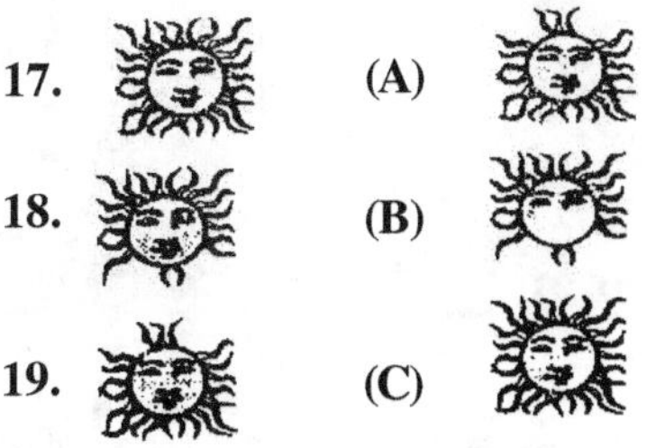

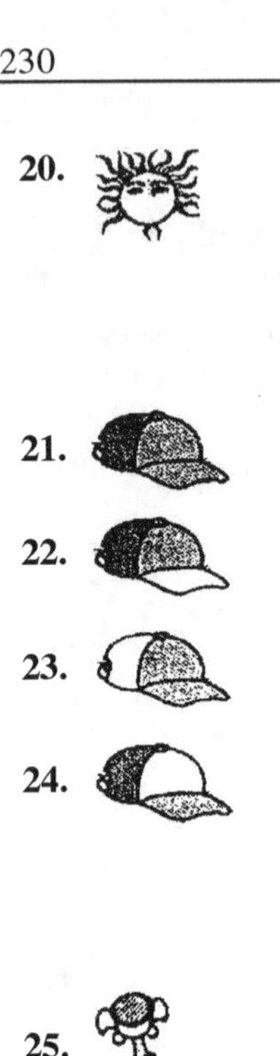

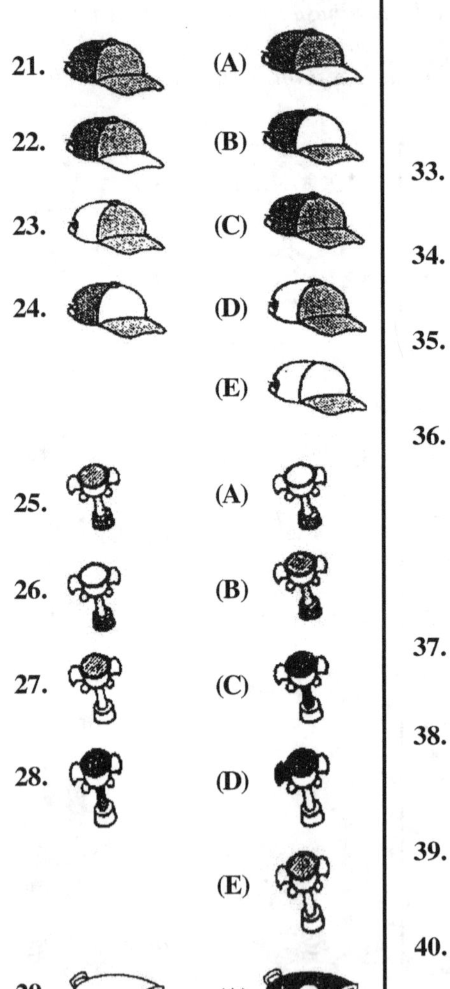

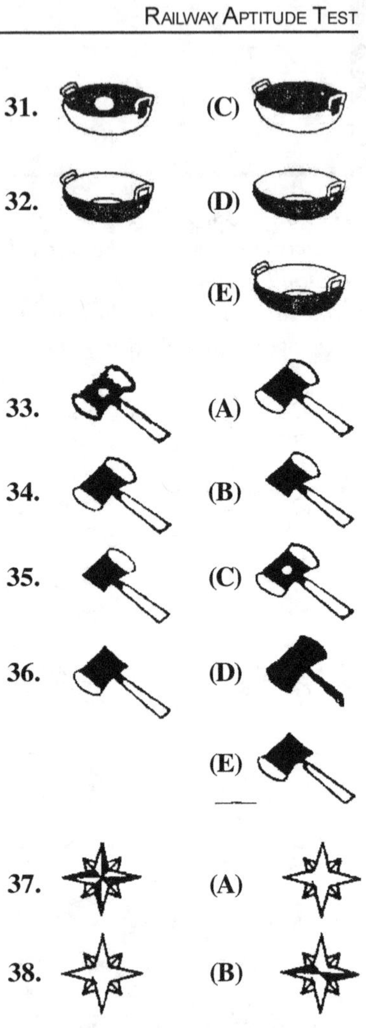

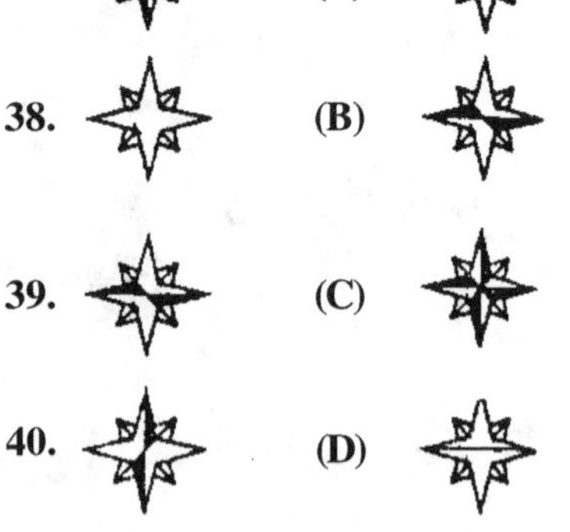

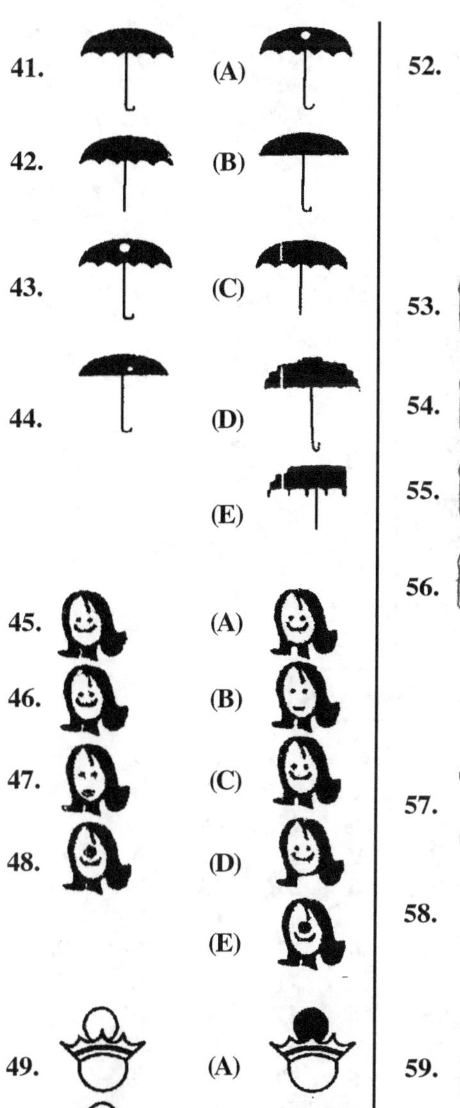

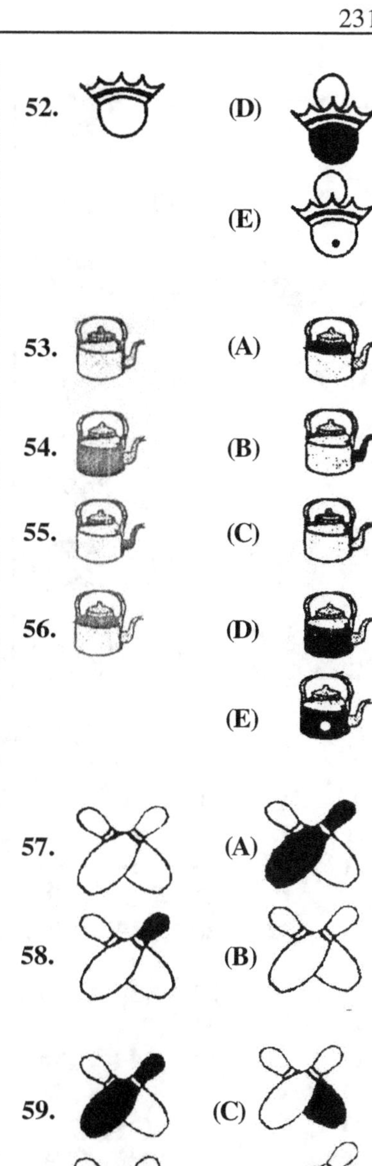

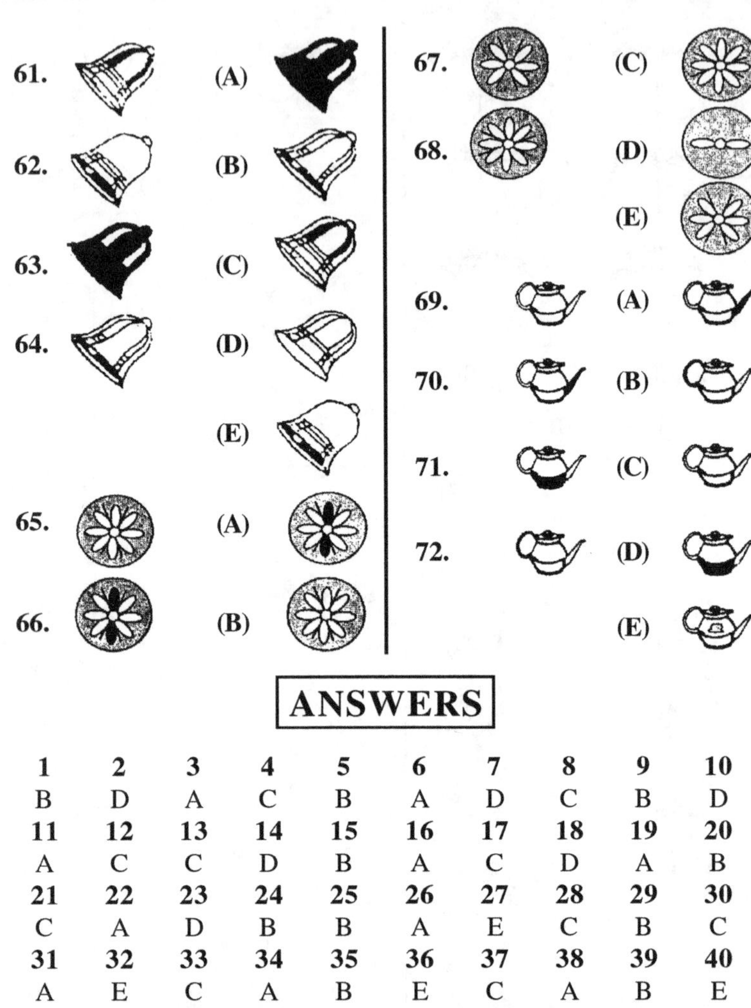

ANSWERS

1	2	3	4	5	6	7	8	9	10
B	D	A	C	B	A	D	C	B	D

11	12	13	14	15	16	17	18	19	20
A	C	C	D	B	A	C	D	A	B

21	22	23	24	25	26	27	28	29	30
C	A	D	B	B	A	E	C	B	C

31	32	33	34	35	36	37	38	39	40
A	E	C	A	B	E	C	A	B	E

41	42	43	44	45	46	47	48	49	50
D	C	A	B	C	A	B	E	C	D

51	52	53	54	55	56	57	58	59	60
A	B	C	D	B	A	B	E	A	C

61	62	63	64	65	66	67	68	69	70
C	E	A	B	B	A	E	C	C	A

71	72
D	B